# REFLECTIONS OF THE
# *Voiceless* BRITISH

Education is the wealth of an
individual and the nation.

Thanks for reading

All the best for the future

HBAlbhl

Oct 2022

# REFLECTIONS OF THE
# *Voiceless* BRITISH

At times empathy goes a long way to help foster a fairer society

## HASSAN AKBERALI

First published as Paperback and eBook on Amazon (2021)

Published on-demand by Amazon

The moral right of Hassan B. Akberali to be identified as the author of this work has been asserted by him in accordance with the Copyright, Designs and Patents Act of 1988

ISBN: 9798763779240

For the *voiceless* in Britain and the world over

People should not feel deprived of opportunities, peaceful co-existence because of the actions of others. Like-minded people need to respect one another irrespective of race, creed, class, sex or age. What the Covid-19 pandemic showed was that it didn't appear to understand social borders fully; similarly, when race, faith, class and divisive politics start to mix, that's equally invariably fatal.

Now that we have arrived in the twenty-first century, we should not find it hard to have the debate about what we have become. Our very desire to be seen as 'civilised' people to uphold democracy, justice, fairness should not stop us from talking about our same 'civilised' beliefs. We should all be given a fair start in life to fulfil dreams irrespective of where we are born.

# CONTENTS

# PROLOGUE

Home is where you launch your life, land that feeds you, where you pay your taxes.

Home is not where you are born. Otherwise, you would live there. Why emigrate?

Home is where you live in social harmony, making a positive contribution, not just a birthright.

And in the globalised world we now live in; you can not pick your home any more than you can choose your family. And people should not look at each other or treat others differently based on skin colour, faith, creed or sex. Like we saw during the Covid pandemic, national borders became obsolete, affecting us all, some more than others. Yet there were also positives like what we can achieve by working together. So, why not live in social harmony instead of hatred in fear of each other!

Before the partition of India/Pakistan, Palestine/Israel and the carving up of the Middle East for strategic commercial reasons due to the discovery of oil, people of different faiths, sects, and cultures generally speaking lived in peaceful co-existence. Likewise, it was no different in other ex-colonial countries like Kenya, Uganda, Darfur, Myanmar, Nigeria, Rwanda. With Kenya and India until recently becoming shining examples of democracy in the post-independent era, where people lived in social harmony respectful of each other's beliefs and cultures.

When I was growing up in the 1950s and 1960s in Tanganyika, under colonial rule and post-independent Tanzanian era, a person's skin colour was an acceptable, more flexible concept based on mutual respect. A lesson on the merits of social co-existence as well as secularism for its citizens. In East Africa, it was mitigated further by shared human values, working together to the best of one's abilities towards the ultimate good of society - without imposing on others.

Of course, no one can deny it was perfect. Yet, we managed to get along and made the best of unchangeable differences related to skin colour, ethnic heritage, faith, and inequality. Unlike the genetics-plus, colour-plus, culture-plus, language-plus, attire indoctrinated atmosphere prevalent in 'civilised' Western democracies, I discovered after arriving in the UK in 1973.

I am second generation East African Asian born in Tanzania. My ancestors were Gujarati Indians born into Islam; who migrated about one-hundred-fifty years ago (*circa*1871 A.D.) to East Africa to escape a famine-gripped region in India in search of a better future. No different to some perilous migration journeys embarked upon in the twenty-first century by those fleeing regions struck by natural disasters and illegal wars inflicted by man on fellow human beings.

Like many South Asians who migrated to East Africa, my ancestors would not have been successful, let alone survive, without the goodwill, charitable deeds of fellow human beings on the way and on reaching their destination. Something the migrants did not forget, wait to do until they had amassed wealth before helping others, nevertheless did so in whatever capacity they could as a businessman or as labourers, for they didn't forget what it felt like to suffer. My family also took every opportunity to share their good fortune to benefit others, especially the people of Mombo. They built a school, mosque, health centre, living quarters, cultivated land for their employees. In 1966, the family donated a fully operational sawmill by forming an African co-operative of workers at a ceremony attended by President Julius Nyerere, making it the first act of its kind.

Like my ancestors who migrated to East Africa, I am also a migrant. Fortunately, I didn't have to make an arduous journey across oceans to escape hardships. Instead, I flew in comfort to Brittan to pursue further education. And after forty-eight years in Britain, I do not feel part British, part Tanzanian. I am wholly British, with a Tanzanian background. My loyalty now is total to Britain, my home, just like my ancestor's loyalty was to their new homeland, Tanzania.

That doesn't surprise me, bearing in mind that I am now seventy years old, spent more than twice my life in Britain, and only twenty-two years in Tanzania. So, to those with racist tendencies, I have to say why shouldn't I be British. What else can I be or pretend to be? Some would like me to 'Go Home'. But where would I go? All I can say is this is my Home.

Whether we are born in Britain or elsewhere, we all like our mother countries of birth to be a hero. Something we would like to boast. But we need to be honest with ourselves. Not see the world through the prism blaming others while turning a blind eye to our actions by making unsubstantiated stories and covering up failings of politicians. Whether in Britain or those ex-colonial countries with diabolical human rights records, therefore, before questioning others, we need to speak out against those abuses and not keep quiet if we want to be listened to as a credible voice by others. Similarly, the white people should not look at non-white people who have made Britain their home as the 'other tribe'.

I believe the onus should be on white and non-white people to put their own houses in order by not taking each other's goodwill for granted. They should stop listening to backward thinking religious or political leaders - democratically elected or not - with ulterior motives who preach hatred and division. My main criticism of those who believe otherwise would be; if you disagree, why live here? But they still do. Why? Because they know too well that despite racism and structural inequalities, they enjoy better civil rights in Britain and will be treated even worse in their countries of birth because of high levels of corruption. And to seek justice comes at a price, with innocent people often ending up in prison and forgotten. Now I am not saying that it doesn't or can't happen in Britain. Of course, it can and does. But the chances to address such injustices are greater even after years of cover-ups, although justice may seem to have come too late for the victims. Also in-spite-of the findings of many costly public inquiries held after major public disasters to learn lessons, the same mistakes get repeated whereby initial pleas of help still gets ignored by politicians, the 'establishment'.

At the same time, it should not be an excuse in Britain for politicians to exploit the sentiments of white people with a populist agenda based on right-wing extremism, nationalism that treats non-white people as second-class citizens in their adopted country. Especially when those from the Commonwealth made significant contributions during two world wars, helped rebuild Britain after WWII; and considered Britain their home. Divisive politics gets humanity nowhere. It should not be a battle of supremacy. Who is better than whom? It should be about oneness. We are where we are. We need to work towards an even better future by working together.

Of all the ingredients that make up my complex identity, being British has profoundly affected my thinking. Not only after coming to Britain but what I benefited from before coming to Britain that has propelled me to swim upstream while simultaneously making me aware of the dark moments from past colonial history or those that crop up now and then. Yet, I still feel proud, happier to call it home because it is here in Britain; I live with my wife and two British born daughters. I also realise that their experience, together with that of my grandchildren, will be very different. Not like mine and others who have had bad experiences of blatant as well as subtle racism. However, like me, the notion that they are not quite British enough, that they are the 'other tribe' in their own country, will seem ridiculous to know or experience that some white people do have that mentality to think otherwise.

The debate of our age should be about multiculturalism, not an identity debate based on a prominent definite colour like white, black, brown or a tertiary one, inciting hatred. Britain should not find it hard to have a conversation because of the common thread that runs through our shared colonial past, which helped coin the phrase "the sun never sets on the British Empire." The outcome will not seem that daunting but very productive by talking to many people, especially the *voiceless* people. It will allow us to harness the good bits, not repeat those dark abhorrent acts from our shared history. It's up to the politicians to rise to the challenge, change their twentieth-century colonial mentality thinking for self-serving egos, and it's up to the ordinary people to make sure that they do for an even better future in the national interest.

I have always considered myself lucky. However, like most, I have had my fair share of regrets along with disappointments. I often reflect on how far I have come, not in worldly things but family, friends, even simple things like discussing inequalities that need an urgent overhaul. I do my utmost, most importantly, to treat people like I would like others to treat me. I was born surrounded by parental love, a mother who always instilled the importance of truth, education, moral values, and role models who understood and practised scruples to respect people as human beings, not based on their skin colour. Of course, it was not always easy, yet I had a very happy upbringing and tried my best to make a positive contribution to society, however big or small it may be, that has helped lead a contentful life.

This book charts what it means to be a white or non-white *voiceless* individual with an ordinary upbringing, exacerbated further if one belongs to the latter group. It examines what it feels like not to be listened to, treated as second-class citizens, patronised by politicians who think they understand people's real-life concerns because they don't. Politicians can no longer afford to bury their heads in the sand, remain delusional to believe underlying issues will disappear. It won't, and subtle discrimination will become even more entrenched and challenging to address if ignored longer. It's a timely reminder of unravelling events in the world today seen from a layperson's perspective, no different from the divisive politics of the old order when people fought two world wars to establish supremacy. Except, instead of fascism, it is now unconscious bias, under the disguise of culture wars and nationalism preached by 'civilised' political leaders born in the twentieth century in their quest to get elected with consequences of their mistakes affecting the lives of twenty-first-century generations such as illegal wars, global warming, poverty, civil unrests, migrations, genocides.

By writing this book, I want to shed light on how the *voiceless* British feel and what goes on in real life. But more than that, I want to articulate why we should care, illustrate what can we achieve further if we try. I'm probably not the sort of an author or even well-known as a celebrity usually invited to publish a book. I am not reliving a curriculum vitae bursting with the tremendous weighty achievements of our time. I profess no particular specialism or expertise in my or any other field. I am a retired family man, an ex-academic, ex-businessman, ex-manual worker. Nor a politician, a philosopher, a historian or a scholar. I'm also a stranger to any gilded lower or upper echelons of the 'establishment'. But what I have in common with the *voiceless* is that I have spent the best part of three decades ignored by the same 'establishment' meant to listen to them. I want to write this book while still a relatively fresh face to this warped game by remaining optimistic that we can do even better before the delicate balance between idealism and cynicism tips too far.

At the beginning of each section, the reader will notice a brief abstract that summarises the essence of the chapter. The book is an attempt to speak for the *voiceless*. It is structured on real-life experiences, observations, news and political analysis. I will also do my best to explore some of the prevalent public concerns that need to be tackled collectively in our multicultural Britain to enhance social co-existence.

# 1.

# THE VOICELESS

In most cases, the *voiceless* do not have time to engage with politicians due to daily work and family pressures, and feel it has nothing to do with them. At times, the public also just put up with the situation, even if it affects their daily lives, such as anti-social behaviour, public services and so forth. It's because people place trust in politicians, look up to them with a firm belief that they know better, duty-bound to resolve matters in the national interest.

It never ceases to amaze me how few MPs and ministers take the time to engage directly with constituents from disadvantaged backgrounds. Rather than take the *voiceless* for granted, politicians should speak out more often on their behalf, not when it suits them. Have an inclusive debate to encourage more people to come forward instead of just listening to a selective audience of advisors, party loyalists, journalists and workers during stage-managed visits for photo opportunities.

I have long wondered how people, irrespective of their colour, faith, sex, creed or age, perceive their places in the world. Especially those trapped inside. Anxious because of poverty, mental illness, disability or homelessness. When the humblest, most everyday needs or even a modicum of success in life becomes an upward struggle, a never-quite-defined danger or failure, too scared to ask for help. And if they do ask, it becomes an enormous challenge, wondering whether those in authority will listen to them? Would strangers even raise their heads to look? And if they did, what would they think?

As it is, life to the *voiceless* feels like constantly walking in oversized wellingtons through knee-high wet mud, and they have already been through a backbreaking, emotionally draining, and gloomy, painful journey. Therefore, there is no point in prolonging their agony; more importantly, deter them from seeking help from the 'establishment'. If you think about it, it is hard enough for ordinary people to get heard; imagine how much harder it must be for those even worse off! I think people at the grassroots level do want to change the status quo by engaging more in the democratic process. And believe there should be a greater focus on compassion, an understanding of the responsibility on the part of those elected to represent through regular informal interaction to keep abreast to prevent the situation from worsening further.

For the *voiceless*, not knowing where to go for help when needed must be utterly heartbreaking. More so after plucking the courage to contact the 'establishment' only not to hear from those in power. It takes a lot of guts to open up to a stranger, but getting ignored doesn't inspire much confidence to engage. Therefore, those who have plucked up courage should not be made to feel out of place by those in authority rattling off a list of standard questions from the computer or by long-winded bureaucratic replies. It makes matters worst for them. Making them feel unwanted, not taken seriously.

Uncertainties exacerbated even more when at a time, the debate of our age remains focused on nationalism and divisive populist politics with questions constantly centred on one's identity. Who are we? Who are they? What do they want? Why do I like this group? And not that group? Why do we do what we do? Does belonging to a particular political party make a person more entitled than those with no allegiance? Does placing their bag on an adjacent seat on public transport make the person feel entitled to the space? Where does the sense of entitlement come from? What about the *voiceless*, the ignored? Who will listen to their cries for help? All important questions, not addressed directly, not often enough by involving those at the receiving end.

It seems these days; we accept national scandals as if it's a normal thing. But it should be more about early intervention, listening to the pleas of help, being pro-active, not waiting for the loss of lives, human suffering to happen, followed by political sound bites and knee-jerk reactive responses. Instead, we should also ask. Is it good enough for me? If not, then something needs to change. Why should it be alright for the *voiceless*? Those in authority are often quick to remind others what they should do without asking themselves what they are doing wrong. And instead of a community effort, it then becomes a finger-pointing exercise. Perhaps politicians should ask themselves why black, brown or white people feel left behind, not listened to by those in power. How have the politicians contributed due to failings on their part?

Just like those who use drugs or drink are certainly not all drug addicts or alcoholics. If anything, evidence suggests many drugs end up in the hands of the wealthy middle classes, those who work in the City of London. Eminent politicians have openly admitted to taking drugs and binge drinking. No doubt they have all thought police should do a lot more to make streets safe, without ever asking themselves. How have they contributed to the problem that has led to increased knife crime and anti-social behaviour? How many deaths have been caused further down the food chain to bring them their drugs? How this crime affects everyone, black, brown or white, proving to be colour-blind? So, perhaps before telling others what they are doing wrong, they should ask themselves what part they may have played? Middle-class drug users should share the blame for the deaths of Black children "pimped" out by crime bosses on Britain's streets. Of course, there's a discussion about youth services. There's a discussion around parenting. There's a discussion around gang activity, but we ought to understand that the drug business is central to why these young people are dying. The affluent drug users are equally a part of the problem.

The situation we are facing is that politics has become an algorithm. Even more so now because of social media. It decides what politicians would like to hear, ending up creating a simplistic binary view of society. It becomes a case of either you're with us or against us. And if you're against us, you deserve to be forgotten as collateral damage. By not listening, people simply feel less important, get more withdrawn into their shells. Being ignored is terrible for the victim, but it's disastrous for the victim's community because these communities need to see that their concerns get heard, debated, taken seriously, and acted upon, not politicised point-scoring exercise brushed under the carpet. Doing so will restore trust in politicians; the *voiceless* will feel part of the process and participate as US, not THEM.

*

Politicians often order individuals to take responsibility, but they are never accountable, despite having infinitely superior levers to pull to combat the spread of structural inequalities. Primarily, though, blaming, placing the onus on a significant proportion of the population it's their fault suits politicians. It is highly convenient for those in power to suggest that the grim depth of this stage of inequality is down to individual failures, as opposed to larger strategic ones over the years that has been the fault and responsibility of politicians and nobody else's.

The scale of what is happening now is not the fault of individuals; it's the fault of a government that appears not to learn absolutely nothing from past mistakes highlighted by various public inquiries. Instead, go on to almost repeating the same error by not listening. Well, yes, everyone has to play their part. But if the government of the day would listen to, not ignore, those at the receiving end, then people might rightly have something to say, how much of it is down to their fault, not the victims. Politicians need to be involved in the bigger picture by keeping abreast of the situation rather than just an isolated part of an ever-steady increase in bureaucracy. Being involved with a hands-on approach at the grassroots makes better use of resources to do things effectively and differently for those in need. It gives a sense of mutually beneficial integration between the community and those elected by them.

Whereas stage-managed visits, seen as doing something speaking to a selected audience wearing clean overalls for the cameras and TV audience, do not accurately portray whether the government is achieving its objectives. Such visits may serve a purpose during an election or party leadership campaign but are meaningless, of no value to those who are literally in dire straits through lack of help when needed most. Therefore, it is hard to see how the government can be achieving value for money to improve the well-being of those needing the most help. Yet, there are more straightforward, less costly ways of improving people's lives if their concerns are not ignored in a bureaucratic tangle but heard. It is not rocket science.

We can often learn a lot more by speaking directly to those affected the most instead of relying on unaccountable 'experts' or those with vested interests, with one eye to make the honours list as well as money out of someone else's misery. Like, those high-end professionals – special advisors (SpAds), lawyers, journalists, professionals, accountants, media moguls and entertainment figures – who have become insulated from the broader society. The ever-increasing numbers of elites are now having a great run milking the system at the expense of the taxpayer. The situation has become so extreme; they have started undermining social norms with the resultant breakdown of institutions. Who gets ahead is no longer the most capable but the one who is greedy, willing to play dirtier?

Perhaps not surprisingly, some of the best conversations one can have are held face-to-face than through third parties and thick dossiers. Sitting down with those facing daily struggles and listening to their side of the story in all their raw glory can open proper communication channels to find solutions to alleviate real-life concerns. Many people from disadvantaged backgrounds tend to relish just the chance to get heard, something they don't get to do very often. That's when one can realise there are far better, cheaper ways of providing help to those who need it most, instead of the same constantly revolving door of poverty, homelessness, crime, drug abuse. At times simple processes such as listening can change somebody's life dramatically, making them feel wanted, but the system often lets them down by not engaging directly.

Meeting people from disadvantaged backgrounds gives a more genuine connection than a part of statistical data. It feels like being wanted. Develops an affinity without fear of being judged or stigmatised. A regular meet-up with people finding life difficult can give a better understanding of their reality. It will provide deeper insight through open, honest interactions with others, safe in the knowledge that nobody would think any less of them. Such a strategy will be far more productive than waiting years for the outcome of expensive public inquiries held after each disaster costing the taxpayer. The findings published in complex glossy thick dossiers, apart from window-dressing exercises, only get forgotten, gathering dust until the next public catastrophe.

Another common problem is a generalisation based on isolated events. Just because you are white or non-white doesn't mean that attending specially designed seminars, refresher courses will make us behave or understand a problem better. Because isolating people into different groups would be counterproductive when we want to be accepted by one another on merit, not judged by skin colour. The reality is that – as with all relationships – things aren't always so easy or black and white in real life. Sometimes working together or putting in somebody else's shoes gives a better understanding of the reality faced by those from a more impoverished background. It helps someone feel heard, understood, inspired to speak out to get help. At times a few kind words can make a lot of difference to people. Yet what is even more important is not to make empty pledges, then not honour them. The government's argument always seems to be that there are adequate financial measures to help the poor. That may well be true; however, completely misses the point. If so, why do structural inequalities still exist? Why do those from low-income households struggle to feed themselves, stay warm, do less well or keep clean?

One way of achieving it would be to select disenfranchised community members acting as independent advisors to the government. Not an angry protest or a monitoring group; shouting abuse at the platform during public meetings or outside the Houses of Parliaments. But I mean politicians regularly meeting a respected group of ordinary people with real-life experiences leading everyday life inside the communities. Doing so will give a far better understanding of the issues, unlike during election campaigns when they scramble over each other to shake hands with the public during their stage-managed visits, not to be seen again until the next campaign.

On the other hand, working closely with outside advisors on an equal level, letting them have a say, getting heard will encourage participation. It will help break barriers that, at times, to the voiceless, feels an impenetrable monolith of a complex, mysterious system of self-serving ranks of politicians and SpAds with its rigid way of looking at things and people. A strategy which to the *voiceless* seems deliberately adopted for mutual benefits to maintain the status quo at the taxpayer's expense. At the same time, it is equally essential to keep some barriers of authority and power as a boss or politician because everyone feels more comfortable when the barriers are in place. However, it requires balancing because being alone with like-minded people develops a 'yes-man' mentality, more power grab and further isolation with lesser interaction at the grassroots level. And even greater reliance on facts deliberately selected by SpAds for comfortable listening to preserve the egos of those advised without being seen as not good at their job.

*

It's a sad reality that immigrants are more likely to suffer due to alienation, language barriers, separation from friends, family, and everything familiar to them. At times they are left feeling humiliated, mortified, like a criminal. Not helped by TV programmes that sensationalise, exploit the poorest in society on top of insults directed by extreme right-wing politicians and media. Many of the migrants are talented people, who put their lives at risk to cross the English Channel after travelling thousands of miles across Europe to escape conflicts, illegal wars fought on their land by foreign powers. Who in their right mind would risk the lives of their loved ones? How must they feel when they try to get heard only to get ignored? Is it any wonder they feel isolated? Who do they turn to other than their own? Is it any wonder they live-in enclaves - safety in numbers?

Likewise, British citizens of non-white immigrant backgrounds from the Commonwealth, unlike fellow white migrants from Canada, Australia, New Zealand, get treated with contempt by those in authority as if they are all spongers on welfare benefits. It may not be blatantly obvious, yet you can feel the undertones of racial prejudice when accessing public services or seeking justice to which they are legally entitled. Even formal complaints regarding NHS appointments and standards of service get ignored. Despite such handicaps, I remain optimistic because in Britain, compared to others, we have a better culture of coming to the aid of the underdog. Nevertheless, we take much for granted at times, and we should not become complacent and forget about how the *voiceless* might be coping with their daily struggles.

The government is always keen to point out that there are safety nets for the *voiceless*, including regulatory bodies, ombudsman services, charities, to raise complaints to deliver justice for those who seek it. That may well be true. Though the reality faced by the ordinary person is different. To access benefits or services, they need the awareness, the know-how to use it, not leave the disadvantaged to their own devices with meagre resources to challenge the 'establishment' and big companies or at the mercy of others to do it on their behalf. When they can't stand on their own feet, what hope will they have to succeed against big people without professional help? Thus, it leaves the many who need a 'level playing field' facing the utmost difficulty exercising their civil rights. Simply because to access justice costs money, a colossal effort often having to rely on charities who themselves are struggling due to financial constraints. The ordinary public does not have a voice; for the many, it is often too late when their pleas for help get heard.

Even with all the information on government websites, leaflets in different languages, support, charity groups, it can seem incredibly challenging, confusing, ambiguous to seek help when needed at the right time. It's partly due to cultural background and upbringing, which go hand in hand with social problems because it's even harder to interact, let alone maintain friendships when you lack the confidence to mix with others outside your comfort zone. Also, it takes longer for the many to build trust; this is when you need people around you willing to listen, not forms filling exercises or writing letters to MPs. I know what it feels like not to be listened to by the 'establishment'. At times it becomes a constant struggle to prove that you are in Britain on legitimate grounds, someone who has paid taxes all their life, not an illegal immigrant on welfare benefits. I feel fortunate that I can stand up for my rights, but mind you, it can be a mindboggling effort to deal with the Home Office, employers, health providers, local councils, or utility companies. I am pleased I have successfully challenged the injustices for myself and others in tribunals or by referring them to an ombudsman.

Still, it is not easy, however easy it may sound because of the various layers of bureaucracy one gets subjected to, a deliberate ploy to wear you out. Perseverance often leads to the correct result in the end. Yet it can be stressful, an exhaustive ordeal; the main reason people usually give up, don't bother to fight for their rights since it can be very time-consuming. I hear too often that people left on their own to seek justice with no support or information say that they don't have enough time in the day to attend to their daily chores, let alone argue for their rights with those in authority, even if they were able to write.

Politicians, when confronted about their appalling immigration, welfare, housing, education, health policy failures along with shortcomings, are quick to dismiss the evidence insisting there is nothing wrong. Only to resign later for misconduct in public office or moved elsewhere during a cabinet reshuffle. In contrast, the victims feel there is no justice, just massive flaws to get heard. There is a distinct disparity between the haves and have-nots, not only income-wise but also to get heard, leaving them overwhelmed with a sense of helplessness that the situation is beyond their control, and they can talk to nobody. Therefore, what is the point of even trying if nobody is going to listen to you? I can't help but wonder if they would get patronised or ignored if the person in question were influential, well connected or with financial means. So, why should it be acceptable to ignore those from disadvantaged backgrounds!

How often have public inquiries concluded that the' establishment' could have averted the disaster if victims' pleas for help were listened to by the 'establishment'? There is an endless list of costly public inquiries. Apart from lining the pockets of lawyers and other professionals, the 'establishment' still consistently fails to implement the main findings (lessons), one of frustration, whereby victims continue not to be listened to by those in power. There is a distinct lack of visible interaction by the authorities when it matters most, with an eerie silence from mainstream media to report those concerns when brought to their attention. To top the frustration, those few who question get targeted by high-profile individuals, company executives and media, underlining their unprecedented control and influence over politicians.

The bottom line is that money in politics and media is a potent force with widespread lobbying – the polite form of corruption reserved for stigmatising third world countries. So much for 'free speech' and democracy. If the government is serious about tackling injustices, it should listen to those who have the experience of fighting them. Otherwise, it will follow a long line of failed past policy initiatives to tackle the "burning injustices." And only serve to raise more scepticism that becomes extremely difficult, more unlikely to dismantle the social structures underpinning such inequalities however hard we try or spend money to fix it. Understanding where and why they emerge is a crucial first step towards tackling them before wasting taxpayers' money.

*

Politicians believe they know better. They are clever people. Think they belong to a world of privilege by attending top schools and universities. Except the only skill they possess is how not to answer the question by being vague. Good at bluster with a mentality do as I say, not what I do. There is a kind of school boys' club-type behaviour in parliament because it is still more like an ex-public school or an Oxbridge university club than anywhere else you'll ever see. And if everyone around you is constantly telling you're fantastic, it's easy to get believed even if you're lying. Therefore, it would feel demeaning to listen to the truth when ordinary folk speak other than those from their close-knit circle. Especially listen to those who have not attended top schools or universities and have never been part of the world of privilege. Particularly to those whose immigrant parents worked hard to feed the family, doing low-paying menial jobs that other British people thought were beneath them.

But by most standards, Black and Asian people are equally competent, yet such attitude can lead to self-doubt, an inferiority complex. A feeling of - impostor syndrome, a lack of confidence in professional ability. Not because of qualifications but because of the racist mentality, an unconscious bias of those in authority who cannot accept others can be equally good or even better because of a colonial mentality that believes their cultural values are inherently superior to others. Impostor syndrome is real; anybody can fall victim, including the white working-class, albeit affecting significantly more non-white men, along with white and non-white women. When asked, Michelle Obama told students: "I still have a little [bit of] impostor syndrome, it never goes away, that you're actually listening to me. It doesn't go away, that feeling that you shouldn't take me that seriously. What do I know? I share with you because we all have doubts in our abilities, about our power and what that power is."

Even if those ordinary people broke the traditions and qualified from well-known universities still face an uphill struggle to convince others of their worthiness. The most intriguing reaction being one of disbelief. Based on the assumption that all non-white people must have a criminal past. Must be an illegal immigrant, lazy or at least lying about having so many qualifications. To the extent have doubts that degrees and diplomas obtained from foreign institutions are not worth the paper it's written on. I speak from my own past personal experiences during job interviews mentioned in my first book. As well as in the 2021 local elections, I contested as an Independent candidate when a troll on social media was more bothered about the authenticity of my academic qualifications and business credentials than of other candidates!

Such a mentality can make people feel less confident and lonely despite being more qualified than those passing judgment. To some rejections, aloneness may not seem hard to bear than others and can affect them positively. These frustrating, tiring experiences at times can help build resilience, make people even more determined. It has helped me develop strength. I believe the determination has come by being ignored when I felt I belonged to the democratic process whereby the political class should hear people. Not a prerogative to whom they should listen. Especially as a British citizen, like many, I have great reverence for our nation's values, freedom and democracy. However, it can become an energy-sapping ordeal to reach the goal.

*

I first became interested in politics in 1992 when I wrote to prime minister John Major. I highlighted the difficulties faced by the small family retailers because of government policies such as increased Uniform Business Rates, unfair trading practices enjoyed by the newspaper wholesalers and rising rents. I felt it was the right thing to do to place trust in politicians. Especially when they often say that they entered politics "to make life better for others." I also formed the Society for Independent Retailers (SIR) to tackle issues affecting the sector. SIR was a voluntary organisation and successfully campaigned on behalf of the *voiceless* retailers.

My earlier baptism into politics told me that a significant number of the *voiceless* British people, for some reason, did not directly engage with politicians, the 'establishment'. What it did was make me wonder why? It was revelatory that most people found it a mundane process, not worth bothering. Many felt that even if they tried to speak up, nobody listened, something I must agree with based on my own over twenty years of bitter experiences I have faced when attempting to do so. It is a pervasive experience felt amongst ethnic minority groups and white working-class people who believe no one listens to their real-life concerns.

About twenty years ago, I had also written to PM Tony Blair well before the tragic 9/11 event, followed by more attempts before 7/7. I highlighted the underlying concerns within the context of multicultural Britain. The importance of social cohesion to prevent exploitation by religious and political leaders who exploit weaknesses. For me, the most remarkable thing that transpired from those experiences was the contempt with which the politicians treated me. Bearing in mind, the pledges "New Labour" had expended what they would do for disenchanted voters post-Tory world of 'sleaze' and voter disenchantment. Regrettably, as an ordinary voter, it felt no different. Is it any wonder a large population of the people have lost overall trust in politicians?

Yet, I have remained undeterred, continued ever since to raise awareness of cross-party politicians and four other prime ministers on behalf of the 'silent majority', the *voiceless*, the law-abiding people like me. It's because often, very few seem keen to raise their heads above the parapet. And ever since, I have therefore decided to articulate an expression of something rarely touched. Namely, what does it feel not to be heard by those in power? What can I do to help fellow *voiceless* who vote only to get forgotten once the elections are over? What happens to their democratic right? How can they exercise their civil rights if they don't fit into any privileged identity circles? What about those *voiceless* who don't vote? Who listens to them?

Ironically, over two decades of unsuccessful efforts to persuade politicians to listen has helped me understand what it feels like to be ignored by the 'establishment'. It has been arduous work requiring great determination, which has helped me understand why many people do not bother to vote and are less enthusiastic about exercising their democratic right or don't even believe in democracy. Perhaps at times, it is easier for those at the receiving end to recognise injustices, making them see the wrongs better, inspiring them to do something about it to improve the situation for others. Otherwise, it leads to half-hearted attempts to tackle injustices by those who don't understand what it feels like not to be listened to. Preconceived assumptions that exist are often wrong, misleading and hinder progress. It would serve better to acknowledge them to address real-life concerns of the *voiceless*.

*

I have been considering various options for serving public duty ever since my MP, Jonathan Lord, in 2016 gave me the ultimatum not to waste his time. In addition to what he had already said in 2010, "if you feel so strongly about local or national issues, you are always at liberty to stand for election yourself or get involved with appropriate pressure groups or charities." I decided not to join protest groups as I was conscious that I would get stigmatised as a radicalised Muslim, an *Islamist* or a *jihadist* because of my beard and Muslim background. Not only that, but I believe in democracy, and those elected should do so by putting constituents' interests above anything else. It, therefore, left me with the following three dilemmas: forfeit my democratic right by not bothering my MP, relocate to another constituency, hoping for a more sympathetic MP, or stand for elections.

After two decades of being ignored by my MP and other cross-party politicians, I became one of the many disillusioned voters. However, instead of giving up, I decided to do honest politics to restore trust and promote social harmony without divisive tribal politics with a US and THEM attitude. Support politics, reach across the aisle to make life better for all, not compartmentalise people along party political lines. So, I contested the 2017 election as an Independent using personal meagre financial resources without a cat in a hell's chance of winning against my sitting MP in one of the safest seats in the land.

Even though I lost, I felt encouraged by some poignant positive messages whilst noting the negative ones from Knaphill residents. It made me wonder. Why can't we do this all the time; why can't we always support each other in this way? What can I do? How can I help other *voiceless* like me? What was uniquely mine to offer? What can a retired person like me do in his 'old age' to help others? What could I do to bring people together? What can I do to rid those strands of racial prejudice, structural inequalities that run deep in some of us? The constant struggle to belong. The questioning, the subtle currents of insecurity that we experience in our lives. The doubts. Do you quite fit despite having the same shared values and aspirations in life? I have often wondered if this is a journey from the negative to the positive. What small part I can play that had my name on it? What makes me different from others? How can I use my personal experience?

Most importantly, to do so peacefully to bring down some of the barriers. How can we balance the need for different groups to have their voice heard without resorting to civil unrest, join this, or that protest group or political party? Unlike most MPs, I am not a career politician but a community-led person though I can say with absolute certainty that politics is an integral part of our human society, affecting all aspects of our life whether we like politics or not. So, as voting public, we must engage in the political process, play our part and take responsibility if those elected to represent us fail in their duty to listen to their constituents.

Although I was not getting anywhere, I did not give up. What always swayed me was that it was about time those in power started listening to people who have elected them. By standing in the 2017 general elections, I became more interested in doing something myself and started writing in the local press on wide-ranging problems. Together with social media, it gave me a platform to bring issues to the public's attention. I also wrote to the national press, and as an unknown entity goes without saying, I consistently got rebuffed. It didn't matter because local people were offering support; most except a few were kind and friendly, making the whole experience more satisfying. At the same time, I was realistic not to expect anything except to do my best. And as long as people shared similar views to mine, I could build upon them by working together.

That experience meant I fully empathised with the *voiceless* and decided to turn my attention to get them heard. As mentioned, I may not be a career politician, author or journalist by profession. However, my desire to serve public duty is more to do with my roots, an upbringing based on Hope, shared values, a community-led individual who has absorbed this world by osmosis. Something I still absorb in our multicultural Britain because, just like the silent majority, I feel the *voiceless* are often not listened to and ignored. It seems inconceivable that people's lives are less deserving, their views less worthy because of their disadvantaged backgrounds.

As I knew, I was not the only one who felt ignored. I was, therefore, prepared to do something. I'd seen others give up, compromise as somebody else's problem. I knew I was strong enough to go on. Do my best to contribute to society in some meaningful way to help those who need help most. After the 2017 general election, I contested three local ones as an Independent in 2018, 2109 and 2021 using my limited resources. I came second each time, increasing my share of the vote and closing the gap on the favourites.

One thing is for sure. We cannot afford to be complacent, and we need to do more. By that, I don't mean being less optimistic, but I mean more realistic. Especially make better use of our resources to make people less dependent on charitable and welfare handouts. Instead, equip them with the right tools to get out of poverty. By that, I mean quality education to inspire in all aspects of life to benefit the individual and the wider community. We can attain much more by working together, listening directly to people's actual needs, not through intermediaries.

I believe we are responsible for raising awareness of all issues affecting the *voiceless* - no matter how difficult it may seem to accomplish - as it costs us nothing as individuals compared to what we gain as a society. Kindness is something we often feel is lacking these days, although it is still very much around us if we care to look for it. Not from the point of view as a duty or monetary gain but more as part of a natural process. Because entirely through no fault of the *voiceless*, often when they feel ignored, not wanted,  they can become inward-looking, as all their energy gets spent on day-to-day survival. Sometimes to the point where they think, what's the point of trying if nobody will listen. Yet, if we take time to listen, try to help, we can achieve even more.

# 2.

# BRITAIN - A BLESSED LAND OF IMMIGRANTS

No place in the world other than in Britain, people of all faiths enjoy more religious freedoms unless you belong to that land's religion. Even then in those countries, people of lower castes or incomes despite belonging to the same religion or those of other minority faiths or of no faith living there, feel persecuted with doubts about their future citizenship status and civil rights.

Love for your land of domicile, neighbours, environment is an essential doctrine of all religions or those of no faith. Religion should not only be about prayers, meditation, fasting, but striving for betterment in this world and the world hereafter. Any religion, if practised righteously, is not an enemy of humanity; the enemies are the perpetrators who come in all colours, sizes, shapes, disguised as religious and political leaders with self-serving interests living in our midst.

The cycle of events, life and death, is a fact. A mere particle in history accountable for its time in the world with no escape from it. However small or big, its record goes down in the deep archives of history, witnessed or not, read or not. The evidence of its actuality, especially life-changing milestones, never gets forgotten; sometimes, some episodes are always remembered and repeatedly reminisced. Something that can be learned from, for its impact during its lifetime was as profound because its relevance is eternal. Hence, their memory becomes immortal and significant; their existence in the mere records of time becomes more prominent and influential than life itself.

Time documents - each event that passes in the calendar of existence – some more than others etched precisely and remains indelible. The transition of power from one corner of the world to another; governments, superpowers rise and ebb like tides. Civilisations, empires, wars, famine, floods, festivals, pandemics come and go, year after year, a decade after another, a century after another shall continue. Yet time hasn't; it shall never look back for any or all. It is the might of time to which our world and life eventually succumb, a stage for one life after another until it is time to go.

Similarly, the past and the present history of the United Kingdom reflect a land of immigrant activity. During times of sorrow and joy, people with different histories, cultures, beliefs, languages have been coming here since the beginning of recorded time - a timeless union of events. With good outcomes, purpose served. Benefits gained which too often conveniently forgotten, with greater focus placed on a few bad aspects. Therefore, it is pertinent to give credit where it is due, harness the positives, learn from the negatives to progress further.

Yet, with a steady rise in nationalism in Brexit Britain, one might think or even feel Britain is not a country much more inclined to hear migration stories. Whatever else can be read into the referendum vote to leave the EU was a hostile period. The Brexit debate at the time, characterised by manipulative politicians and their cohorts with self-serving political ambitions lying about the imminent threat of people arriving from the EU, played heavily on people's fears of immigration.

And like in the past, politicians had their version of scapegoats, called immigrants they readily exploited. Immigrants got blamed for everything. For our struggling services. For stealing our jobs. For sponging on welfare benefits. For taking money out of our country. For not speaking our language. And our 'free press' equally relaxed to refer to them as "hoards" like they're rats or cockroaches. At the same time, some people feel comfortable abusing them in the street. We tell them to "Go Home," even happy to vandalise their property. We show limited empathy towards them when their children drown in the sea.

Thankfully, the Brexit debate is now water under the bridge. Best forgotten. We are where we are. Though what cannot get overlooked is an immortal memory of events, a timeless episode, archives of history, written in golden ink, which only becomes more apparent, dominant with the clock's ticking, which has been the post-war era of multicultural Britain. This unison, this timelessness, this shared history, this shared values need to be appreciated. The part played by Britain and the migrants from the Commonwealth in the twentieth century since these are the most recent events, fresh in our minds based on experience, easy to recall, therefore more relevant.

It was a period when thousands arrived as refugees from wars, famines, or civil and religious persecution in their own countries. Including many invited who answered the call made by the British monarch and the government to settle since they had particular skills which Britain was desperately in short supply and needed their help to rebuild after WWII. Some were brought here against their will, as slaves or as servants. Some came to study. Throughout the ages, Britain has been a magnet for those seeking a better life, in much the same way as Britons have emigrated, in large numbers, to other parts of the world.

In the last century, Britain has done more to provide refuge to the dispossessed through a combination of steadfast faith in human values, justice and fairness. The progress can be attributed directly to the fundamental goodwill, democracy, decency of HM's Governments, the British people, and what is salient about the vast majority of the immigrants who believe in respecting the law, hard work, family values, and enterprise. The British benevolence has been paid back manifold by the immigrants not only in terms of monetary gains but a Beacon of Hope, an example of what can get achieved if humanity works together in social harmony.

Britain has always been a model of tolerance for most, including immigrants, a freedom that people should not take for granted. Although at the same time, many white and non-white people have deep concerns about the seemingly reckless pace immigration has recently been allowed to proceed and needs to be controlled. And feel the country may have already reached a tipping point beyond which it can no longer say to contain a single nation. Should that point be reached, although not true, then, ironically, in its evolution, critics would say Britain has become a nation of immigrants; and ceased to be a nation of one race. However, we cannot turn the clock back and must work with optimism, take advantage of the many benefits of a multicultural society, and look ahead.

I have always believed Britain is a blessed land. I say that because if we look at our multicultural Britain, we will see people virtually of all faiths in the world practised freely on this land. If we think about it, the citing of prayers, reading of scriptures by thousands from Holy books at all times of the day worshipped in Churches, Synagogues, Mosques, Temples, Gurdwaras, and homes; makes Britain the land that is given and protected by God. Its stature is no different, if anything, on par with many Holy places revered in various faiths. Britain is just perfectly made for cultural diversity and religions.

Britain is unique by recognising people of all religions or those of no faith. With all the prayers recited in the places of worship during the troubled times, uncertainties the country was facing during the Covid pandemic, Brexit or other crises, it has always been reassuring to feel optimistic that, as always, Britain will pull through the situation. What is equally crucial is that despite differences or points of view people may have on many issues from marriage, abortion, divorce, we must all obey the law of the land and respect others. Likewise, it is also imperative not to take our religious freedoms or civil rights for granted but continue working towards social cohesion. Since loyalty to the land of domicile, compassion towards fellow humans, regardless of sex, creed, race, or class, are the basic tenets enshrined and preached in all faiths. At the same time, be mindful that the principles of peaceful co-existence, not hatred, are the foundations of every genuine religion since hatred breeds more hate.

It is only appropriate to bestow plaudits upon Britain for playing its longstanding, significant part in allowing all faiths to practice freely without hindrance, which serves as a nucleus in the overall peace of our country. It is sublime to see the splendour of Churches, Mosques, Synagogues, Gurdwaras, Temples in our midst become part of the most prominent centres of worship for communities. An outstanding achievement that every respective member of the various faiths can take immense pride in. I never tire of admiring the enterprise, self-reliance, unity, and civic duty that are the cardinal values of all religions that would serve the country's greater well-being well if harnessed further. Such as bridging West to East, East to West, with love, culture, tradition, work ethics, family values, knowledge, and wisdom.

Perhaps, thinking of the common good is the right way to end what I regard as a particular moment of Hope, to steer humanity away from religious and political extremism, not inflicting unnecessary hardship and suffering on each other. I have always said, and firmly believe, no lasting harm will come to Britain because of the prayers cited by so many faiths allowed to practice freely. Some are enjoying more rights in this country than in their own country of origin. All the prayers said on this blessed land will protect us from the permanent harmful effects of atrocious acts of inhumanity. That is why I remain undeterred; more importantly, I will continue to persevere in doing my best to get heard with more vigour and effort.

*

Migration has always played a crucial role in the success of pre-and post-colonial Britain. Just like the Windrush generation heeded the call in the 1960s, the directive of the mother nation. Likewise, Indian immigration to Kenya from the sub-continent was also encouraged by Britain during colonial rule, at times enforced because it was in Britain's interest to do so. Many Indian workers died in their thousands building the Uganda Railway from Mombasa on the East African coast to Lake Victoria, known as the Lunatic Line, in the late nineteenth century. Six hundred sixty miles of it through scrubland, malaria-infested swamps, where collateral damage was inevitable. However, it was a price worth paying for Britain, which people paid with their lives in the piercing heat, marauded, killed by man-eating lions. Like slavery and apartheid, these are some of the dark moments from Britain's colonial past best not repeated anywhere again.

The migrants to East Africa worked hard to build a better future for themselves and Britain. They succeeded in doing so by helping each other. During the first weeks or even months after arriving, migrants stayed with relatives, friends, or in communal houses, if they had none. These informally organised communal houses were often the business premises of an Asian trader, who had already become established in East Africa. It was because many migrant families did not forget what it had been like for themselves when they arrived pennilessly. There were many instances whereby some Asians had lost everything, yet with the help of others, they became successful businessmen and engaged in philanthropy helping others.

Religion, culture, family heritage are essential sources for personal development, whereas performing charitable acts for the less fortunate meant a lot for those pioneering souls. Something we can all learn from because humanity as a whole needs each other, not only when in need but also in times of plenty. Hence, further reflecting humans have the same fundamental shared values; the same overall objectives to provide a better future for their children to lead a prosperous life than the previous generation. In a way, no different to conservative (Tory), socialist (Labour) and liberalism (Lib Dem) ideologies all put together. Whereas, the only irony being these values are categorised (segregated) as tribalistic political parties in the West by politicians who think they know better by dividing people with an US and THEM attitude!

However, what those pioneers to East Africa believed in most was humanity. Most importantly, not to forget what it felt like to be on the receiving end of hardships and inhumanity. If we look closely, such values have been practised universally to varying extents since the beginning of humanity in one form or another. In the process, the past migration from the Western shores of the sub-continent to the East African shores achieved acts of liberalism, conservatism, socialism, reformism, and traditionalism. These shared values are universal, and if people are allowed to practice freely, they can control their destiny, own well-being. While the role of the government should be to make it possible, alleviate obstacles so individuals can realise their dreams, aspirations.

What is more noticeable is that to the people practising these shared values, it felt normal. Values passed down through generations, which raises an important question. How did they learn to practice liberal, socialist, conservative ideologies, usually associated with Europe? They had not attended schools or universities nor visited the West. How did they learn to practice such doctrines? It shows that humans share similar survival instincts, beliefs, work ethics to leave a better legacy for their families to succeed if they are allowed to do so in a safe, not conflict-ridden environment.

Various Asian business communities built, funded places for religious worship, schools, hospitals, sports and other amenities. Most Asian migrants, including Africans, depended on the goodwill of wealthy migrant families. Everyone needs each other and caring for children, spouses, immediate family is a basic human instinct. The first step in philanthropy is to go beyond the boundaries of close family, loved ones. It means surpassing the extended family or one's self-defined community. The second requirement is acceptance of a certain degree of self-sacrifice, not to expect anything in return for the charitable contributions or voluntary work one has given, not even respect or social prestige. The final step is to allow all communities, races, or nationalities to access the charity, which amounts to humanism in its purest form.

On the surface, it may appear South Asian families play no vital role in political developments or socio-economic changes since it usually doesn't get well documented. However, on closer examination of various aspects of African history, newspaper accounts show that this is not entirely true. South Asian families, like my family and others, have played crucial roles not only in the economic development of East Africa but also in the political role in the independence movement, post-independence progress, welfare of their workers and the general well-being of the local community. In short, South Asians, just like my ancestors, have played essential roles in loosening racial, religious boundaries in East Africa. They served the colonial officials and the people of Tanzania. In the end, from the small seaport of Morbi in Gujarat in India, they ultimately became 'world citizens', well before the term multicultural Britain was even invented or heard.

The pioneers arriving at the shores of East Africa arrived with an enterprising attitude, hard work with the minds of a prototypical businessman to pursue wealth to improve life, not only for themselves but also for others. What it shows, without doubt, we humans are ready to face life's challenges, tragedies, make sacrifices, and if given a degree of chance, we can all achieve something in life. It's a testament to the tenacity that the migrants of Western Gujarat managed a peaceful, prosperous existence in East Africa for more than one-hundred-and-fifty years without firing a single shot or bloodshed. I feel privileged, fortunate to be part of a history of those shared values, multiculturalism, social cohesion, a racial co-existence, well before such concepts became acceptable in the West.

*

Sadly, the British multicultural society has been exploited cruelly by the political and religious leaders over the years. However, I remain very optimistic for my adopted country because whichever political party is in charge, the resolute British commonsense, in the end, seems to prevail. Fortunately, in the UK, we are also blessed with a healthy democratic process, the Mother of all Parliaments. Equally, the resolute British values always allow us to overcome natural or abhorrent difficulties. Like it helped us rise when people stood together during two world wars to fight the rise of fascism and recently during the Covid-19 pandemic when people from all walks of life, race, and faith came together.

Therefore, politicians need to stop playing dirty politics. We need to focus more on how Britain and the British Empire, forged from different strands, was indeed an immigrant Empire of nations, and through that, had found the strength to rule nearly one-third of the world. It should serve to remind those with racist ideologies of the crucial role of the coloured immigrants, then and even now. Also, remind them further that Britain has been a land of immigrants since the Romans in 55B.C.; followed by Huguenots fleeing persecutions in 1719; Irish families in the 1840s forced to leave Ireland during the potato famine, Jewish refugees escaping fascism in the nineteenth century. Likewise, there is nothing to fear from the post-war new migrants from the Commonwealth who may not be white and, most recently, those from Eastern Europe. Of course, there is no doubt some underlying problems from the past that have got ignored need to be tackled, though these are not existential threats, not impossible if anything solvable with the proper political will.

Let's be honest. The shortages in hospital beds, schools, housing, employment, increasing national debt are not the fault of immigrants but down to wrong policy decisions made by unaccountable politicians. It's also true Britain has always relied upon migrant workers. Therefore only advantages to be had if we manage migration in a 'civilised' manner because Britain has always faced a shortage in the skilled labour force. That is why the Home Office offers work permits for people to fill labour shortages. Those with work permits then get their visas extended due to the continuing lack of professional labour Britain faces. Then tempted by the immigration rules that encourage skilled people in the first place to come, migrant workers like me and many others obtain British residency to make Britain their home. Otherwise, these people would have no incentive to wind up one house, set up a new home for a short period, only to pack again. Let's be realistic. Many who migrate do so for a better future, often risking their lives and those of their loved ones. And after years of investing in building a home for themselves, it will not be that easy to go back for those who came to Britain. And go where? Other than staying in Britain, the country they had helped rebuild. Also, this time can't expect them to pack their worldly possession in one suitcase or a rucksack like they had done when they first arrived.

For the past five decades, a highly polarised, fiercely argued, still by no means concluded debate has been taking place by politicians, especially during elections and referendums, about how damaging immigration has been on public services. Quite often, sentiments reach a fever pitch during the debate on immigration. Though what the politicians fail to tell during elections, referendums, in hate speeches is what an economist would say about the economic benefits of immigration. That immigration is, in aggregate, an economic necessity, beneficial for countries like Britain with an ageing population. At the same time, immigrants, to some extent, tend to pay taxes at a higher rate than they use benefits or public services, work for low wages with greater productivity – which helps to pay for our public services, retirement pensions for all our elderly. Similarly, many successful immigrant business owners, managers in British today who have arrived and settled here provide employment. In 2014, there were 8.3 million people in Britain employed in businesses started by immigrant entrepreneurs.[1]

Instead of scaremongering, right-wing politicians, groups and newspapers should engage in an honest debate based on factual evidence. Like many before, they use the sensitive subject of immigration as cheap fodder for self-serving interests to cast doubt by asking: "What have migrants ever done for Britain?" The answer, according to them, is precisely nothing, that they represent a net drain on the economy, claim benefits, abuse public services, steal, generally loaf around in parks. It can be nothing further from the truth. It does not accord with commonsense or experience because immigrants came to Britain long before the modern version of the welfare state existed. So not all immigrants could have sponged, lived on benefits other than toil hard to earn a living. Also, anyone who has used a minicab, visited a hospital or called a plumber or gone to retail food outlets will most likely have found themselves in the company of a hard-working individual. Someone who has travelled halfway around the world to make a better life for himself and his family. Therefore, it is dishonourable for politicians, including the media, to construe facts to create social hatred for personal gains.

We have reached a moment in the national discourse whereby the time has come to ask. What have been the benefits of immigration for Britain? What have immigrants not done for Britain? Because the most severe critics of immigrants are only happy to spread obnoxious lies, not speak the truth about the immense economic, cultural contribution made by the immigrants and their descendants who have settled over the years in Britain. If only the followers of those critics of migrants would take the trouble to find out for themselves, they would soon learn beyond any doubt that without immigrants, Britain would lack much that makes the country it's today. Britain owes so much of what forms an inextricable part of the cultural landscape to the immigrants. It's hard to imagine how Britain might have been today if it had not received any immigration since Norman times.

Indeed, much of what we believe is quintessentially British is down to the contribution of the immigrants. It's an endless list: From Punch and Judy to Madame Tussaud's, from Selfridges to Marks and Spencer, from Handel's 'Water Music' to the poetry of John Betjeman, from the classic 1959 to Thunderbirds, from the arts Orbit sculpture of Anish Kapoor at the Olympic Park to the director Steve McQueen of the 2014 Best Picture Oscar, from curry, Cobra beer to the Great British Bake-Off the most popular TV programme won by Nadiya Hussain in 2015 who baked *sari* decorated cake followed by the honour to make one for the 90th birthday of HM The Queen, from the wealth of world-class football players, athletes to the knighted Somali refugee Sir Mo Farah, from the NHS staff comprising even today from many different backgrounds. Whilst not forgetting the Black nurses invited by the then Minister of Health Enoch Powell between 1960-1962 from the Caribbean to come to Britain to heal and care. One abiding legacy we can thank Enoch Powel for, sometimes forgotten by the right-wing groups and press. Lastly, The House of Windsor, the embodiment of the British nation rebranded by George V during the First World War, is a multicultural reality with German, French, Dutch, Danish and Greek influence. A never-ending list of immigrant contributions to life in multicultural Britain.

Having said that, it remains the case that, until only very recently; even at present, although the numbers have increased, the immigrant population, including their descendants, only ever comprised a relatively small proportion of Britain's total population. In order to flourish in white-dominated Britain, many immigrants and their descendants have had no real alternative but to successfully adopt over the years its customs, manners, their dress, language in countless other ways but at the same not abandon whatever distinctive, compatible to their own culture; values and practices that they or their ancestors brought with them to Britain to help lead everyday lives. And precisely because of that accommodation made by the immigrants to Britain has achieved with their host population, the country has enjoyed an enviable record of social harmony combined with a large ethnic and cultural plurality in multicultural Britain. To say this is not to deny, ignore tensions, conflicts or unconscious bias that have flared up from time to time which has soured relations between communities. Because of which regrettably, that relatively high level of social harmony is now under severe risk due to the recent creation of varieties of populist politics of nationalism that threaten to unravel the social fabric, disunite the country into a set of contending racial-cultural separation and communities.

Therefore, we must not fall under the illusion that resentment towards immigrants, especially those of non-white type, does not exist or pursue an open-door immigration policy. Hence tackling illegal immigration should be of utmost priority. That means managed immigration. In fact, the only uncontrolled immigration has been from the European Union, and they are not non-white in the slightest. After Brexit, one hopes it gets sorted; otherwise, I wonder who the right-wing Tory rebels will find next to blame! If truth be told, we can see that some draconian immigration rules have specifically targeted non-white people over the decades. How can we forget the Windrush saga and "Go-Home" van posters?  Likewise, we are putting significant obstacles to prevent or apprehend refugees using all necessary means, legal or illegal, to send them back by tightening immigration laws. Therefore, it is dishonourable for politicians who prefer addressing one another as honourable members willing to sacrifice high standards in government for short-term political benefit by peddling biased misinformation about levels of non-white immigration.

So, immigration should not be an issue about race anymore. But some still do conflate it for a reason. We need to call out divisive politics that encourages racism, discrimination, social tensions. Also, it's essential to tackle real-life concerns of many white and non-white groups of people left floating, malnourished, at the back of the UK's economic queue who feel their problems have compounded because no one speaks for them. And when they do, no one listens until a disaster happens, followed by more suffering, more public inquiries. Only to be forgotten until the next time when repeated elsewhere.

There are two kinds of people in the world, those who leave home and those who don't. Unlike other immigrants in the 1970s or before, who left homelands with dreams of a better life following stories they had heard from relatives, friends or watching films that the streets of Britain's are paved with gold for those prepared to work hard, mine was different, not planned, different in a sense. It happened in pursuit of better education. Just pure fate, Britain is what I now proudly call my home. Ask any British citizen like me and many others with an immigrant background, which is the best country in the world to live in. Without hesitation will say Britain is the best country in the world to live, work and study. There is, of course, always room for improvement, and as long as we recognise these lacunae in our society and communities, as long as if we are prepared to address them, then all will be well.

# 3.

# BEST OF BOTH WORLDS

While growing up in Tanga, it was natural to form close friendships with people of various backgrounds. We mingled freely to study, talk, play, attend parties as equals, with no inclination; we belonged to a different race, creed or class. This black, white, brown thing based on skin colour was entirely outside my personal experience. I was not aware of derogatory, racist names for the Black and brown people until I came to the UK.

I was born in 1951 in Tanga, Tanganyika, an ex-British colony. Hence, I grew up under colonial rule for most of that decade as a British subject and the next decade after independence in 1961 as a Tanzanian citizen. Events were bringing a change in Europe, Africa and all corners of the World after WWII. Historians regard the twentieth century as the most explosive in the history of humanity because, for the first time, the entire population of the world was affected directly or indirectly by two world wars, one after another, changing the face of civilisation. The West would never be the same again, neither would be the Third World countries.

Soon after the colonial empire dissolved, the world got engaged in a storm of rage, confusion, uprisings. For Europe, practically centuries of supremacy and complacency came to an end. Suddenly alone, the Third World countries found it equally hard to embrace, manage alien ideologies of democracy and Western concepts. The world could no longer be regarded as one single idea, one correct colonial standard, while other differences, just mere native discrepancies of no relevance.

Like most towns, Tanga also has a fascinating history. It was famous for the sisal plant that went around the world because of its maritime use, where Germany and Britain fought – 'The Battle of Tanga' in WWI. With a population of 70,000, Tanga was then the second largest town in Tanzania, with a multi-ethnic polyglot community of Africans, Arabs, Indians, and Europeans. The Africans formed the majority, followed by Arabs, mostly of Omani origin. Indians, the third-largest, comprised of various sects from the Indian sub-continent. The last group was the Europeans, primarily the British, followed by Portuguese, Greeks, Germans, Italians, American peace corps. They all went about their daily lives in their close-knit white communities as colonial masters with special privileges.

The prevailing colonial political, socio-economic environment meant that the Africans, Arabs, Indians and Europeans led segregated lives in designated areas with separate residential areas, schools, sports centres, and other amenities. Before 1951, there were two primary schools. The Germans built the Tanga School in 1895, not necessarily driven by an ideology to educate the local tribes. But more to satisfy their needs as a colonial power to communicate with the local people (Africans) to exploit their land's natural resources. With its safe harbour and proximity to the Usambara Mountains, Tanga was ideal agricultural land with great potential for planting cash crops, such as coffee, tea sisal, etc. Catholic Missionaries ran the Tanga school for Christians of African and Indian origin. A second school was built in the 1940s by the philanthropic Karimjee Jivanjee, an Asian family, with the central intake of Indians from all sects, few Arab and African children.

In the 1950s, the Ismaili community and the philanthropic Taibali Sachak family built primary schools, which I attended from 1956 to 1963 for children from their respective religious sects. If I recollect, the annual intake was about thirty to forty children attending each school. These two schools allowed the second school to increase its in-take for African and Arab pupils. Later, the same Karimjee Jivanjee family built the first secondary school in Tanga for non-Europeans, with an annual mixed intake of about two hundred from all communities and races.

The only contact I had with the Europeans was at school. Mr Cook taught geography, while Ms Gardner, a temporary teacher for six months, taught English before "O" level exams in 1967. The rest of the teachers, less than fifteen, were Indians, with one African teacher for Swahili, later another for physics. They were all great teachers. I can still name many of them. Apart from teachers, the only contact with other white people was distance-based or during cricket matches when asked to play against or in their team, when short of fixtures or players. Mr Hornsby, our headmaster, was also British, a strict disciplinarian, not impartial to using the cane. I was at the receiving end on a few occasions. Not for academic reasons, but dress code and misbehaving outside school hours when riding a bicycle on the right-hand side of the road instead of the left. As I found out later, that side was for pedestrians and horse riders to see oncoming traffic. A lesson I never forgot! However, one never publicised such incidents. I would not have dreamt of telling my mother. Even if I had complained, she would have said that I must have deserved it for misbehaving and if I misbehaved at home will inform the teacher to punish me. A no-win situation, so best to keep such matters private.

After independence in 1961, the top priority for the Tanzanian government, under President Julius Nyerere, was to provide free primary education, irrespective of race, class, creed. He was an eminent graduate of Edinburgh University, a teacher himself, referred by Tanzanians as Mwalimu (teacher in Swahili). The newly independent Tanzania had very few schools, teachers and insufficient resources to educate everyone. However, the president developed a platform for all Tanzanians to receive primary education by building more schools in bigger towns and villages, dramatically increasing African pupils' intake.

The atmosphere amongst Tanga residents was that of broad-mindedness based on conversational education, not one of harbouring prejudices, driven by national or international politics because historically, this is what divides human beings. No one questioned differences based on race, creed, class and made the best use of the prevailing situation, giving opportunities to one another. We were also always taught a clear moral message at home that we must respect our elders, teachers, property, and others to live peacefully in a society. We were reminded constantly of the difference between right and wrong. Then endeavour to do the right thing. Discipline and respect came naturally. I can say it has done no harm, has served me well. How simple, reassuring it was to know that a clear line existed between good and evil, which side I should choose. I have often wondered that as grown-ups since: we are brought up to recognise good from bad; how to behave in a way that demonstrates such 'civilised' virtues, likewise carry out parental duties so our children do the same; then why is it difficult to adhere to these values? Is it because simple values are getting compromised for self-serving interests by those in authority?

Growing up in Tanga in the 1950s,1960s invokes memories. Tanganyika changed its name to Tanzania in 1964 when it formed a union following a military coup in Zanzibar. I did not attend nursery school; it was not common them days except for a few. Yet just like others who did not, it felt no different. I went to primary school when I was five years old. I attended secondary school in 1964 after passing the national territorial exams, completing "O" levels in 1967 with first-grade, "A" levels in 1969, followed by a BSc (Hons) from the University of Dar es Salaam, a PhD in marine biology from the University of Manchester in 1977. We got top-class education in state-funded schools built by philanthropists, making most of the opportunities we got.

My path was therefore laid out automatically due to my academic results. What better gift than that of ignorance? For the rich, learning may be an embellishment, another asset among many others to have. However, for others, it could represent the promise of a different life. I do not know what would have been my fate if I had not succeeded academically. It would be for sure I wouldn't be calling Britain my home if my lecturer Dr Mike Pearson at Dar es Salaam University, had not motivated me in 1973 to consider a PhD at the University of Manchester. And if my research had not been novel, Professor Trueman, my *guru,* would certainly not have offered a job if I had not published my research paper in the prestigious *Nature* journal, equivalent to the *Bible* in the scientific world. Moreover, as a post-doctoral research fellow at Manchester, I wouldn't have published thirty research papers in reputable scientific journals, including a major review published in the "*Advances in Marine Biology.*"

*

Of course, like many immigrants, I have faced the trials and tribulations of discrimination in the world of academia, business, employment. Even subjected to racist name-calling, which still makes me wonder why I was called *Paki*. I used to think I was called *Paki* because people thought I was from Pakistan. So, I used to reason that I am an East African Indian. I even asked my friends what it meant; however, no one has given me a logical explanation to date. I still don't know why? Except I know that all those who look like me is called one. It makes no sense. Most often, I ignore it, wonder what do people gain by being nasty. But then, if it makes them feel great, who am I to deny them their one-second moment of glory, except feel sorry for them what they are missing by not being nice.

But one thing I have learnt for sure since my arrival in 1973 is that being non-white in Britain meant being different. While blatant racist, derogatory name-calling may not be fashionable these days due to legislation to curb conscious bias. Sadly, however, the historical mentality of superiority over others, the unconscious bias based on the colonial past, still lurks amongst people, which gets exploited when it suits them. I am therefore determined to do my best to heal differences to counter racism, discrimination based on colour, creed, class, sex, age.

I believe mutual respect; equal status can be brought about through education, sports and social activities at a community level to enable white and non-white people who may work quite happily together. Yet when they get home, they will probably each go their separate ways, not mix until the next day at work. Understanding is much deeper than knowledge. There are many people we may know, but very few we may understand. Informal get-togethers help foster a better understanding that people - irrespective of their colour and faith - can be clever, trustworthy, capable of achieving anything they want or want to, never too late to do something in life.

Insults are about how you deal with them. About whether you take them personally. About whether you want to be hurt by them or choose not to be. It would be wrong of me to say I don't get affected or offended. Of course, I do; after all, I'm human and have feelings. However, I do not let fury blow my top; I don't allow pain to rule me at the best of times. Instead, I become more focused to do well at whatever job I am supposed to do. So that people will have to define me, others like me in fairer terms, not in the generalised held view that people of colour and Muslims are all the same; lazy, *terrorists*, *Islamists* and *jihadists*. Despite a cultural shock of how people are perceived, I have always believed in pursuing incisively, calmly, the channels of authority to defeat racism. After all, it's a form of injustice. In addition, in a 'civilised' society, such behaviour shouldn't be tolerated. I want to try to put things right for people when the very system meant to protect them fails them. To be a victim of skin colour doesn't seem right.

Luckily, when it comes to discrimination based on race, faith, creed, I have a thick skin since I know who I am and my values. I believe in humanity, do my best to leave a better legacy for our children and grandchildren because Britain is a great country. Accordingly, I would like to play a positive role in a country that has been my home. Britain can be "Great" once again, not with a colonial mentality, repeating the bad mistakes but harnessing the good things from our shared colonial past. I think we can still do that on the grounds Britain, compared to others, has a better record for social harmony than most countries, even those countries, immigrants call their motherland or 'home' country, most don't dare go back to settle.

*

My 1950s,1960s upbringing has played an essential part in my life, forming a ring of Hope, solidity, shared values, and acceptance. The good old days when everything seemed perfect in place. Not a worry in the world. We had what we needed, nothing more. Nothing less. We had motherly love, food, a roof over our heads. A foresighted mother who valued the importance of education, who made sure, unlike them, I was not denied that opportunity. So, all I had to do was graft, pass exams to qualify for the limited places available to further my education. At the same time, those students from wealthy families who failed national entrance exams and didn't secure a place in state-funded schools attended fee-paying private schools or went abroad. However, having an expensive education does not automatically make you clever.

For some reason, I can recall that Tanga primary and secondary school days were full of fond memories not based on nostalgic sentiments but more because of the quality education we gained from top-class teachers. We were young, awkward at times, yet overtly enthusiastic, respectful in everything we did. We were not entirely saints, played occasional mischief fully expecting to be disciplined though never destructive. We fell in love, got hurt by it. The school I attended had the best standards in academia and sports. Not in terms of facilities but no different to the best British grammar or public schools. If anything, it was better because we were encouraged to respect one another from an early age, not brought up with unconscious bias, a snobbish attitude towards others based on race, creed or class. The school had a fantastic record of producing brilliant students. We received education from teachers who took us on a journey of academic enlightenment, moral values that taught us that we wouldn't learn and miss out if you do not respect people.

Looking back, we were lucky. Tanga produced a generation tolerant of others, not taking anything for granted. It was as simple as that. All we cared about was to do our best academically, and if we did just that, the rest took care of itself. We learnt to share at an early age. We didn't have much. What we had, we made the most of it. What we had we shared with others. What we didn't have, we didn't feel deprived or missed it. It helped us appreciate the little things in life. Looking back, I believe it has served me well in all aspects of life, even in my varied vocational career and retirement age. Also, we were not that materialistically oriented as long as we had good textbooks, which the school generously provided. I don't remember having toys, but we did acquire bicycles if we passed specific essential entrance exams. We took part in school activities, belonged to cubs, scouts, played all sorts of sports, swam in the sea, and after finishing homework, off to bed looking forward to the next day.

To progress, all we had to do was work hard, do our best, get good results, be pleased yet not astonished by exam grades because hard work pays. No one had low expectations, the school, teachers, parents, including the student themselves. That way, it made it easier not to think of anyone as inferior or treat others in contempt due to one's poverty, race and creed. It was all down to us to have high, not low, expectations. All that was required was hard work, good behaviour, excellent results, so no one was surprised when we did well, academically, sportswise or otherwise. We didn't get stigmatised or dented by our skin colour that you can only be good at certain things and bad at most. If anyone had low expectations, you just proved them wrong, made them change their attitude about you. It just made us more determined. We had ambition instilled in us, brought up to work hard, not an entitlement to expectations based on privileged upbringing. Therefore, it did not let race, creed or social class hold us back.

Based on my own experience, the Little and Big school days were the least traumatic. It provided quality education for those fortunate ones who had worked hard to secure admission for the limited places. We knew why we were there, and the teachers made sure we realised our full academic potential. We had good friends circle, peer group relationships. It not only helped to socialise but more importantly, such interactions benefited us academically. After independence, the interaction with African pupils increased with the arrival from other schools to study "A" levels at my school. To the extent, when I was in National Service and Dar es Salaam University, I would say 10%, or even less, were Asians. There were no 'in groups' or 'out groups', no winners or losers. Everyone did their best.

Teachers set high expectations for us to follow, and by working hard, we reaped high rewards for all to share, not low ones to the point of oblivion. The school didn't divide children from various backgrounds; we all shared the same facilities. We had role models, markers of status, figures, rules, standards to emulate. We were not cynical yet hopeful, expectant, left school with a positive attitude. We all got along with the job on hand to enhance our academic achievements, which reflected upbringing, respect for one another for what we are. It was not a barrier. Even before independence, my family had a good relationship with Africans. I have to thank my family, teachers, friends for breaking down barriers based on race, class, creed. I am glad both our daughters are no different. They invited friends of all races home and went to theirs. I think this is the way forward for the future, not suspicion and hatred.

*

I remember well arriving at Heathrow airport on a cold September morning in 1973. My first experience travelling on a plane, let alone set foot on foreign land into air twenty degrees colder I was used to, the light greyer, different smells and people. I was not overwhelmed by the strangeness of the place because, deep down, I believed if I were respectful, polite, others would reciprocate. I had never been surrounded by Caucasians before, although that did not intimidate or bother me in any way.

I recall with great fondness the first experiences of the British people at Heathrow airport; they lived up to my expectations, as they were helpful, friendly and courteous. After asking for directions, I took a coach to Victoria Station, then a train to Manchester. Looking out of the coach and train, I could not believe I was in the country from whose education system I had benefited from during the colonial and post-independence era. I arrived at Manchester Piccadilly Station with my green suitcase; it was raining. Manchester lived up to its reputation as a rainy city. I was twenty-two years old, a successful science graduate.

My arrival in Britain wasn't a part of the mass immigration from the West Indies, India or Pakistan. I was not even a part of those who had come to Britain to answer the call from the motherland for bus drivers, NHS workers, skilled labour and manual jobs. I was also not part of the East African Asian exodus. The victims of independence, who as former British subjects were slowly being squeezed out of Kenya in 1964 by President Jomo Kenyatta, the anti-colonial campaigner, to anchor his newly independent country. He called it 'Africanisation'. Kenyan jobs for Kenyans. Whereas, President Idi Amin in Uganda chose a more ruthless anti-Asian business policy by expelling British Asians in 1971 to settle a feud with Britain. At the same time, Tanzania chose an African variety of Socialism called *Ujamaa*. The ensuing political uncertainty led many students from well-to-do Asian families to go abroad, mainly to Britain, to pursue an education. In contrast, those like me and many others left behind had to make the most of the opportunities.

Thanks to my lecturer Dr Mike Pearson, I pursued a different path, which motivated me to consider a PhD degree during my BSc course. On his advice, I wrote to Professor Edwin (Ted) Trueman at Manchester University. It was the only university I wrote to for a place because of my research interests. Also, I had heard of Manchester, connected with a local lichen species (a type of green algae) growing there, which had turned black during the Industrial Revolution due to smog pollution. Sadly I had also heard of Manchester following the tragic loss of lives of the Manchester United Football Team in the Munich air crash.

Education brought me to Britain, the natural route I followed because of what my late mother said I had to do if I wanted to prosper in life. I worked hard and succeeded because of my research findings, which led Ted to apply for a Natural Environmental Research Council grant worth £33,000 to employ me as his post-doctoral research fellow for four years to conduct more scientific investigation. And in the process, I established a working model on the toxicological effects of copper on the whole organism down to the tissue and cellular level by studying marine animals' behavioural, physiological, and biochemical responses to environmental stress.

For forty-eight years, Britain has been my home. I am committed wholeheartedly to this beautiful land. The best place in the world to live despite some problems which I am optimistic will get sorted if we put our hearts and minds. I believe it must have been fate that made me choose Manchester in search of further education because it meant that the UK would become my future home. In a way, it was my destiny, just like it was for my great-grandfather, who had heard about sandalwood from Omani Arabs, so he landed in East Africa in search of it, which became his home and my birthplace.

I am now a proud British who came here to study. So, here I am, paid all my taxes. Apart from teaching, I have contributed to scientific research, was in a retail business, set up a pickle manufacture cottage industry, did manual jobs, made lots of friends from varied backgrounds, served public duty. So, why should people have the audacity to question my loyalty and even contemplate repatriation of people like me and others who have worked hard. Britain is my home and that of my family.

# 4.

# TOP-CLASS EDUCATION

---

Quality education reflects the wealth and health of the individual and the nation. It promotes social cohesion, strong ethical values for the well-being of society at large - an excellent engine for personal development and social mobility.

It is through education that a child from the ghetto can escape poverty: a child from the inner-city can become a teacher, a child of a labourer can become a doctor or a son of parents like mine, who never went to school, can attend university, contest elections in a great nation like Britain. Quality education not only improves career prospects but gives someone opportunity, confidence, opens minds to prevent falling victim to those who preach hatred. In contrast, a lack of education can be a significant barrier.

Not long ago, the British education system led the way, considered top class, the best, the envy of the world. Like many others, I am one of the grateful beneficiaries. Britain's educational excellence powered the Industrial Revolution and colonial rule, including inventions that have benefited many far-flung nations. Regrettably, British children have now been overtaken by these very nations due to a significant drop in academic standards, leaving many youngsters worried about their future.

Education should open doors. Education should be about making effective use of what we have learned at home and in schools for a better future, not about separating one person from another. Likewise, children mustn't become limited by lesser facilities because of their background; their social mobility should not be hindered by what they read, think, or dream of achieving. Indeed, education on its own will not bring success. In addition, what is also needed is hard work, sacrifice, determination. What quality education does is that it allows an individual to apply commonsense - the knack for seeing things as they are, doing things as they ought to be done.

Education apart from improving career prospects should allow an individual to make informed decisions, not fall victim to extreme varieties of religious or populist political indoctrination that preaches division and hatred. Similarly, referring to someone with a university degree as an *educated* person does not mean being *literate*, while somebody without a degree is *illiterate*. Because we often see people with just quality elementary education, or not even attended school, can be *wise* as they often possess a higher *degree* of righteousness and commonsense.

Besides preparing a child for better social mobility, education should also open up their mind to apply logic in their specialised field to understand humanity in all aspects of life. Leaving formal education should not mean you stop learning and *reasoning*. It should not only be about success or failure. Instead, education should equip you to study anything which interests you. Also, just because someone has attended top-class universities doesn't mean they are more educated, enlightened and tolerant of others. It's because education is not the same thing as wisdom. After all, wisdom is the combination of experience and knowledge; therefore, a person needs both to have the ability to think, to act appropriately to make correct decisions. There are some very educated people globally, yet they can lack wisdom, therefore, can be useless, filled with hatred. I hasten to add we see examples of eminent leaders who have had impeccable education; nevertheless, this may not have given them the correct values of righteousness, therefore very capable of inflicting extreme atrocities and pain on others.

Equally, we need to find ways to engage the young and old to participate actively in politics in a unique way to harness both talents. The elderly have the benefit of experience, what worked, what went wrong for them. Whereas, the young are showing interest, vigour in their's and planet's future, which should be encouraged. It would also help alleviate some of the blight of modern society: such as loneliness, mental health, anti-social behaviour, social mobility, social harmony, by bringing awareness through quality education at an early age, with subjects like civic studies in the school curriculum, so they can learn the importance of serving public duty. The main aim should be to give an overview of topical political events at the local, national, international level of social interest that encourage awareness with well-informed discussions to provide better insight into the world's problems. Such an approach would yield impressive results in terms of a well-informed worthy society, not easily swayed by hatred preached by religious and political leaders with a populist agenda, targeting vulnerable audiences for their gain.

Likewise, religious education shouldn't distinguish between spiritual doctrines and current knowledge of the world but, where possible, combine the spiritual, intellectual, physical, and mental capacities simultaneously. We should not abandon the field of religious discourse - what it means to be a good follower of any faith - as a separate entity from contemporary education. Instead, combine both. So while acquiring wisdom, the scholar gains knowledge; experiences nature's handiwork in the Universe, in the world of soul, religion, and humanity to give a holistic outlook in all aspects of life without compartmentalising knowledge.

For human aptitude to flourish, mere principles will be inadequate. To acquire contemporary and spiritual knowledge, we need a disciplined atmosphere, an education curriculum to bring about awareness and mutual respect. The centres of learning and upbringing should allow virtues to develop and blossom, abilities enriched, so that the individual and society as a whole share its fruits. It's equally essential children have a stable home and a learning environment where life and personality first get shaped, followed by success, decency, law and order.

*

Unfortunately, the number of unprecedented educational reforms for close to six decades since the 1960s by successive governments has not helped. Instead of transforming school excellence, we have seen education standards drop, leading to a tolerance of mediocrity. Employers and universities often complain about students scoring lower in maths and science than their foreign peers. It's because governments are only interested in tinkering around the edges at the expense of the child's future. More concerned about performance tables, rather than the quality of education. Only for the next government to change it with the cycle repeated, wasting billions of pounds. It is unbelievable to think how politicians would survive if they squandered their own money in the same way. But then why should they worry? It's not their money or their lives at stake; it's that of the ordinary person!

The trend over the six decades, especially during my life span, has been towards a culture of school's performance league tables and student grades. How can anyone assume on what basis students should fail? Or a school is not performing? If you want to identify blame, it is politicising education with the disgraceful league tables this country operates. Its very nature means that schools try to climb the table every year by pushing outstanding schools down the league. As a result, the bottom school could have a consistent history of being a good school, yet parents will only see its position to decide its crap, putting the school under ridiculous pressure. At the same time, tempt some teachers to act unprofessionally by giving higher predicted grades not to give a bad name that will reflect poorly on the school and their professional duty.

Similarly, during Tony Blair's era, his Education, Education, Education mantra that all children must leave school with a qualification created an illusion, giving false hope. Before that, children who weren't academically minded had gone into an industry to acquire the necessary skills. Until that time, we had not believed that all students should have degrees; also, not many students were interested in studying "O" or "A" levels. Regrettably, successive governments have only been interested in top-down reorganisation in education, including most other public services with an unaccountable management hierarchy. Such reforms result in retiring the top-brass with attractive pensions and financial compensation packages, costing the taxpayers a fortune. Only to return to take similar posts elsewhere or get hired as 'advisers' to the government of the day.

If anything, Blair did the non-academic kids, and the country no favours by insisting they should all leave school with qualifications. There were plenty of vocational qualifications that were more relevant for them to acquire relevant skills, of which there has always been an acute shortage of skilled labour in the country. Instead, despite having university degrees, many students are now finding it extremely hard to find jobs or doing jobs they didn't contemplate doing or enjoy. Lumbered with student loans they can't repay will only end up being written off by future governments to become a part of the ever-growing national debt. Instead, that money could have been invested wisely in acquiring practical skills to help young people get a better job, not struggle to find one.

Similarly, exams have questions that require correct answers. It doesn't matter whether a student is from a poor background or not; a correct answer is a right answer; anything else is a wrong answer. Why should pupils be allowed an upgrade in their exams? If the answers are accurate and marked correctly, they should get a qualification. If wrong, then you need to work harder. Therefore, it is crucial that everyone, whether from rich or poor backgrounds, get top-class education. That way, people will have practical skills and commonsense. Not stuck with blinkered educational upbringing into adulthood, of no use to them in the real world. These days there is far too much pressure put on youngsters for little gain.

Whereas, if every child received the best education with facilities to match from a young age, it would serve them better. It will give a better foundation to gain hands-on experience to get a job in a relevant field. At the same time, those who want to gain further education will also be well equipped to attend university. That way, it will help them learn new skills; switch careers due to changing circumstances. Like it served me when I needed to change from academic to business, even manual employment. The entire education system is outdated, in dire need of a rehaul. In the past, for me and others, education meant learning new things in life to help in whatever vocational career they chose while at the same time help appreciate humanity in the broader context.

Our task then should be to identify where we are going wrong now. It shouldn't be that difficult since we already have evidence of what we did right in the past. Instead of ignoring those practices as *old fashioned,* not fit for the twenty-first century, why not deploy some of the past teaching methods that had the highest impact on student achievement whilst eliminating those current teaching programmes that don't produce results. Most importantly, let teachers spend their time on what they are good at, teach, not occupied filling forms, ticking boxes, generating meaningless data gathering exercises devised on a whim by the government and bureaucrats, only to change by the next one. It is a never-ending cycle of changes, costing more in the end, making it worse without improving the academic attainment levels of the children.

*

What is also needed is not drastic overall changes to the education curriculum. Other than putting in place those tried tested systems that served exceptionally well in the last century. Education curriculum should not be all about pandering to growing calls to make the national curriculum more diverse, making curriculum changes based on a single issue or purpose prevalent on the day. Instead, those responsible should design the curriculum with more emphasis on understanding the basic principles, facts, and concepts, especially in teaching the *three R's,* allowing a child to open up their mind to apply logic to think outside the box. Since not everything, especially commonsense, cannot be taught as a "GCSE" or "A" level subject to equip the child better.

Perhaps revisiting some of the *old* teaching methods will improve our understanding of what is required to rectify the situation for better results. Learning from past experiences will help design courses to give teachers and schools greater flexibility to teach effectively, spend more time on academic excellence, less time consumed preparing performance tables. Teachers know best what and how to teach. They are also often the eyes that spot signs of abuse, the ears that hear stories of neglect and abuse. They need to be allowed to do their professional duty to give a grounded, solid knowledge in maths and science to help develop a logical mind. Prepare the child to understand those subjects to help them in vocational careers they may want to pursue later to give a holistic aspect of society and their environment. So, it does not become a morality tale, get influenced, vulnerable by some quasi-religious or political ideology instead enable them to apply logic. Thus protect the individual from the evils by not easily getting swayed by extreme political and religious views purported by individuals or groups on social media.

What's missing is not money, but quality education, a sense of national urgency to address the shortcomings in teaching reading, arithmetic and writing, the *three R's*. Of course, money is essential, and equally, the government should not deny any child of high educational standards and job prospects. But not by throwing more money, setting performance targets. Instead, revisit some of the past syllabuses, especially maths, to help overcome most present-day students' phobia about logically based subjects. Many teenagers now can't understand fundamental functions, multiplication, division or lack confidence to perform mental arithmetic. Although more students than ever are attending further education, more students are getting top grades in the "GSCE" and "A" levels. Yet only a tiny percentage enrol for science, maths, and engineering degree courses and we need to ask why.

We need to unlock the phobia towards maths at an early stage in primary schools. In that respect, we need to embrace an education curriculum with more comprehensive benefits, especially during the early formative years of a child's education at home and school. If necessary, revive and deploy those effective teaching methods from the 1950s,1960s to teach maths, science and literacy skills. A challenging, rigorous syllabus would overcome maths phobia, serve pupils well to develop thinking based on applying logic in future vocational careers and assist in problem-solving in real life.

*

Another aspect of our higher education system that requires closer examination is the reasons behind the unprecedented success rate of inventiveness, including, the ground-breaking discoveries during the Industrial Revolution. Likewise, revisiting the merits of pure scientific research will give a deeper insight into its vital role in past scientific breakthroughs. It was the direct result of an atmosphere in universities that prevailed at the time, which served scientists' quest for primary research that led to those scientific advances. Regrettably, here too, our higher education policies have been moving in the wrong direction by the twentieth-century born politicians denying others academic opportunities they were beneficiaries of state-funded university education. The truth is that through years of pure research pursued by a scientist in a laboratory, significant discoveries, that *Eureka* moment comes about, even those most seemingly stupid, innocuous ones, have had a direct, measurable effect on technology. From theoretical physics research to astronomy to space exploration to biology to geology to palaeontology.

Every theory, every discovery, every sliver of knowledge that has either impacted our lives directly in a huge way or contributed to a path that eventually ended in something that pushed humanity forward have come from pure scientific research. Years of dedication in a laboratory by a scientist have brought tremendous economic, technological implications at the core of our personal and everyday existence. Research funding for pure research may not have instant commercial benefits yet ultimately can lead to significant scientific breakthroughs. A lack of research funding means scientists need to spend more time filling forms to raise research funds with less time on research. As a result, more promising research avenues get cut off each year, especially the high-risk, innovative research that may ultimately yield immense rewards.

Therefore, it also means that if we want more Einsteins, Newtons, Darwins, Brunels, Attenboroughs, Hawkins, then we need state funding to invest in pure research to unleash the world-class potential of British scientists. A lack of state-funded research has led scientists to seek financing from industries, emphasising applied research to yield a quick return for investors. It has often led to a drop in the quality of research, as seen by an increasing number of public inquiries and a decline in major scientific breakthroughs. Also, scientists are under ever-increasing pressure to publish findings on suspect research data to boost publication output, not quality research, to attract funding to improve their promotion prospects. Thus disincentivising scientists in pursuing risky or long-term investigations, which might necessitate a period of low publication output.

One of the many stark realities of the shortfall in pure research highlighted during the Covid-19 pandemic was the difference in opinions due to the lack of coherent scientific data. It resulted in politicians ending up throwing billions of pounds to bring the pandemic under control, irrespective of whether the research yielded results or gave value for money. Whereas, if allocated to pure research in related fields over the years, a fraction of the amount would have served in good stead. Instead of private companies and scientists exploiting the situation to further their cause pocketing £7,000 consultancy fees for short term unproven research with no guarantee of success.[2] But, why should politicians worry? It's not their money! During the Covid-19 pandemic, political leaders often spoke of the "new normal." We are where we are; let's hope one of the lessons we will learn is not to repeat the same age-old mistakes in all aspects of everyday life affecting ordinary people.

*

Looking back to my 1950s,1960s school days, what's also missing is the *fourth* R. A subject not taught as such, yet played a crucial part for those fortunate to attend school who were the beneficiaries and did well. Especially when their parents never had an opportunity to attend school, most parents, including mine, could not even read or write to help their kids with their three R's homework. It was also an era with no parent and teacher evening meetings to discuss progress. But more importantly, those parents realised the value of education to succeed in life so that their children did not face similar handicaps.

Those parents and teachers need applauding for instilling the *fourth R,* which stood for *reasoning* to apply logic, *responsibility* based on an ethic of hard work, *respect* for elders, teachers and each other. What was most striking, despite not attending school, parents had a sound understanding of arithmetic, proficient enough at performing basic calculations mentally, which served them well to go about their everyday business at work and home. Highlighting that arithmetic is one subject, however fundamental grasp an individual may have of the subject helps them apply reason in their daily life, giving a broader outlook to perceive society. Similarly, the past generations were good at administering logic, as evident from a legacy of inventions and scientific discoveries based on random observations to start with, followed by dedicated research that has stood the test of time.

Most parents show interest, pay attention to what gets taught in their children's schools, but some tend to absolve themselves of all responsibilities. Thus, we need to look from a different perspective, learn from the past by asking the right questions. Such as, How did those children whose parents never went to school manage? Who helped those children with their homework? Why did their children not become radicalised? Why there was less or no blatant/ subtle racial hatred corrupting young minds? Is it something to do with a lack of conversational education at home? Are we missing something?

Maybe it goes much deeper than just throwing more money at schools, changing syllabuses, or setting performance targets, hindering some children. We also need to look at the real-life pressures parents face today; could it be something to do with those pressures? Could it be because parents now have less quality time to spend with their children in their child's early formative years? If so, we need to address this and other aspects of a child's life and the parent's social mobility.

It is no secret that most women play a pivotal role in developing and shaping moral values, particularly giving their love and tenderness, including their unique quality to nurture life within their own body and after birth. A mother's love for their child does not diminish, even when they reach adulthood or have children of their own. In short, a mother's love is true love, unconditional. Mothers make extraordinary sacrifices for their child's education, relinquishing personal comforts for their children at a personal cost. Maybe we need to find ways to realise the full potential of women's roles within society. Something men will find hard to understand or be capable of fulfilling. A child's education – academic or spiritual – is much better served by women. They are ideal for showing good habits to do well in life and fortifying children with a love that could withstand whatever the wider society might throw at them. Likewise, in politics and generally speaking, women usually show greater concerns, empathy relating to human values, environment, upbringing, culture, education, health and seem less ruthless, more accommodating than men since they think more about what's good for humanity.

Despite the tremendous progress made in the last century in many areas to uphold peace and human rights, we need to ask why there is still so much discord despite the lessons learnt from the two world wars. We need to focus more on education, discipline, mutual respect from which flows everything - prosperity, respect, law and order. If we let troublemakers in classrooms become diligent students, our whole society and educational system benefits, including the pupils and their classmates. In many ways, the disorder in society is often the result of what the younger generation learn, perceive as right and wrong, set by their role models at home and those in public life. Likewise, the blame lies not entirely with the children but with the adults who guide them in their early and later formative years.

# 5.

# WHAT IS BRITISHNESS?

Britishness is the spirit of the Commonwealth, a unique bond of men, women, children of different creeds, races, skills and aspirations. An illustration of the binding force based on shared colonial history that brought us together.

Britishness is about how well the immigrant minority can successfully become an integral part of Britain despite different traditions and beliefs from the host community. An incredible legacy to leave behind for the twenty-first century, an opportunity that should not be missed or taken for granted but strengthened for a better future.

In all honesty, it isn't easy to define what we mean by Britishness. To think it is easy is being naïve. It isn't easy because of Britain's colonial shared history with other countries. It is made even harder to define when the debate on immigration constantly gets used as a political football by politicians during the election and referendum campaigns when they blame immigrants for their policy failures and the resultant shortages in public services. It also depends on who you ask, when you ask, who is asking, and why it needs asking?

Now, if you ask someone like me who was not born in Britain, who spent the first ten years of his life in a British colony, followed by twelve years in a post-colonial country and forty-eight years in Britain, now retired, Britishness has a different meaning. Whereas someone born during the dark periods in Britain's colonial rule at the time of slavery, apartheid, famine, partitioning, conflicts, massacres, Britishness will mean different. Forget going that far back. Britishness will mean different to the twenty-first-century victims of Windrush, Grenfell fire or other injustices. Whereas, if you ask Black or brown politicians, athletes, football and cricket players proud to be selected to represent England, Britishness means getting called racist names, hearing monkey noises on the field and putting up with racial abuse on social media.

At its simplest, being British is a legal status of citizenship, conferred by birth or registration after completing residence criteria and a test. In a sense, Britishness is defined, with emphasis on a set of conditions that allow the acquisition of British citizenship, which can even get revoked at the discretion of the Home Secretary. Or, in the case of the Windrush generation, after sixty years of nation rebuilding, paying taxes, setting up home in Britain, their Britishness can no longer matter. And through no fault of theirs, they can even get deported for not being issued with the proper documents thanks to the hostile Home Office environment created by the then Home Secretary, Teressa May. Who later got rewarded by becoming party leader and the prime minister.

Such behaviour doesn't inspire confidence after prime ministers from both sides over the years, especially in the last decade, have been at pains to urge what Britishness means by putting in place explicit policies instituting conditionality to invoke a sense of national unity. For example, as Sajid Javid said on becoming Home Secretary in 2018 following the Windrush scandal that British citizenship is "about signing up to those British values (of democracy; the rule of law; individual liberty; mutual respect for and tolerance of those with different faiths and beliefs) that we share and live by together. It's about integration, not segregation." But the politicians then have the audacity to renege, leave the victims of their policy failures stranded, at the mercy of expensive lawsuits! Over the years, due to double standards on their part, Britain has always found it hard to have a mature debate on Britishness.

Yet Britishness should be more about our shared Commonwealth history, not what politicians want; after all, they are here today gone tomorrow while the victims have to pay for their misjudgements and lies. Bearing in mind, we are where we are, thanks to their policy failures. Equally, we cannot turn the clock back on Britain's colonial past. Nor can we repatriate non-white immigrants, their children born in Britain, by displaying government-sponsored "Go Home" posters on vans costing the taxpayer or directing racist chants at them on the streets. Also, say if it is possible to send them back 'Home', whatever is meant by 'Home' where would we send them back after all these years? For some, that "Go Home" narrative may be applicable. For others, not that much, because their country of birth is for visiting purposes. Not their 'Home' and glad to return 'Back Home' to Britain just like any white British feels who go on foreign holidays. While, for many others, "Go Home" is not applicable since Britain is their 'Only Home' by being born here in the UK. So, for them, what is 'Home' is the first sticking point in the debate on Britishness.

To make sense of the first sticking point, we need to recognise the second sticking point. We need to understand why the Britishness of those British citizens, especially of Black and Asian origin, is always under question and close scrutiny? We need to find out how offended and segregated they must feel by this. We need to hear their side by actually asking them to take part in the debate on Britishness. Something we ought to do with greater urgency to make sense about what we mean by Britishness. And not just listen to the right-wing politicians or media who always jump on the bandwagon keen to incite hatred to get elected or sell newspapers by questioning the loyalty of others. Instead, before asking others, ask themselves how they have served Britain other than sitting in comfort in their ivory towers?

Whereas, if you ask any Black or Asian British citizen, and they will say Britishness to them means more than just the privilege of being white:

*For them, Britishness was about being invited to the shores of Britain to help rebuild after WWII. For others, Britishness was to help build the British Empire, maintain railways, including other infrastructures during the colonial rule for mutual benefits; however, racially biased it may have turned out to be after completion with separate carriages and amenities, etcetera. For many others, Britishness was fighting side by side in the two World Wars and other conflicts to uphold British values. For students, Britishness was choosing Britain as the first place of choice for further education. Most of all, Britishness to everyone meant what they were used to when their 'Home' was a British colony. For them, it meant belonging to the Commonwealth; even today, after all the mistakes, horrors of past colonial history, they still feel a deep sense of awareness of the bonds that unite, bringing the young and old together.*

Whereas, if you ask any Black or Asian British citizen in the twenty-first century multicultural Britain, they will say:

*For them, Britishness is also about being proud of the royal family, public institutions, beautiful parks, lush countryside, seaside holidays together with other cultural references. For many, Britishness is about making an economic contribution, creating jobs. For others, Britishness is about NHS doctors, surgeons, nurses, pharmacists, teachers and other public sector workers. For many others, Britishness is about not shirking from duty during the Covid-19 pandemic. For the rest, Britishness means athletics, cricket, football, fish and chips, chicken tikka masala, British humour, music, plus much more.*

*For the remainder, Britishness means outpouring emotions, coming together during royal weddings, royal births, HM Queen's Silver and Golden jubilees, London 2012 Olympics,1966 World Cup victory and other momentous occasions. An endless list of what Britishnesses means to them that identifies them.*

Despite all their contributions, these non-white British citizens can't understand why they still get targeted by racist "Go Home" posters or racial hatred? Despite feeling as British as they come, they can't understand: why someone can still get treated like an alien in their own country, they call 'Home', leaving them somewhat upset, stigmatised, stranded and exhausted. That they still have to challenge the inclusiveness of society at all times. That even now, they have to prove their loyalty. When, in their hearts exists a profound awareness of the sanctity, dignity, desires, regardless of race or religion. Hoping, if only those doubters would look beyond the framework of race, below the surface, they will find that Britishness does exist in these communities and a desire to live in peaceful existence in social harmony. But at times, it seems no one cares about their Britishness or listening to them what it feels when questioned all the time about their loyalty.

Is it any wonder sometimes there is an outpouring of outrage on the streets like the 1981 Brixton riots, 2011 London riots and recently the 2020 Black Lives Matter protests not only in Britain but worldwide? However, I have always believed there would be no need for civil unrest if politicians - within reason – focused on people's real-life concerns instead of self-serving egos and party interests. Equally, protests should be peaceful, not an excuse for destroying and looting property, costing the taxpayers like them and others. Similarly, gestures of taking the knee during sports venues, banning Nazi salutes made by right-wing groups or pulling statues of slave traders will not solve racism. Other than attracting more hostility, it will not draw righteous political attention or public support to tackle racism by doing something different.

What is worth bearing in mind if making gestures works? Then why since the 1968 Olympics protest by Black athletes' racial discrimination or apartheid, ethnic cleansing still exists! Because making symbolic gestures will not solve racism, bigotry, knife crime, poverty, or structural inequalities, but society, councils, and governments can. Besides, it also depends on what our interpretation of racism is. Though, it will not get addressed by focusing the debate on whether to make gestures, pull down statues because it suits culprits inciting racial hatred. Since it works in the interest of those responsible, helping them divert attention away from the problem of knife crime, jobs, housing, and education affecting young Black kids. Making gestures has passed its sale by date, has not worked in the past, so why will it work now. As discussed later, we have to consider new novel approaches to tackle the old problem of racism.

Correspondingly, we will not solve racism if we think by giving a few token Blacks or Asian people places allowing them to rise into the upper echelons of society while neglecting 90 per cent of people are under-represented. Making election pledges, chanting slogans, or token promotions doesn't help understand how complex racism is, and solutions are even more complicated. If anything, it only gets exploited by the 'establishment' to deflect policy failures and structural inequality, not only for non-white but also white working-class people from disadvantaged backgrounds. Gestures ( civil protests), in other words, show us the world as it is, yet it does little to make the world the place we want it to be. Gestures do not represent progress for the public other than highlight signs of heinous policy and moral failures. The proper way to honour pledges to tackle racism or injustices should not be about making gestures instead having a mature political debate that wouldn't require making them.

Protests should not be divisive but inclusive for white and non-white disadvantaged people living in the slum estates under deplorable conditions. It should be about preventing the sick or the disabled from being treated as second-class citizens. In doing so, the spotlight will be on the *voiceless* to say it's time for a meaningful change. To help recognise that certain sections of our society feel that the democratic system works against them. Therefore we all have a responsibility to fix it. Otherwise, it's only going to serve the purpose of those right-wing politicians and media hell-bent on stoking further division based on race who want their opinion to prevail. Integration should be a two-way street, not a betrayal of trust. There should be zero tolerance towards racism, rapists, child abuse, poverty, with no ifs and no buts or empty words. And if we are serious, it can be tackled through education, including tackling structural inequalities. Also, differences should be heard, settled in a more 'civilised' manner. Not by ignoring but by listening, for there is a limit to how much people can tolerate. Just like there is a limit to how much pressure can be applied to a bottle before it explodes!

*

Britishness should not be about people against people. It should be more about people working together. Ironically, there are essential differences in the ways UK passport holders relate to and identify with Britishness. A study in 2005 found that all the participants knew they were British citizens. Though only non-white people are more likely to describe themselves as British. Besides, unlike in England, non-white people living in Ireland, Scotland and Wales, identify themselves more strongly with those countries than Britain. While those living or even if born in England feel comfortable identifying themselves as British due to the reluctance of the white English to accept them as fellow English people. Whereas the white UK passport holders are more likely to identify themselves as English, Irish, Scottish and Welsh.[3]

What emerges from the study is that people think about Britishness in different ways. For some, British people included all British citizens (that is, UK passport holders), regardless of region or ethnicity; for others, the British exclusively means the white English people; and their mentality criticised by white Irish, Scottish and Welsh people. Because to them, Britishness should include British people of every diverse ethnic origin. Therefore, the challenge for the future should be to keep it simple with one identity of Britishness for everyone. Or recognise English identity for the increasing sections of the white English population making claims to multiple and diverse origins, which will be even more complex to relate to and more divisive.

However, it's debatable if it will serve any useful purpose. Other than what such definitions will ultimately tell us about is what links - or separates - people? While the law defines the rights and limits of citizenships, it attempts to define its core values by setting up citizenship as a club with rules though the membership card checked or disputed more often for some than for others. Perhaps instead, we need to focus more on shared values interconnecting those living alongside each other, whether 'British' or not. Attempting to teach Britishness or British values in schools also ignores the reality that children learn about the diversity and complexity of society, including what it means to be British through their *experience* in school. Children are becoming British anyway. What constitutes being British is a 'flexible menu', whereas pinning it down to core elements results in a level of generality that is not very informative yet more divisive.

Britishness should be more about recognising the embodiment of what binds the white and non-white British people from the colonial days - not about distinguishing dominance based on race - to form the foundation to enhance unity and identity. Our very Britishness shouldn't stop us from talking about our very Britishness. It should be an inclusive dialogue intrinsically tied with nationhood, multicultural Britain, social cohesion about uniting people, as well as communities. Nationalism is about flag-waving, fear and division, whereas we can have national pride, namely Britishness, without the populist politics of nationalism.

How can we ever forget April 1968? When Dr Martin Luther King got murdered on 4 April, after his famous March 1963 "I Have a Dream" speech for uniting people. Only to be followed sixteen days later when Enoch Powell delivered his divisive speech on 20 April in Birmingham, some 4,112 miles from Atlanta, Georgia, dubbed the "Rivers of Blood" speech. Without going deeper into the motives or political semantics, the two speeches are a universe apart, both in terms of distance and content-wise. One speaker was trying to unite people of all races, faith and creed. While the other doing his utmost to do the opposite with subtle undertones to incite racial hatred for his self-serving interests to increase his waning election majority by using his command of the English language, oratory skills to arouse the emotions of the faithful. And not surprisingly, in 1970, Mr Powell succeeded in increasing his majority to nearly 15,000 two years after his "Rivers of Blood" speech.[4] In contrast, Dr King got assassinated after giving his speech.

In a way, the two events have defined an era of hostility towards people of different races, faith and class. In America, the fighter for emancipation got gunned down, creating shock around the world. While in Britain, the use of enchantment of oratory skills to articulate a calculated political argument against substantial, non-white people immigration became more fashionable. Articulation of apparent anger. That has waxed and waned but has never found peace as such and never wholly disappeared.

Ever since Enoch Powell's speech, it has become legitimate to direct hostility during election campaigns towards non-white immigrants, their UK born children and grandchildren, even becoming acceptable for the so-called 'journalists' to call them "hordes" or "cockroaches." Along with becoming acceptable for racism to raise its ugly head by any Tom, Dick and Harry reincarnations, including the variants of UK's fractious far right-wing groups and press. Even allowing mainstream political parties and tabloid press to exploit racism for self-serving egos during election campaigns, Brexit debate, or the 'send them home' brigade who believe Britain 'should remain a white country'. At the same time, some have the cheek to say that they are not racist since they know many non-white people. While conveniently forgetting that being acquainted with them and living a life of prosecution and persecution like theirs is not the same.

I am also a realist, under no illusion or naïve that racial tensions did not exist before. Of course, they did; however, there were clear boundaries. Not under the pretext of when on the one hand, politicians tell us we are all equal with the same democratic, civil liberties except when it comes to exercising, only to find out the extra hoops one has to jump through. In fact, in some instances, racial tensions are deliberately allowed to exist in Britain and elsewhere. Where we see politicians deploy whatever means to win. They will stop at nothing even if it means encouraging civil unrest by stigmatising ethnic minorities, like in 2018, fifty years after the 1968 speech by Enoch Powell, or even when the world was struggling to cope with a Covid-19 pandemic (about which more later).

Politicians should not forget that these non-white immigrants they despise so much have played a crucial part in Britain's success at home and abroad. Like their white ancestors, theirs also fought side-by-side during two world wars to defend civil liberties, 'free speech', which they take for granted though they are happy to deny others. While conveniently forget to say during the 'immigration debate' that through the ages, non-white immigrants have played a crucial role in rebuilding Britain's economy and infrastructure after WWII. Besides, immigrants even now play a significant part in the NHS, public sector; their contribution to the economy runs into billions. The real question to ask should be how Britain, in a globalised economy, should seize the relentless tide of talent currently sweeping across the world.

Equally, politicians readily forget to mention during the 'immigration debate' that integration between communities is possible if we allow it to happen in a 'civilised' way, albeit not by deploying a divisive approach like theirs. Since multiple loyalties are possible whether you are white or non-white, and one identity - I am British or that – does not necessarily clash with another. Like in my case, part of me is East African Indian and a Muslim. However, I can say without any doubt; it has never affected my loyalty to Britain; if anything, it has strengthened it even more. Britain is now my home; I am a proud British, so are my British born children. I am equally proud of my Asian parenthood, culture and Tanzanian upbringing, which has taught me to treat people as fellow human beings. I also believe that to discard one's cultural identity to fit in with the crowd to appease them that you are one of them is false loyalty. Because by betraying one's birth culture, what guarantee there is I will remain loyal to the new one, except a pretentious one by being a misfit.

Similarly, it makes no difference what so ever, or means nothing whether I support the England football side, East African or Indian cricket squad. I will support East Africa in their cricket fixture against England, England against other teams; after that, no one, as long the match embodies good sportsmanship. So, the only occasion I wouldn't have wanted the England cricket team to win; would be when they played East Africa; however, if I can recall correctly, it has never happened in a major tournament. Now that my childhood love of cricket has since waned, it's more about England but at the same time enjoy watching a good match won by the best team. Whereas, for my English born children and their families, it's England all the way.

However, it raises the question. Why the controversial 'cricket test' coined in 1990 by the Tory politician Norman Tebbit about the perceived lack of loyalty to the England cricket squad among South Asian and Caribbean immigrants as well as their children did, or does, not apply to the English, Scots, Irish or Welsh fans. Does it mean they are not loyal to British society when they support their respective teams? This sort of subtle racial connotations by politicians only drives a wedge amongst people of different races. Why does Britishness not come into the equation when some Scots, Irish, Welsh, might not like the English, let alone not support the English cricket, football, rugby team or in whatever other sporting event including politics and vice versa?

*

Likewise, why does the Britishness, language and culture of non-white Asian migrants from the sub-continent come under greater scrutiny than that of Chinese, Vietnamese, South Koreans or Japanese immigrants? Because just like the non-white people of Black or brown Caribbean, Indian, Pakistan, Bangladeshi and Sri Lankan heritage, they are no different if we examine their loyalty closely in various aspects of their lifestyle within the context of the 'cricket test'. They also live in close-knit extended family groups and do not mix freely. Also, they are less fluent in English which right-wing extremists would not have failed to observe in Chinese take-aways and Chinatown. Similarly, they must have heard of traditional organised-crime groups like the *Triads*, which is no different from *Yardies*. But we don't hear right-wing tabloid press or politicians attacking or questioning their loyalty. Crime is not colour blind; criminals and terrorists commit it, affecting everyone, white and non-white alike.

We also need to ask, as discussed later. Why is it that the Chinese, South Korean or Vietnamese people don't feature - even seem to be affected like non-white people of Black and other Asian origins - or bothered by public debates and public inquiry reports into racism or structural inequalities? Are there some different narratives for them to push than the rest of non-white people? If so, why? This type of discrimination, inequality, prejudice, and stereotyping also needs to be understood why non-white people of Chinese origin are not part of the debate despite leading a life of isolation. It leaves the many others involved in this debate wondering why? Is it because there are different sets of rules? Are such attitudes relating to the Chinese *et al.* perceived as fabricated fiction? Or is it we don't understand Chinese culture, hence do not bother to dig into the unknown due to legal constraints, thus proving more challenging to impose white superiority over the Chinese? Therefore less easy targets for right-wing groups and media to attack. So, best left alone since it is harder to demonise them as the 'other tribe' on racist grounds than Blacks and other Asians!

What is also different and quite rightly so, that right-wing politicians and press do not tarnish the whole of Chinese or those of similar origin that they are all the same. Like they defame when it comes to non-white immigrants and Muslims of Black and brown background. We need to ask why? Is it because China, Japan and South Koreans have more robust economies, therefore more equal than the 'other tribe'? Or is it they are not as dark as the 'other tribe', therefore look more like US than THEM, and best left alone for the time being. Likewise, we also need to understand this sort of discrimination as to why the contributions of white people from Commonwealth countries during the two world wars get more noticed. Only by being fair, open-minded right across the board, what we mean by Britishness will we address racism.

*

What is equally worrying is what happens to the British identity if the Scottish, Welsh, English, and Irish nationalist's clamour for Independence is successful? What would be the identity of the non-white people of immigrant background and their children born in Britain? Those campaigning for the break-up of the UK need to have a grown-up discussion with those who will become collateral damage. We need to address it now, not kick the can down the road. We cannot keep stoking problems for the future because of the short-term, self-serving egos of politicians. It is not that we haven't learnt lessons like what happened to the Windrush generation once they had served the self-serving interests of nation-building after WWII.

Britishness has become more complicated on people's sense of identity post-Brexit. Before Brexit, many in Northern Ireland subscribed to the mixed identity expressed by the great poet John Hewitt, who said he was a Ulsterman also Irish, British and European. Wonder how will Black and Asian people be identified? Brexit has denied many their sense of being Britishness, despite proclamations made by our town crier Nigel Farage that 23 June should be Britain's 'Independence Day' holiday. What did he mean by that? Independence Day for the select white English. It is now back on the political agenda. An unexpected outcome of Brexit will be problematic to avoid. The challenge is not to rewrite history as Brexiteers like Boris Johnson, Nigel Farage, and Tory EU rebels appear keen to focus on their disruptive, polarising campaign to achieve their vision of "Little England." Instead, we should focus on building a fairer, peaceful, prosperous society, where every citizen wakes up with an equal opportunity to flourish. I believe we can achieve much more as the United Kingdom, made up of nations, whereas whether we will be better off outside the EU remains to be seen!

However, we are where we are. So, why not make further gains by learning from past mistakes for the good of the wider society. Not by erecting borders and more obstacles because we know what happens when we create them. We can only move forward. We cannot turn the clock back. I am an optimist who believes we can overcome prejudices if we are prepared to learn, not repeat past mistakes of living in fear and insecurity. Only by speaking to the victims, by listening to those who have experienced injustices, will we realise what it feels like to be on the receiving end of hatred. Those politicians with a populist agenda should not be allowed to exploit the situation with unscrupulous dialogue, dehumanising bonafide immigrants as convenient fodder during election and referendum campaigns to cover up policy failures relating to immigration, NHS, housing, education, employment.

*

A few decades ago, lots of people often changed their names. Grown-ups, children alike felt that their names would sound foreign and funny. Instead, they used short English names to give them a feeling of acceptance, fit in with people they did not know so as not to stand out, and feel humiliated if asked to spell it out. Or have to try to explain what their real first names meant and feel alienated. Also, for that generation of non-white people who fought for similarity was a confidence thing for them. Because the language of being proud of your culture, who you are, where you came from had not yet become part of the everyday talk about race and identity in Britain that was to come later. Glad such cultural consciousness had gone by the time when my children went to school in the 1990s since they did not face hostilities or come home from school asking why they have different names from their peers.

Just how Asians had to suffer mickey-taking about their names was summed up well in the 1998 *Goodness Gracious Me* satire sketch when you turn the tables. In the sketch, Asian actors told Jonathan, a white actor who insists on using his English name, it would affect his promotional chances if no one can pronounce his ridiculously long-winded name. And if he insists on being called by that, he will be singled out as a troublemaker. So, Jonathan, when asked for the last time, comes up with an Indian name Joginder Pal Shivarama Guru Patinus. It was wickedly apt for the creators of this show to turn the tables to project reality faced by Asians, also choose a title so reminiscent of the stereotypical portrayal of Asians that the British media had blighted the older generation for decades. I am glad young people don't think names are 'funny' anymore. Comedians are intelligent individuals; who can cleverly convey real-life experiences to expose hypocrisy.

These are encouraging signs of integration; people can feel proud of their cultural heritage without the fear of intimidation. However, what did get mentioned to my daughters was their colour. When out of the blue, I was asked by my older daughter why she was of a different colour. So obviously, such playground talk did take place. How do you explain a four-year-old? Except, say we all tend to go darker in bright sunshine, whereas those who need sun cream for protection call it a suntan instead of colour.

Also, in 2001, after the 9/11 attack, my younger daughter asked me if it was true Muslims were terrorists. When I asked why she said her history teacher told us in the history lesson. So, it seems young people must hear from grown-ups who get brainwashed by the political discourse of the time (discussed later). How do you explain a young child? Except, explain we are Muslims and not terrorists. However, some terrorists are also Muslims, just like some terrorists are also non-Muslims. And like us, your non-Muslim friends are not terrorists. That doesn't mean all Muslims, just like your non-Muslim friends, are terrorists.

It has been a long journey from those decades of suspicion and hatred to today, 'names' just one minor eddy in that big pool of progress that makes this country what it is. I believe in a few more decades, future generations will wonder what all that fuss over racism was about; why did people not just accept one another as fellow human beings? As I have always said that Britain is the best country in the world. A blessed land. It seems we are gradually overcoming some of the many micro-aggressions which were keenly felt daily in the past. However, we have to work harder to make further gains to leave a better legacy for our children.

*

Realistically, I would feel out of place if I described myself as English as I was not born in England, although it's been my home for forty-eight years. It is also true of other ethnic people. Now my children are born in England. But who knows whether they will ever get accepted as English is a sixty-four-thousand-dollar question? Just like David Lammy was confronted by a white English caller on his LBC radio phone-in show who claimed that he couldn't call himself English despite him being born here because he is not white. Of course, Lammy politely disagreed with the caller without shouting. [5] Because England is a country with cultural and political identity. So "Englishness" is a nationality, not a race. Besides, the English have many different ethnic groups, albeit generally speaking white Scottish, Welsh or Irish ancestry, who consider themselves English and British. Otherwise, unless "Englishness" or being English is confined only to white people, it shouldn't matter if you are not white. Anybody can be English if born in England, just like people born in the UK can be Scottish, Welsh, Irish, or Mancunians, Scousers, Geordies, Brummies... It is your loyalty to that land that matters most.

But like many others, white and non-white alike, not born in England, Scotland, Wales or Northern Ireland, I feel I can relate more to being called British, a proud one too because of my Commonwealth roots. Being British is a brown, Black, mixed or any other coloured thing, including a white thing. It is more comfortable being British living in multicultural Britain. Even the national census recognises the various categories of being British. I would feel the same if Scotland, Wales or Northern Ireland was my home. Being British is like being part of a more prominent, inclusive, reconciled family, not exclusive and separate. It makes being British unique, gives

Britain its strength to be white and non-white Welsh, English, Scottish and Northern Irish if you are born in those parts of the UK, even if you are not born there. So, why not develop what unites us, being British, towards even a better future!

That is why I have always been a strong advocate of the Commonwealth and the United Kingdom; a Union made up of England, Northern Ireland, Scotland and Wales, not of the European Union. It was the main reason I voted leave in the 2016 EU referendum, not because of the misinformation pedalled on the red Brexit bus and racist UKIP " Breaking Point" posters. I was also against the UK joining the EEC in 1975. Likewise, I can comfortably identify myself as brown Irish, brown British, brown Scottish. But not as brown English or brown Welsh, for that matter. Because being English or Welsh in multicultural Britain has been deliberately manipulated by extreme-right wing groups, media and politicians with racist undertones of nationalism to make non-white people feel out of place, become easy targets to undermine social harmony.

For non-white people like me to feel accepted as brown Scottish, not alienated by my colour and religion, bodes well for the Scottish people. Unlike the English and Welsh nationalists, it seems the Scottish are far ahead in understanding what Britishness actually means. It shows Scottish society is more inclusive, sympathetic to racial integration and social harmony. Therefore, the Scottish people need to be mindful of this valuable quality, the elephant in the room. What being British will mean if Scotland becomes Independent? Because there is no doubt what nationalism means in England and Wales. It is all about being white and nothing else. So, what will be the consequences for non-white people living in England, Northern Ireland and Wales if the UK breaks up? Who will get targeted next? Will it be Jews and other white people even though they look white? I hope that the British people will not allow politicians with divisive agendas based on nationalism to break up the United Kingdom without considering the full consequences of what will happen to not only non-white but also other white people?

Similarly, Britishness should not be about whether the flag of St Andrew's Cross, St George or The Red Dragon is fluttering at the top of a pole in someone's garden or the car or getting faces painted with appropriate flag colours. It is more to do with the cultural norms that give the UK and the Commonwealth strength we can rely upon, stand together, build upon, not whether you are white. I feel no less British because of my colour and religion yet proud of my shared values that bind us together wrapped under a Union flag. A common cause for the common good. However, I am not proud of an education system that holds back some people, a judiciary system biased against non-white people, institutionalised racism and a lack of non-white or women of all colours in executive posts. That, to me, is not Britishness.

To me, Britishness is also about compassion, making an even kinder, loving society for all to live in peace if harnessed positively. I believe there is still goodness left in the British people, which I have witnessed regularly. But, we cannot afford to be complacent or take it for granted, allowing divisive politics to hijack the inherent British virtues. I believe in social cohesion that unites people and communities. I still recall with great fondness first experiences of the British people's helpful, friendly, courteous nature that has lived to my expectations since landing at Heathrow forty-eight years ago. I did not feel overwhelmed by the strangeness despite never being surrounded by so many Caucasian people. Nor did I feel intimidated or bothered because deep down, I believed that others would reciprocate if I were respectful and polite.

Let me make it absolutely clear. By British, I mean the ordinary 'man in the street', not the 'establishment'. There are certain innate qualities unique to the British: honour, wit, wisdom, credibility, compassion, fairness, warmth, self-awareness, benevolence, innovation, and most importantly, support plucky underdogs like Robin Hood, Oliver Twist, Dick Whittington, Nelson Mandela, Dr Martin Luther King, refugees and David, not Goliath, greedy fat-cats or bullies. Another distinctive British characteristic is not to evade responsibility but help address the situation that matters most, not succumb to tyrants as seen during two World Wars and other conflicts. Equally, in 2019, we saw emergency services and ordinary public help victims by not running away from danger but towards it during the cowardly terrorist act on London Bridge. Also, during the Covid-19 pandemic, we witnessed frontline public sector workers risking lives despite the shortage of PPE and not the politicians who were working from the safety of their bunkers or busy posing for photos.

Likewise, I have experience of British courtesy when I first wrote to a British prime minister in 1992, reinforcing my trust in British justice, administration, accountability, which allowed an ordinary person to exercise their democratic right. But that was then. Regrettably, over the last two decades, I have experienced a distinct conflict of innate British values amongst the elected politicians, to the extent, not even expect an acknowledgement as a matter of courtesy when I have written to them. Similarly, the BBC World Service news from London heard on Murphy or Phillips receiver once upon a time was a must for people living in remote places. It was the only reliable daily news connection.

Regrettably, it's no longer the same old "Auntie" BBC, the trusted voice of reason, a reliable, unbiased news coverage. Due to the recent damning findings of an inquiry into the handling of Martin Bashir's Panorama interview with Diana, Princess of Wales, in 1995.[6] At the same time forced to set up dedicated complaints page for

Israel-Palestine coverage after hit with complaints from its viewers over its output on the mounting situation with many people taking to social media to slam 'biased' reporting.[7]  While I agree with Boris Johnson, the Diana interview was a sinister deceitful act of journalism by the BBC, I couldn't help thinking there was one thing he *didn't* say: and it's something that, equally, has been spoken about extensively, especially during the Covid pandemic – the spread of fake news by politicians like him and others who use the media to their advantage, and the reluctance to call for an urgent public inquiry when it involves politicians. Perhaps the prime minister will take a leaf out of this, commission the long overdue independent inquiry as a matter of urgency into party donations, cronyism, cover-ups because trust and honesty are critical to the survival of not only the BBC and the 'free press' but also for democracy. Therefore, it's vital for politicians and media such as the BBC not to lose that trust, especially when choosing public duty as a career. They should not consider it a privilege but a civic responsibility for which they get paid handsomely by the taxpayer, including in their retirement.

Today, the paralysis of political leadership is the most reliable certainty to the extent British values get compromised for self-serving egos with the politicians dancing to the tunes of the so-called free press controlled by the media moguls. Journalists to whom holding politicians accountable was of utmost importance. Yet nowadays, journalists often allow themselves to be used as propaganda channels for political leaders to spread fake news by peddling lies, smears in exchange for perks: places on state visits, honours and news exclusives. The BBC management needs to ask serious questions, stop behaving arrogantly like politicians without accountability. Because in these days of fake news, we need a state-funded source of genuine journalism, unbiased news coverage to hold the government to account, not an arrogant old school boys' network which has been allowed to exist over the decades in BBC.

Over the years, we all know the right-wing media love to promote ridiculous anonymous, hateful stories with racist undertones. It is not the first time the publication in question has run stories about "no-go areas." [8] If you are wondering which story to believe. Then perhaps I can help by telling you that the 'no-go areas' story, long and detailed as it was, was not based on original reporting but a book by an "ex-Islamist" with self-serving interests and greed. Whereby the author makes several controversial claims that support his thesis of a divided Britain. Subsequently, these disturbing stories get teased into media headlines based on exaggeration with a loose factual relationship that undermines Britishness by stigmatising the faith of Islam with labels like *jihadists, Islamists, terrorists or radicalised Muslims.*

Also, there are some parts of the British press that, for a long time, have not simply reported the news instead done their bit to create it so that it conforms to a preexisting narrative. Because of such complacency, it is how we become numb to the extent of the distortion and its dangers. Once the account is made respectable by politicians, the press, the discussion then passes into the realm of "difficult truths" that must get addressed. It puts on a different, more respectable shirt. The 'no-go areas' tale becomes a perennial story that some papers have been pushing for years, and to them becomes a "row", a "controversy", a "debate", immigrants are "cockroaches", something spontaneous, organic, rather than manufactured and recycled. And this isn't just one example but a myriad behind which those with evil, divisive populist political agendas hide behind in the name of democracy and 'free press'. It doesn't bode well on our ability - or the media's belief in our capacity- to focus on difficult political conversations?

Unfortunately, the present hostility and catastrophe of entrenched populist agenda fanning division have not helped. It will dominate, define domestic life for years to come. Yet, I remain hopeful from what I have experienced that the British are astute, fair-minded people with plenty of 'commonsense', contrary to Jacob Rees-Mogg's comment about Grenfell victims in 2019. I believe there is still goodness left in the British. However, we cannot afford or allow political complacency, chaos, a lack of effective leadership to hijack inherent British values. Britain can still play a crucial role in the world as a Beacon of Hope, a place for fairness, justice, not a place inciting hatred and division.

Speaking as a proud British citizen fervently against the break-up of the United Kingdom, it is worth bearing in mind that the cause for preserving the Union, the first duty of all true patriots must be: to acknowledge that, just as Britain would never have achieved all that it has done without having been a country of immigration; so too it would never have been able to achieve all this; unless its immigrants had been able to take their place within and become a part of what never has been a nation without immigrants, nor ever could become one or maintain its international influence without destroying itself in the process.

What Britishness means is a miracle of cumulative human endeavour, wisdom on par with the notable achievement of science or any political, religious, philosophical ideology known to humanity. For it enables millions who have never set eyes on one another to act together in peace and mutual trust. There can be no more authentic service than to preserve such a Union, prevent those millions from dissolving into antagonistic and destructive groups.

# 6.

# INSTITUTIONAL RACISM

Isn't it time that 'civilised' politicians and people in authority are guided more by the limbic system for the overall good of humanity? Let go of the ancient urges linked to the primitive survival instincts of some long-buried lizard brain that evolved way back. Since we no longer live in the same world as our ancestors, who relied on aggression to overcome their fear of others for survival.

The sad reality is that empathy is a word not conducive to the culture developed amongst politicians steeped in divisive populist agendas encouraging fanatical curtain-twitching behavioural tendencies. Though dog whistles may win votes, it destroys humanity, and the voice of the few drowns the needs of the many.

Times are changing. Instead of changing with times, when it comes to racism, politicians are stuck in the past with their old colonial mentality and unconscious bias. We're here now, in the present, not only in a new century but millennium, and it's up to us what we hold on to, what we let go of, what we reach out to progress in the new world order of 'civilised' democratic values we want others to embrace!

Ye need to ask: What are the underlying root causes of institutional racism? What leads an ordinary person to adopt racist behaviour? What makes them remain in denial? What makes them turn a blind eye when they witness it? We further need to ask: Why do public institutions meant to play a vital role in looking after the well-being of citizens irrespective of race, creed, class, sex, or age attract racist behaviour? We also need to ask: Is it because those seeking professional careers in health, education, judiciary, Home Office and police are racists at heart? Or is it due to the onus placed on them to implement policies imposed by those in authority that leads some to pursue racist behaviour when executing professional duties?

By the same token, ordinary people are not born racist. It is the prevailing conditions, influences that allows them to practice the abhorrent practice which needs addressing. For decades, we have seen politicians of all persuasion relaxed to pass laws for short term self-serving interests sleepwalking through draconian policies. And what we are witnessing now is the consequences, culmination of those abuses of power by political leaders with a populist nationalistic agenda targeting minority groups because of their race, religion or social class in countries with the oldest, biggest democracy such as Britain, India and the USA.

Likewise, the British people are fair-minded. The root cause of institutional racism and social tensions is not due to them. But down to the subtle divide and rule politics deployed by politicians who use immigrants as cheap fodder during elections to cover up policy failures to stay in power by blaming them for shortages in jobs, hospital beds, school places, social housing, and changing neighbourhoods. It not only dehumanises immigrants but makes them more prone to racism. If that is not enough, politicians are equally quick to jump on the bandwagon to condemn ethnic minorities even when it's not their fault. Like we saw the two MPs mentioned later, who wrongly blamed ethnic people for the spread of Covid-19 yet conveniently kept quiet when white people behaved irresponsibly or blatantly violated national lockdown measures. Also, not speaking out who introduced Covid-19 into the UK! It's not that politicians should be encouraged to pit one group against another, which many often do under the pretext of democracy and 'free speech'. But it beggars belief as to why they don't get reprimanded, called out by their masters for inciting hatred!

To tackle racism, we must recognise prejudice-especially those innocent types and varying degrees of biases. For example, how quickly we express our likes (love) or dislikes (hates) for material and non-material things. Statements such as I love tea, cricket, chicken, this or that colour, fresh air, football, so on. Equally, how quickly we express our feelings for things we hate. Therefore, we need to understand: Is prejudice a natural process? Is it innate? Is it something deep inside us that can be traced back to our hunter-gatherer ancestors when it mattered to know what to eat or avoid, the 'in tribe' to belong and the 'other tribe' to avoid, which could mean the difference between life or death?

How can you 'love' a cup of tea or coffee. Instead of 'like' a cup of tea or coffee. Yet, we often say it. We also have our prejudices when it comes to material possessions. We often don't 'like' the colour of a shirt, car, behaviour, people's attitude. We also have different tastes. Nothing wrong with that. But on no account, it should become acceptable when discrimination and prejudices get roused because of one's skin colour, faith, caste, culture, sex or age, that it turns into the vile form of racism. Indeed, something we, especially in the West, should not accept when we want others to embrace our democracy and 'civilised' culture.

To do that, we need to understand how those in power manipulate innocent prejudices. Namely, the twentieth-century born politicians and their cohorts - the 'establishment' - to sustain their positions and the semblance of order in the twenty-first century. Have those in power been smart enough to understand how to maintain their grip? Have politicians recognised that they can usefully harness subtle forms of the harmless, innocent hunter-gatherer prejudicial instincts to stay in control? Such as instil suspicion into the 'in tribe' of the 'other tribe' based on race and faith to maintain a hierarchy that supports their self-serving interests. And accordingly, we then witness the consequences of their subtle divisive politics, the unconscious bias, filtering down into the wider society, affecting those at the bottom the most.

And, it has now become a problem to draw the line without being perceived as racist and not getting caught! Because the 'old fashion style' blatant form of racism is an ugly, horrible word as it reminds people of images of violence, slavery, apartheid South Africa, Mau Mau uprising, Opium war, racial segregation in America, racist murders, police custody deaths in Britain. Also, we consider ourselves more 'civilised' than the 'other tribe', and in the twenty-first century, we should not be encouraging or seen doing such vile acts. The easiest thing to do for the 'establishment' to stay in power is to be against all that nasty racist stuff of the past, pass legislation banning the sharp end of discrimination by putting in place national and international commissions of racial equality to monitor the blatant forms of prejudice and racism. And the victims, if they can afford it, can seek justice in long drawn out expensive legal battles in tribunals or courts.

Now, it may seem we have resolved the most extreme forms of racism to absolve our collective and individual responsibility that we are not part of it. That might well be true. But what about the subtle routes cleverly exploited by the 'establishment' to incite hatred yet remain well within the laws enacted by them or their predecessors.

By understanding, we can all be prone to subtle forms of discrimination; we can begin to recognise how those in power manipulate us to do their dirty work by stirring subconscious confusions of our innocent prejudice, which can eventually lead to racist behaviour and attitudes in us.

It is because we all own this stuff called prejudice. However righteous, upright 'civilised' citizen, we may believe ourselves to be. And for some, racial hatred becomes an established thing. Therefore, it's our responsibility not to be complicit and fall into such devious traps directly or indirectly. To observe and say nothing is wrong is as bad as being complicit, even worse. And, by not saying, you become complicit. It also does not help when politicians deliberately resort to unwise, unthoughtful, unscrupulous remarks with racist undertones designed to win people's trust by appealing to their innate prejudices to instil doubts directed towards the 'other tribe'. By arousing passions to manipulate people into making decisions with which they wouldn't usually be morally comfortable.

So, it may seem what's the point of even trying to tackle racism. After all, we all have innate tendencies of the innocent prejudice type. Of course, I do not deny it. I'm also aware that it can be manipulated by those with an evil plan, whether white or non-white, democratically elected or not. But the point I want to make here is that although we are all likely to exhibit prejudiced tendencies, it can be a valuable tool to understand where the two opposite sides of the debate on prejudice and racism are coming from or where they stand. Because some of it is subconscious, some conscious, some unconscious bias, it does not mean we are racist from birth. It means that in the world we live in, we are controlled and manipulated by built-in myths and narratives to help navigate our lives and maintain hierarchies for our good, which at times gets cruelly exploited by politicians to divide us on racial grounds.

Many twentieth-century born politicians, those who attended posh public schools, often find it very difficult to let go of their colonial mentality when Britain had an empire and a credible voice. Yet, remain shackled, extremely mindful not to appear blatantly racist as it's not fashionable to be associated with those uncivilised abhorrent acts of slavery, apartheid or inciting racial hatred. And therefore, politicians tend to be very duplicitous, subtle with their racist undertones because of their unconscious bias. Well versed, wilful, yet exceptionally cautious about using the right choice of words not to sound blatantly racist.

When challenged over their unconscious bias, covert rather than overt racist undertones, politicians or their cronies are quick to respond, claiming we aren't going to learn very much from the past if we erase too much from our history by confronting it. They then vehemently try to justify that the critical thing in this debate should not be whether the language was acceptable, civil or not. Because "colourful language" will always play a part in British political life, while those using it get referred to as outspoken mavericks who mean no harm!

But the irony is when their victims practice 'freedom of speech', it's considered inappropriate; at the same time, politicians running scared when invited to participate in a grown-up debate to allow the victims they attack to question them about their subtle racist overtones. They deny those innocent victims they attack their 'freedom of speech' to reply. Also, the very 'free press' will not give them the time of day or an opportunity to pen an answer to their puerile vile claims, despite living in the same liberal democracy. One would expect politicians would not run scared; most of all, first, check facts by engaging in debates with other scholars to allay fears instead of spouting nonsense by hiding behind press articles or speech lecterns.

When political leaders abuse their privilege spreading dangerous misinformation construing facts about a particular faith or minority group to incite hatred in their handsomely paid newspaper columns is not 'freedom of speech'. When the same 'free press' use isolated incidents to criminalise minority groups or portray images in satirical magazines demeaning minority groups is not 'freedom of speech'. And when they tarnish their whole faith as radicalised Muslims, construing facts is not 'freedom of speech'. These are double standards.

'Freedom of speech' applies when the minority speaks to the 'civilised' majority hoping they will be listened to by those in power. 'Freedom of speech' applies when the minority can speak, and the bullied are given a chance by the bullies to respond. 'Freedom of speech' is when the truth is told to those in power and heard by them. 'Freedom of speech' is when victims can challenge lies. It's not 'freedom of speech' when politicians use dog-whistles or when a majority of over 90% try to shut out the minority. How can a Muslim minority of 4% or any other minority shut a majority voice? How can the 96% feel intimidated that their 'freedom of speech' will be affected? How can the majority remain silent, unable to speak? Likewise, 'civilised' honourable politicians in the name of democracy should not encourage rift between societies, the majority and minority; that's not 'freedom of speech' but thuggery!

Similarly, instead of facing the media or the victims, politicians often send an ethnic spokesperson to do the dirty work to justify their actions by making desperate claims the politician has immigrant ancestry and holds no such racist views. Attempts like that made by Kwasi Kwarteng, an ethnic business minister when he was sent on 18 February 2020 to do the TV studios and radio stations round to pacify Andrew Sabisky's past comments, as 'offensive' and 'racist', who had resigned after being appointed by Boris Johnson and his advisor. [9] Likewise, not to feel left out, our ethnic

Home Secretary Priti Patel decided to do media interviews on 19 February to defend the prime minister following the remark made by Rapper Dave at the Brit Awards about Boris Johnson's judgement to hire Mr Sabisky. She said the comments were "utter nonsense," adding, "I don't know what those comments are based on. As in the prime minister's case, it's wrong to judge individuals when you don't know a particular individual. He's not a racist at all, and I just think those comments are highly inappropriate." [10]

Such arrogance raises a few questions. Why do organ-grinders send ethnic ministers to get them out of the hole? Is it one of the roles of their appointment to do the dirty work? Why should the prime minister hide not defend himself after causing controversy? A few handpicked ethnic ministers may be suitable for illusion's sake, a charade which one can easily see through it. These are past practices of divide and rule best left behind where they belong, as the painful lessons of our colonial history, which we must not practice or need to re-learn. It shows that the politicians don't care because, unlike the ordinary ethnic public, they do not have to face real-life consequences in neighbourhoods, workplaces, schools with chants of 'Go Home' or monkey noises on football pitches. Unfortunately, politicians, after making bullish remarks in newspapers or speeches: such as Muslim women look like 'letter boxes', Black people with 'watermelon smiles' and gay men as 'tank-topped bum-boys' to name a few, then decline offers to engage in proper face-to-face debates with those they have insulted, or blamed for their failed policies or actions.

It's this mindset, the unconscious bias of the twentieth-century born politicians and those in authority, that needs to be understood to tackle the scourge of institutional racism and its effects in real life on those affected by it. What also needs to be understood is that knowing a handful of non-white people or being casual friends is not the same as understanding racism. Because racism is mostly unwitting, very few people think they're racist or admit it. Also, politicians will be quick to absolve themselves to have played a part in inciting racial hatred. By implying it may be so among football and other thugs who talk about non-white people in a racist manner. That's how certain people in our society talks about immigrants, but we honourable members are not like them; we are 'civilised' and do not stoop down to their level.

However, they conveniently forget that their racist comments in speeches, Houses of Parliament, newspapers articles, and media interviews usually leads to increased racial violence directed towards innocent women, children, and people who look different. It proves there's a link, whether it be conscious or unconscious bias towards racism. And for politicians to say dog whistles is just "colourful language," a teething problem is an insult to non-white people's intelligence. Tell that to those affected. The 'establishment' needs to help alleviate the pain of racism in wider society.

*

*Politicians have perfected the use of dog-whistle politics. They often use harmless coded language that appears normal to the majority yet communicates specific things to their intended audiences. They often use broad generalised phrases: like family values, immigrants, ethnic people to send signals to white supporters that a politician believes in Christian values without alienating non-Christian and non-white people or sounding racist, homophobic, misogynistic, Islamophobic and antisemitic. In general, accusations of dog-whistles are hard to prove also may be false by their nature. Because they often get used as broad generalised statements with an 'authoritarian personality' that tend to appreciate the order of superiority which are socially conservative. They also tend to resonate with the 'in tribe' by making the 'other tribe' more conscious that they are different. For example:*

When politicians constantly refer to proud British citizens like me, including our children and grandchildren born in the UK as immigrants of ethnic origin BAME-Black, Asian and minority ethnic. Why do immigrants need to be constantly reminded or tagged? Is it to remind them that their British values are different and not acceptable? Therefore, they should not expect equal treatment as the 'in tribe'! When confronted, the politicians are quick to respond by saying that it helps government agencies target specific policies to benefit the immigrants. However, it raises the question if that is true, then one would not see immigrants living in deprived inner cities in low paid jobs facing structural inequalities!

What message did prime minister Gordon Brown send to employers and right-wing groups when in 2007, in his speech to the Labour Party, made a rallying call "British jobs for British people?" What did he mean by that? Did he mean those British workers from the white working classes who no longer had it so good? Or did he mean Black and brown British workers like me? When challenged, he insisted he was not referring to non-white British people, but he needed to be careful handling dog whistles. Because, during a series of wildcat strikes outside refineries and construction sites, there were many displaying placards against the hiring of 'foreign workers'. And it did not stop the extreme right-wing group, the British National Party, to claim victory, calling it an excellent day for nationalism and patriotism?

What did David Cameron, in his role as prime minister, mean when he blamed non-white communities for 'passive tolerance' of unacceptable practices in a speech in Germany on 5 February 2011? What did he mean by claiming that such an approach had only served to help radicalise young Muslims, and he urged a new 'muscular liberalism' to promote British values more forcefully? He should have realised that preaching or making divisive speeches will not address institutional racism. If anything, it encourages those with racist tendencies to practice more!

What message did David Cameron send when he got shouted at with cries of being "racist" at the prime minister's questions in the Mother of Parliament of all the places? When he joined on 26 April 2016 in the dog-whistle politics with Tory MPs with an unfounded attack on Labour's London mayoral candidate Sadiq Khan had links to a supporter of Islamic State? Cameron's attack on Khan echoed those already made by Zac Goldsmith, the Conservative mayoral candidate, who had claimed his Muslim opponent would be soft on crime because he "provided cover for extremists." If a prime minister and an MP openly make wild accusations without proof, what example are they setting to others? That it's alright to victimise (apprehend) or hound someone because of their race or religion based on wild rumours without evidence?

What message are leading politicians sending when they deploy subtle routes to sow the seeds of doubt with an US and THEM racist, misogynistic undertones of an 'authoritarian personality'? What did Boris Johnson, the current prime minister, have in mind referring to a section of British citizens as "piccaninnies", "watermelons", "letterboxes", "bunch of Black kids"? This use of casual racist phrases, however unintentional, does have an impact. It has a corrosive effect on the fight against racism. When cornered and asked, Boris Johnson has the arrogance to brush it off as "satire," harmless "colourful journalist language" best forgotten.

Although an independent probe led by Professor Swaran Singh to look into allegations of Islamophobia within the Conservative party has cleared Boris Johnson over a complaint following a Daily Telegraph column in 2018 describing Muslim women wearing the burqa look like "letterboxes" and "bank robbers." However, the report said it did give the impression the Tories were "insensitive to Muslim communities." Despite a pointed message directed to the prime minister that the leadership "ought to set a good example for appropriate behaviours and language," Boris Johnson, in his usual arrogant bluster, refused to apologise. Except say, "sorry for any offence taken" over his "often parodic, satirical" journalism and went on to say: "Would I use some of the offending language from my past writings today? Now that I am prime minister, I would not." In response to Mr Johnson's assertion, the report said he would not make "discriminatory and unacceptable" remarks now. And the panel, therefore, concluded, "while this could be considered leading by example, the investigation would like to emphasise that using measured and appropriate language should not be a requirement solely for senior people, but ought to be expected throughout the Tory party." [11]

Typically, the author of any official report gives interviews, though Professor Swaran Singh, who led the investigation, was nowhere to be heard or seen on this occasion. What shamelessly patronising has come out of the report that: Boris Johnson admits he would not use derogatory name-calling language now that he is prime minister raises many questions the author failed to investigate. Yet, if the panel had cared to do that, it would have reached a different conclusion. Such as they could have asked Boris Johnson a simple question, why use it in the first place? What was the motive? It is a no brainer. Boris Johnson is not that stupid; however buffoonish he tries to portray because the article served its purpose. A year after his Daily Telegraph column, Boris Johnson got elected as leader of the Conservative party by rousing the grassroots membership with Islamophobic sentiments.

It further helped Boris Johnson win the 2019 general election since it appealed to Brexit supporters that Mr Johnson would be tough on immigration. Now, if this is not racist dog-whistle politics, then what else could it be. Just like fifty years ago, not surprisingly, as mentioned previously, it had also helped fellow Conservative MP Enoch Powell. Two years after playing the race card in his 1968 speech, he succeeded in getting elected in 1970 by increasing his waning majority to nearly 15,000 from 6,585 in 1966.[4] Not only that, but it shows that the same old mentality still prevails, tactics deployed for self-serving interests. It was also fifty years ago; sadly, Martin Luther King got assassinated in 1968. It seems we have still not tackled racism!

Professor Singh, by saying Islamophobia or discrimination is not in the Conservative party is for the birds, misses the wood from the trees, an insult to those who experience it. As Baroness Sayeeda Warsi, a former minister who has campaigned against Islamophobia within the party said, the report found "an inadequate, inconsistent and opaque system of dealing with complaints of racism." While the former Tory MEP Sajjad Karim said: "The manner in which this inquiry has been conducted means it is nothing but an attempt to whitewash deep-rooted issues out of sight."

However, Professor Singh's investigation into racism in the Conservative party provides a historic opportunity to reset its relationship with Muslim communities as it wasn't a complete whitewash. Although the investigation's remit was tailored with restrictive terms of reference to minimise damaging outcomes like that faced by the Labour Party over antisemitism, the report recognises serious concerns about Islamophobia within the Tory party. Also excluded from the findings was the term systemic racism since the investigative panel had an adviser who believed the idea of Islamophobia should be "junked." Hence the investigators selected a more sympathetic peer reviewer who came from a think tank that devoted an entire anthology to attacking the very concept of Islamophobia. Nevertheless, the investigation made recommendations to include an overhaul of the complaints process, reopening cases falling short of the expected standard, including an outreaching strategy focusing on meaningful engagement with Muslim communities. And if Boris Johnson is serious, he should stop faffing, accept Islamophobia exists and do something about it. He should now pave the way for a judge-led public inquiry instead of an independent probe to get to the bottom of Islamophobia in the Conservative party to help tackle institutional racism in Britain and internationally.

But don't hold your breath as the chances of it happening is extremely rare as there is no great mystery to Boris Johnson. There is little to unpack. Since the 1990s, as a journalist, his identity, actions or beliefs have always been divisive. After all, he is a politician not only with a self-serving ego but with a childhood dream to be the "king of the world;" therefore, his self-serving interests come first, just like leopards, will not change spots. Anyone who thought he would pivot to being anything other or prime ministerial is an illusion. That's what he is. Like most politicians, an opportunist. At the expense of others. Never mind the consequences for those on the receiving end of institutional racism if they get singled out as the' other tribe' by those in power, even if it becomes a constant uphill battle for them. It may seem "colourful language", but it is not a laughing matter for the victims!

We need to be mindful of how this racist undertones mentality of Boris Johnson that the end justifies the means in pursuit of the rainbow's end for selfish reasons should be acceptable. And whether it should be allowed in a 'civilised' society when politics should be more about building the structure of human destiny by serving public duty. Not for self-serving interests at the expense of others. Not only it is abhorrent, but it encourages institutional racism because the public perceives such behaviour as acceptable to emulate when they see the 'bastions of society' get away with it. The recent rush by Boris Johnson trying to counter the accusations against him of racism and Islamophobia by filling the cabinet with ethnic minorities promotions is a big mistake. He's making it worse if he thinks this is the answer because it isn't. It will cause more resentment amongst the white people, undermine the worthiness of his non-white cabinet ministers and, at the same time, also fail to convince that he is not racist and Islamophobic.

Satire or not, such remarks are not helpful, especially coming from a prominent politician. Ask those at the receiving end who have to endure the extreme discomfort in real life? How are they supposed to react? What should they do? Laugh along? Applaud? How could he think it was alright to laugh at this at all, sort of cheap satire at the expense of others. Especially when knowing fully well, such comments lead to an increase in racist attacks! Or are the victims of his humour meant to believe that the people who follow Boris Johnson's style of satire are laughing at him, not at them?

Just like people watching popular TV programmes screened in the 1960s/1970s like 'Till Death Do Us Part', 'Dads Army' said they did. Namely, laughing at Alf Garnett and Lance Cpl. Jones, not at the Black and brown people! But then those on the receiving end of hate crime would say otherwise.

*

*Equally, why do severe issues in the twenty-first century in Britain affecting employment's rights of the 'other tribe' go unnoticed until a disaster happens? Why it took the Covid-19 pandemic for the local North West Leicester MP, Andrew Bridgen, to speak out about the exploitation of probably 10,000 textile workers as modern-day slavery? What's puzzling why he had decided not to speak before openly? It is not that he didn't know about it. Like he said, "everybody knew about 250 Leicester sweatshops that have gone under the radar for such a long time because the city council don't inspect them." He went on to say, "I would point out that all the factories are in the constituency of Leicester East, which is the hotspot of where the virus has flared up in Leicester and anyone saying there's not a link between those conditions, the poverty wages and the fact that Leicester's in a lockdown, it just doesn't add up." [12] Now, one would think this was associated with a bygone Charles Dickens era, though according to the MP, it seems not.*

So, the question remains, why the MP did not call it out before? Even more worrying, after the MP jumped on the bandwagon to denounce Asian practices, Leicester County Council confirmed that no Covid outbreak was traced back to City's garment factory. Sadly, the MP has not yet deemed fit to jump on the bandwagon to put the record straight. Even if he had, it wouldn't have made much difference. Or, is it that such behaviour by politicians has more to do with political point-scoring, not forgetting the MP has a track record of dog whistles during Brexit as an outspoken member of the European Research Group (ERG)? Is it any wonder ethnic minorities are treated as second-class citizens by the law enforcers and others? Since raising his head above the pulpit, I wonder now that the MP is aware of the existence of modern-day slavery if he has taken up the cause of those modern-day slaves, who, after all, are his constituents! Now that will be expecting a lot from our upright members of the society, especially when those affected are immigrants. Using people as cheap fodder for self-serving interests is not honourable but cheap political point-scoring, not fit for purpose in a 'civilised' country.

If that was not enough, immigrants were even getting blamed for local Covid-19 breakouts by Calder Valley MP Craig Whittaker. He claimed there were "sections of the community that are flouting the rules and not taking the pandemic seriously." When asked if he was talking about the Muslim community, he replied: "Of course." He then went on to say, "because I am white, should I not say these things? I am not going to be quiet just because some people don't like what I have said." [13] Now, this is where it sounds farfetched as if the MP is concerned about Muslims and has nothing to do with dog-whistle politics. It makes a mockery of democracy. Why the MP remained tight lip about high Covid-19 cases in parts of the country with a higher white population?

Because the widespread flouting of rules had nothing to do with religion, and the MP knew it. Since he would have witnessed it himself by walking past pubs, these places were full of people, inside and outside, totally disobeying the social distancing rules were not Muslims. If truth be told, he would have seen naughty people across the UK of every creed, race and religion, including SpAds, politicians, his right honourable colleagues, breaking the rules. Such comments from Leicester North West MP and Calder Valley MP from the safety of their bunkers are not helpful. It is a slap in the face, particularly when ethnic minority communities had suffered disproportionately during Covid-19, including NHS doctors, nurses and care workers of ethnic origin, who were in the frontline saving lives!

What example are we setting if MPs, the lawmakers, are seen singling out ethnic minority groups when many others who had transgressed more obviously: such as sun-tan seekers, beach lovers, pub-goers, illegal ravers, anti-face mask protestors, football cup win celebrators and many others? Do politicians believe it is appropriate to categorise all by race? If so, in MP Craig Whittaker's world, it would mean sowing seeds of hatred. By pitting white-tanned people vs BAME folk? Such divisive nonsense, disgraceful 'overtly racist' comments only encourage those with racist tendencies to do the same. I wonder why the MP did not raise his head above the pulpit when Covid-19 infections had increased in areas with low or no ethnic people and when it grew over the Christmas festive period. The MP remained stumped when there was a significant surge in Covid-19 before and after Christmas in parts of the country, not necessarily immigrant enclaves. But leafy suburbs, not habitats occupied by ethnic people, let alone visited by them!

Equally, why the two MPs were not heard or seen on TV over Christmas. Not a dicky bird, criticising white people violating Covid-19 restrictions not only in the UK but even in a foreign country when hundreds of unmasked British backpackers were drinking, suntanning, dancing and singing in Sydney's Bronte Park. Sadly, it highlights that in the eyes of the MPs, the spread of the virus has racial bias. And it has to do with skin colour, Muslim faith or where you live or work despite the evidence clearly showing that the number of Covid-19 cases in England rose by almost a quarter over Christmas, following the easing of lockdown measures by the government, highlighting the impact of social mixing throughout the festive period. According to the Test and Trace data, a total of 311,372 people tested positive for the virus between 24 and 30 December - a 24% increase compared to the previous week. It was the highest total since the programme launch in May 2019 because people were not following the government's slogan: "Stay home, Protect the NHS, Save lives." [14]

The MPs in question also remained silent. When cabinet minister Jacob Rees-Mogg - who claims to be an upstanding member of the human species with lots of "commonsense" on every account – ignored the government's guidance on travel in a "hypocritical" manner after crossing tier boundaries to attend church. [15] It just seems yet again: there is one rule for us and one rule for the rest of them. I am not a Christian; I am not a Tory; I am not Labour or anything else. I am just an ordinary member of the community who abides by the laws of the land yet, fed up with the hypocritical approach from the people making laws for others to follow. Their spread of racist lies about Muslims puts innocent lives of women and children in danger. Something not easy to forgive or forget, though Muslims like me and many more do it daily for the sake of our country; they find the strength and maturity to put their emotions and anger aside.

Reading and hearing such comments made at an opportune moment in time directed explicitly towards ethnic minorities not only hurts but feels embarrassing. Such criticisms imply pandemics and economic crises are to do with skin colour. Otherwise, why on earth an upright member of society speaks about it? Using constituents as collateral damage by MPs for self-serving egos only encourages others in authority to follow suit.

*

*Whereas, as mentioned previously, the Chinese get treated with kid gloves. Not a single politician, including the prime minister, jumped on the bandwagon to blame the Chinese like the two MPs who were quick to blame Asians and Muslims despite being no doubt amongst leading scientific opinion including the Chinese that the Covid-19 pandemic broke out in Wuhan, China. Also, as reflected by well-documented evidence, there is no doubt that during the initial stages of the Covid-19 outbreak in January 2021, the UK was very blasé in its response to prevent the virus from coming from China. Despite concerns in some scientific quarters, the UK government ignored to put in place quarantine measures for many Chinese students returning to Britain with their families after celebrating Chinese New Year on 25 January. If anything, an eminent scientist had conceded that they would "not be surprised" if people had returned from China with the virus.*

Likewise, Southampton University's study showed that 190,000 people flew into the UK from Wuhan and other high-risk Chinese cities between January and March and travelled freely across Britain. [16] The report estimated up to 1,900 of these arrivals would have been infested with the virus - guaranteeing the UK would become a centre of the subsequent Covid-19 pandemic. Especially when some countries like Italy had already introduced temperature testing at airports whereas others had banned all flights from China or introduced quarantine measures.

In January 2020, while a silent and stealthy killer virus from China was creeping across the world, unusually, Boris Johnson was absent from the first Cobra meeting on 24 January. The prime minister usually chairs cobra, but Boris Johnson decided he was too busy to listen to an earnest discussion about a foreign flu bug. He had other things to do that he deemed more critical, like hosting a reception for the Chinese ambassador Liu Xiaoming to celebrate Lunar New Year, which doubled to discuss a post-Brexit trade deal. And a photo opportunity as he joined in with the traditional lion dance ritual held outside No. 10 Downing Street front door.

Such behaviour shows that the Chinese are not discriminated against when it comes to apportioning blame. And unlike other BAME people, they're not seen as non-white people with a different culture. No one dares to question or speak against the Chinese, whether it is to do with not mixing with others or not speaking fluent English. It highlights the height of hypocrisy from politicians like Calder Valley and Leicester East MPs when they are quick off the mark to condemn British Muslims or the Asian textile workers for the spread of Covid. In contrast, Boris Johnson sees nothing wrong and relaxed referring to Muslims by derogatory, racist names. At the same time, Jacob Rees-Mogg feels comfortable mocking Grenfell fire victims for not using "commonsense" by jumping to safety from the tower block.

We should have the courage to speak out when things are wrong, not by wrongly condemning or blaming certain sections of society. Yet, sometimes I can't help but wonder if we don't do that because we are blinded, worried or scared about not securing trade deals with China or any other country. This attitude by the politicians towards British citizens of Asian and Black immigrant backgrounds shows it is an acceptable practice as long as they are not of Chinese origin. While at the same time, they conveniently forget to recognise the sacrifices made by the Black and Asian people of the Commonwealth during and after the two World Wars! Do we have to be so blinkered by trade deals and greed that we have to compromise so easily our principles of Bristish fairness and justice?

*

*Likewise, why is the treatment of the Windrush generation or Grenfell residents in twenty-first century Britain just two of the many public disasters still allowed to happen? Is it because the affected people are BAME? Is that why; the Conservative-led coalition government, with the help of Lib Dems in 2012, felt comfortable introducing a 'hostile environment' by the then Home Secretary Theresa May. And the Tory MPs had no qualms later to make her their party leader? These events are shameful stains and should not have happened or been allowed in the first place if we are serious about tackling institutional racism. Is it any wonder the law enforcement officers at times show exceptional levels of institutional racism when their 'superiors' meant to set an example behave like this? It is unacceptable when equality legislation, designed to prevent disproportionate impact or unfairness on minority groups, was effectively ignored. [17] So much so that it has had such a profound implication, people lost loved ones and still suffer from those shameful events.*

Also, in twenty-first century Britain, why do we constantly need to be reminded by citing examples of the number of BAME Cllrs, Mayors, MPs, Ministers? It not only reflects an admission of general unfairness towards the BAME people but gives an impression the individual is not worthy. Instead, it should be based on merit, not on someone's race, creed, class, sex, or maintaining the status quo because it sends a wrong message that BAME people will lean more towards their kind. Although entirely untrue, it will not satisfy those extreme right-wing groups and media with a racist agenda to make false proclamations that immigrants are taking over white people's jobs. And the country will get flooded by them, with falling standards as they will favour their own. Not only that, but their appointment gives an impression of special treatment for being BAME and lowering of recruiting criteria along with inadequacies tolerated to keep another token non-white face in the public eye. In the process, it undermines their confidence and the authority to execute professional duties, creating doubts in the minds of the white and non-white people they are trying to serve. It makes it embarrassing for those on the receiving end, even more secluded by skin colour, making them more prone to further victimisation.

Why are we still asking the same questions to tackle institutional racism despite successive PMs fully aware of the "burning injustices and pledged in their inaugural speeches to address them? Is it because we are not asking the right questions to move forward to work for all people who deserve better, and not only immigrants?

Why do politicians prefer short-term policy measures to force ordinary citizens, e.g. doctors, landlords, and bank clerks, to perform immigration checks on their neighbours with threats of being fined, which only helps increase institutionalised discrimination? No wonder the government's "right to rent policy" was ruled racially discriminatory by the high court; however, that will not stop landlords from renting to people with foreign accents, attire or names.

*

*What example are politicians setting for the country's police force? When an independent inquiry, set up by prime minister Boris Johnson describes his Home Secretary Pritti Patel's behaviour towards civil servants as bullying!* [18] *Not only she is responsible for law and order, but she breached the ministerial code. Only for the prime minister to overrule the inquiry findings that she did not breach the code intentionally. So, what's the point of an independent injury? Is it any wonder institutional racism and sexist behaviour has often been a cause of concern in the police force? Is it because the culprits know that at the end of the day, the findings of public inquiries do not matter in the overall scheme to control power to maintain the 'establishment' hierarchy?*

What trust can people have in public institutions if the prime minister of the day feels relaxed by the conduct of his Home Secretary? Is it any wonder the Windrush generation have been treated so inhumanly by the Home Office? Is it any wonder why the Home Office felt relaxed to send vans going around in areas with a high immigrant population displaying 'Go Home' posters; without due diligence, how will those legal immigrants and their children, primarily British, feel?

And this is what the victims perceive: here is a government department responsible for law and order, good at implementing policies targeting some of the most vulnerable people in society, like migrants, refugees, victims of people trafficking, and the Windrush generation. Instead of ethnic minority people feeling confident that the Home Secretary who is leading this work measures up to the highest standards of fairness and accountability, it makes them wonder what to expect next. Will their citizenship rights get revoked on a whim? How will their British born children be treated in the future? Will they get ostracised for not being issued with correct documents? It may sound ridiculous, but the track record speaks for itself, that it can happen!

*

*Equally, what message the government is giving when in the middle of Covid-19 pandemic politicians were quick to bring the issue of race? When BAME people were on the frontline in the fight against Covid-19, saving lives in the NHS and public sector, putting their lives at risk and paying the price whereby two-thirds of the two hundred healthcare workers who sadly lost lives were BAME during the early months of the Covid-19 pandemic. At the same time, with its panel of 'experts', the government was quick to jump on the bandwagon that it's to do with BAME's genetic makeup. Only to be proved wrong by an independent study carried out by the Runnymede Trust.* [19] *It is worrying. If politicians are so quick to spread such racial baseless myth, what can we expect from others? Is it any wonder that we continue to face the curse of institutional racism with such a dog whistle political attitude?*

It's equally dismaying that of all the critical issues facing multicultural Britain regarding racism and racial inequalities right now. The government decided to focus on recommendations about labels contained in the report by the Commission on Race and Ethnic Disparities (Cred) that the term BAME - "Black, Asian and minority ethnic" - should be ditched by the government as it is outdated and fails to distinguish between different groups.[20] Without sounding like I told you, I have raised similar sentiments for a couple of decades as recently as 2018 in a letter to my constituent MP, Jonathan Lord, mentioned in my last book. It would save the taxpayer money if politicians listened to their constituents. However, why should they since it's not their money? More importantly, politics to politicians is not about serving public duty. But more about self-serving egos, a gravy train, a career, how much they would get paid if they worked in the private sector. The irony is that no one has forced them to enter politics; why do it since they are jolly well aware of remuneration in the private sector. Also, why complain, cling to power and face allegations about donations or who paid for foreign holidays, flat decoration and other perks when they could make more dosh outside politics! No one is stopping. If truth be told, they won't last one day in the real world.

However, the equality watchdog accused the authors of the above controversial Cred report into racial disparities in the UK of creating a "false dichotomy" about the underlying reasons for racial disparity, including the UN human rights experts who said it tried to "normalise white supremacy." In contrast, some twenty stakeholders credited in the report distanced themselves from its findings.[21] They believed the reasoning offered by Cred misses the main point. It sounded simplistic without tackling the underlying issue by wilfully misunderstanding the problems. So that we don't tackle the root of racism, instead get distracted by other things like people saying the wrong phrases instead of the systems of power that discriminate that victims experience in lots of ways. By denying structural racism exists, the government is claiming that disproportionalities exist due to the deficiencies of particular communities – it's a form of victim-blaming, divide and rule politics pitting one group against another.

As mentioned previously, I would prefer if people were referred to as British as it's more meaningful to achieve a true multicultural Britain without any label tagged to it. Like their specific ethnic group or, more broadly, as an 'ethnic minority', such as a BAME person. Also, the conclusion reached by Cred that the "country is still institutionally racist is not borne out by the evidence" misses the wood from the trees. Because the reason institutional racism exists is the consequence of the hatred incited by politicians who are the main culprits exploiting sentiments of ordinary people for self-serving interests to get elected with a divisive political agenda based on populism and nationalism.

I think the term BAME, other names or whether to use them or not, is a ploy deliberately chosen to create a divide and rule culture by politicians to get elected or divert focus from their major policy failures by blaming non-white people. For example, the Cred panel, after all, was set up and commissioned to investigate institutional racism in response to the worldwide Black Lives Matter protests in 2021 by Boris Johnson. Therefore, it's least surprising that Cred obliged to divert attention because it worked by distracting media attention away from the serious debate on institutional racism by focusing on ethnic names trivialities. Let's hope politicians will not use the findings to fudge the underlying issues when tackling institutional racism and huge structural inequalities facing white and non-white British people. The lack of understanding of reality by the 'experts' advising the government has often been the major cause of failure. It shows how out of touch the politicians are with the grassroots. Because when you are from a privileged background, you don't have those experiences. Something you can't understand by sitting in ivory tower offices reading thick reports produced by 'experts' who also lack what it feels like to be living in the real world!

*

*And from this flow, further examples giving more profound insight into the colonial mentality of the twentieth-century born politicians and their unconscious bias still busy at work corrupting and indoctrinating minds in the twenty-first century. At times, such arrogance of false superiority makes no difference to these British politicians to look at the broader picture.*

We saw it played out during the Covid-19 pandemic. For example, Britain could have learned from countries like South Korea, Taiwan, Singapore, and even China on how to contain the pandemic, especially their Test and Trace technology. Instead of learning from other countries, Boris Johnson got so engrossed with his colonial mentality of superiority that he insisted Britain would develop her own "World Class Test and Trace" by June 2020 that eventually got launched after delays costing £37bn. Which cross-party committee of MPs blasted in a scathing report that it had swallowed up "unimaginable" amounts of taxpayers' money with no evidence the scheme made a measurable difference in slowing the progress of the coronavirus pandemic. Britain was also late announcing national lockdown measures, travel bans, which caused unnecessary loss of lives and economic consequences, worse than in other developed nations. [22] Also, instead of learning from others, Boris Johnson, in his wisdom, decided to shake hands with Covid-19 patients. At the same time, Jacob Rees-Mogg preached telling the country to wash hands, saying don't panic like Lance Cpl. Jones used to say in satirical TV show *Dads Army*! While the Health Secretary Matt Hancock and other senior ministers tried to wriggle out of the confusion caused by the conflicting messages from Boris Johnson. Look where that has got us? Over 125,000 deaths, unnecessary loss of livelihoods, impact on children's education, effects on people's mental health, billions wasted and much more without knowing the long-term consequences on the economy and the national debt!

Racist behaviour from anyone is unacceptable. One would have thought, especially from an honourable member of the House of Lords. Sadly, not so that would be expecting too much from His Lordship John Kilclooney when he tweeted on 9 November 2020, "What happens if Biden moves on and the Indian becomes President." [23] It beggars belief. What sort of message does it send? That it's alright to make racist comments about Kamala Harris, the first woman US vice-president and an Afro-Indian.

It wasn't the first time our Lordship has uttered such racist comments because it seems old colonial habits die hard. In 2018, he referred to Taoiseach Leo Varadkar as a "typical Indian" because his father is Indian. Regarding a visit, Leo Varadkar had made to counties Armagh and Down without informing a local representative, which he said was "poor manners." If anything, from personal experience, it's the politicians who do not even have the common courtesy to acknowledge letters when I have written to them. So how can he generalise Indians as uncourteous? Unless if he has deep-rooted reversion towards Indians. In 2017, Piers Morgan also called him out for saying that cricketer Moeen Ali was not "racially" English.

Nonetheless, somehow, he remains in the House of Lords, thus legitimising such behaviour and getting paid handsomely for it. Which then gets played out in public institutions by others. How can they claim afterwards that their comments got misconstrued, or this is not what they meant? What they forget the people they deride with undertones of racist names are fellow human beings. When such people get caught out, all they do is remain in denial, believe they are innocent, forgetting the physical and mental harm it causes to others.

At the same time, Culture Secretary Oliver Dowden was similarly swift to defend the England test cricketer Ollie Robinson that his racist posts on social media were "written by a teenager." [24] Such a relaxed attitude on racism shows the arrogance of somebody out of touch with reality. It raises an obvious question. If so, then why make racist comments in the first place. Whether as a politician, teenager or at any stage in anyone's life. It also highlights that as a teenager Ollie Robinson or others like him with similar upbringing must have been exposed to the use of racist language (behaviour) by politicians, 'grown-ups' or role models like Boris Johnson, Oliver Dowden *et al.* with a colonial mentality of superiority based on race as a 'normal' thing to do. Such behaviour shows that politicians like Boris Johnson and others are quick to jump on the bandwagon to occupy moral high grounds, equally quick to discard racist undertones as "colourful language."

Here are some more ways political language experts believe politicians use dog-whistles to send subtle messages: Donald Trump spent years lying about whether Obama was born an American citizen or if he was a foreigner. UKIP's "Breaking Point" poster during the 2016 European Union referendum. Boris Johnson's 2016 remarks about Barack Obama "Some said it was a symbol of the part-Kenyan president's ancestral dislike of the British Empire – of which Churchill had been such a fervent defender." At the time, Churchill's grandson Nicholas Soames, a Tory MP, called the article "appalling, unreliable and idle about the facts." As it is, there is a fine dividing line between segregation and integration. Dog-whistle populist politics has been a convenient divisive tactic for many in the establishment. Not least, for Boris Johnson, Donald Trump, Nigel Farage *et al.*, who have paved a path to political leadership with wildly exaggerated speeches, newspaper columns and slogans pouring scorn on everybody else except themselves. The list is endless and outside the scope of this book.

*

*It seems some of the most brilliant public institutions, populated by the most well-heeled and upstanding people, are those that have got the most out of control because of the uniqueness of power. These individuals feel they are far above the standard moral codes of society, safe from the prying eyes of others. These men are ex-public schoolboys. Everything laid out. They've spent much of their lives forced to follow a strict set of rules that probably didn't end with their leaving school: choices around what university or course to attend, what career to pursue, what sort of house to live in, what it means to make ends meet or what it feels to suffer because of discrimination, skin colour, faith, sex, creed.*

At the same time, those men who did not attend public schools reclaim their council estate upbringing and Trade Union credentials to give a sense of commonality for self-serving egos. In my experience, those who preach respect for the rules and policies they have enacted also take the most enjoyment in breaking them like that seen during the Covid pandemic, MPs expenses, sleaze, or Labour politicians sending their children to private schools. The country needs leadership, not charm by inexperienced men with only a sense of entitlement without accountability. For the life of me, I do not understand why the opposition politicians and those parts of the broadcast media outside the control of right-wing politics play along with the deception and pretend that the world as it is does not exist. It's as if Britain were a Victorian family keeping up appearances. As if not just a government with every reason to conceal, but also the opposition and media are bound by a promise never to wash Britain's dirty laundry in public - even as its stink becomes overwhelming. Is it that they are also complicit because of similar unconscious bias based on their twentieth-century colonial mentality?

Targeted dog-whistle comments from politicians and upright standing members of the society are not only profoundly insulting, patronising behaviour but encourage those with racist bone in them to vent their anger on innocent victims going about their everyday business. At the same time, politicians remain in hiding tucked in the safety of their bunkers, unavailable to defend the wild accusations made by them. Dog-whistles and jingoistic nonsense are not helpful to fight racism. I'm as proud as the next man or woman, though these guys are responsible for legislation, education, social justice and everything in our country. And by the way, they are serious when making such comments. Using British exceptionalism based on people's colour is misleading, only serves to promote institutional racism. That's the problem. These past practices of divide and rule, best left behind where they belong, as the painful lessons of our colonial history.

Politicians are good at manipulating words when making dog-whistle political comments, not to give the game away. Scrutinised them every which way, words they use, construe facts, but in the end imply US and THEM, the 'in tribe' and the 'other tribe'. Words that cause discomfort, pain and unwantedness to the 'other tribe' at the receiving end. Words implying lazy, good at sports, good at music, good at dance and low academic expectations. Not words like hard-working, law-abiding, ambitious, determined, keen to learn, good family values, nation-building and British. Non-white people get continuously judged, always under the spotlight, evaluated not for merit but on their skin colour. At all times, ruled by a series of stereotype impressions formed over the years of every person of colour they had known, heard, read about in tabloid newspapers and not even met.

If such dog-whistle political language gets thrown about routinely, often in a derogatory way. Is it any wonder institutional racism still exists? Is it any wonder words like *Paki, spade, wog, coon* or sometimes even *nigger* can still be heard? Is it any wonder old-timers in public institutions may think likewise? It is no wonder that even the new generation (millennials) also chant racist songs and make monkey noise at football matches. Is an insult still an insult if only perceived, not intended? Ask those (the *voiceless*) who get called racist names in the streets. It's this that leaves ethnic minorities pondering this eternal puzzle in their everyday lives. Learn to tolerate while the government (politicians) work out what, if anything, could be done to improve the situation through mature dialogue because it is essential not to alienate anyone.

An excellent place to start instead of disgust and disdain would be acknowledging the mutual benefits that people could reap by working together. Highlight the contributions and sacrifices made by the ethnic minorities to help rebuild Britain after WWII; the vital role played in the frontline by the low-paid public sector during Covid -19 pandemic. At times empathy goes a long way to help foster social harmony. Not acrimony, divisive dog-whistle politics for self-serving interests. On most occasions, instead of directly facing journalists or the public, politicians will send an ethnic spokesperson to defend their actions by making desperate claims that the politician holds no such racist views. Also, quick to say that they know many ethnic people. At the same time, conveniently forget that knowing someone is different from living a life of real-life consequences that ethnic minorities have to face due to their actions. Instead of engaging, politicians decline 'civilised' face-to-face debates with those they have insulted or blamed after making bullish remarks in newspapers or speeches.

Another ploy often used by politicians and the tabloid press is to make quick comments with a racist undertone on the news relating to incidents of civil unrest involving BAME. But when challenged, jump on the bandwagon to defend that "the point here is about free speech, which has now got reduced to a stage where no one can innocently say anything." And they go on to say, "their views reflect that of the majority, or their words got construed, as they did not mean what they said or wrote." No different to that uttered by no other than Enoch Powell in his 1968 "Rivers of Blood" speech. Politicians then try their utmost best to defend themselves by mentioning procedures they have set up to address racism, Islamophobia and antisemitism. Just empty words to give an impression that the party is a broad church, and the few "bad apples" will be dealt with after the internal disciplinary process has taken its course.

Likewise, people often make racist jokes and comments meant to be funny, offensive, and relevant but simultaneously not to sound impolite, not to offend ethnic people in the audience. So they will begin their racist jokes and comments, "No offence, to you, but......" To invite you to join in and not to take it personally. At the same time, they continue to make jokes or comments to hurt people of colour based on the assumption that they are stupid and primitive. While those insulted if they feel upset or become withdrawn would be told: "Come on, can't you take a joke, don't be oversensitive."

It also doesn't inspire confidence when those non-white people whose mother tongue is not English language but genuinely try their best to speak would shy away, feel embarrassed by their strong accent because some would zoom into and say, "huh ... sorry? Could you please repeat what you said, or ask someone to do it?" Whereas others, to be polite, pretend they understood what was said, while others discard their contributions not worth paying attention to because of their accent. Such patronising comments are unhelpful, make people feel excluded, run in an endless loop, hide and pretend British by name, not blood, and wonder what being British means?

Similarly, white people in public life and institutions are more likely to come in contact with Black or brown public sector worker who will probably be on the other side of the serving hatch: e.g. porters, door attendants, cleaners, retail staff, canteen staff, dinner ladies. Black and brown staff serving white people is the usual dynamic in public institutions. A situation where the only contact many white people will have with ethnic minorities will be in servile positions, only reinforcing their unconscious bias of white superiority. Although, of course, there are so many top-class Black and brown doctors, surgeons, scientists, celebrities, teachers, pharmacists, nurses, even politicians.

There is a vast catalogue of examples of dog-whistle politics deployed by twentieth-century born politicians. They revel in their racist superiority based on the past colonial era of bloodshed and misery. Not a good example to set to the millennial generation, who have far more open-minded relationships, friendships not based on race but shared human values. So why corrupt their innocent minds with a vile racist undertone that serves no valuable purpose in a globalised world when other serious challenges need tackling, such as global warming and the economy post-Covid-19.

Most of the stories we hear about the 'other tribe' are fear-based, how bad they are, the threat they pose to 'civilised liberal values', dress differently, lazy spongers of welfare benefits, smelly and have a hidden agenda to take over. And those stories, repeated time and again, lead to situations of racial hatred, neighbourhood suspicion, police prejudice, a culture of stereotyping to make the 'other lot' feel like second class citizens. It becomes a constant drip, drip of dog-whistle politics with an unscrupulous populist political agenda designed to corrupt people's minds. It's about time politicians put their own house in order by setting the pace instead of stoking the flames with a subtle racist undertone if we seriously want to tackle institutional racism. Where necessary, they should get called out by the people; they are trying to divide by inciting racial hatred.

Despite numerous undercover recordings, investigations and whistleblowers have raised the usual boring questions. If a journalist can unearth evidence of institutional racism, how can the various official regulatory bodies that oversee public bodies fail to do so? What can be so tricky if others can do it? Is it because after making progress, we fall back because the first answer to a question is not the right one? No different to that played by dog-whistle politics designed to bring out the nature of ingrained prejudice. That very odd thing in our heart that brings a reaction to what we consider strange or told it is weird by politicians deploying unsubstantiated facts for self-serving egos to get elected? Thus, making it acceptable for others to follow. These unacceptable tactics based on an ideology of passion instead of reality should be revealed, understood, and challenged, so it doesn't filter into the rest of society because divisive dog-whistles allows society to stand by while politicians make a mockery of the law. It gets ingrained, and it is hard to see how public institutes can eradicate it because of the subtle ugly undertones. It comes back to politicians' responsibility to be able to help society flourish. Like everything else, institutional racism will only get tackled if there is political will. And only if politicians will stop exploiting divisive politics by serving a toxic mix of largely concocted fears over race and immigration, playing into the fears of an identity crisis of a nation that not so long ago ruled the waves.

Politicians claim when they talk about non-white immigration that they are not racialists. And talking about immigration is not the same as talking about race. But there is that persistent context they prefer to refer to about the rising 'coloured population'. When announcing stricter immigration laws and policies seen during the election, including referendum campaigns based on falsified data, scaremongering that it won't be long before there will be more coloured than white people in Britain. No different when Donald Trump announced travel bans from specific non-white countries that he is not a racist! Enoch Powell also made similar remarks like that in his 1968 "Rivers of Blood" speech. UKIP and Nigel Farage also played the race card during Brexit playing to white-working class fears and prejudices, increasing widespread racist crimes that made the lives of non-white people hell. Police own data show an increase in hate crime on immigrants after every divisive speech made by politicians.

Politicians are also often quick to claim what they are saying reflects the views of hundreds upon hundreds of letters (emails) they receive on immigration or shortage of hospital beds from their constituents, asking them to address their concerns. With one striking point, such claims never get substantiated, with a high proportion usually anonymous correspondents, from ordinary, decent, sensible people, writing a rational and often well-educated letter. Years later, investigations or the release of secret documents would reveal that such claims were all made up. Evidence is evidence; reality is reality. Truth is truth. Truth cannot remain hidden forever. Eventually, it comes out to haunt. Even long after the perpetrators have passed away.

So, why not learn from past lessons because the measure of 'civilised' society we like to call ourselves is how well it treats fellow human beings irrespective of race, creed or faith. Politicians will further protest their innocence when they get found out. And claim what they said and wrote was is in the past, said in the heat of the moment, or that is not what they said and were misquoted, giving an impression they are saints, fully committed to the 'civilised' common goal with no racist bone in them.

What such flippant language and behaviour of dinosaur politicians and executives fail to do, is inspire confidence in non-white people that they will be treated fairly by the 'establishment'. It is disappointing, especially when we need to make further progress in tackling racism. It is also worth noting that the 'establishment' has the power to recommend who gets bestowed with knighthoods and golden handshakes. The mindset of these people got exposed when in 2020, the ex-chief FA executive Sir Greg Clarke was forced to resign with a golden handshake after racist, sexist and homophobic remarks he made in one go in front of MPs during the Parliamentary Select Committee hearing. [25]

Despite being found out, he pleaded that he was not a racist but a product of the language commonly used in America. This type of colonial mentality, the language of deceit at the top, needs to change to tackle institutional racism. What does it say about the role models at the top meant to guide, inspire and help mere mortals? It says a lot that ex-public schoolboys have controlled the "establishment" for long. Middle-aged white men at the top who may be well educated enough yet live in the past using offensive language are fully aware of what they are saying and the consequences of their actions. Only to change their tune when they get found. Not even bothered about the pain and hurt it causes to others. When did we start calling Black guys 'coloured footballer' as he did? This sort of stuff is from apartheid South Africa!

Though in such situations; whether it be a politician, executive, president, prime minister or anyone in authority calling for replacements to be black, white, brown or whatever colour under the sun is not going to root out institutional racism or prejudices amongst people belonging to various tribes, the 'in tribe' and the 'other tribe', winners and not-so-winners. It shouldn't matter at what level we think about tribes across the world, country, neighbourhoods and workplaces; the reasons for their existence are the same. However, it will be challenging to eradicate discrimination as long as those in authority have only one thing in their minds: domination and power, control over others as inferiors.

Favouring or promoting people to make up the numbers may allow us to address racism to make sense of a set of variables too vast, complicated for individuals and society to understand. But it does not solve or address the underlying causes of racism; if anything, it exacerbates it and causes more resentment amongst the indigenous population, leading to further alienation of non-white people. What will happen once all the top executive posts get filled in the private and public sectors with non-white people? How will the white people feel? Of course, quite rightly, they will feel discriminated against that the tables have turned against them. So, what is the answer? A mature grown-up discussion and education; an acceptance of past mistakes, learning from them that we are now in the twenty-first century with shared values living in a globalised world, and at the end of the day, that's what matters most. Not by working or accepting each other based on skin colour because racism affects us all. Be it climate change or Covid-19, rich or poor, non-white or white.

In the UK today, there is a structural, historical bias that favours specific individuals, which doesn't just stand in the way of BAME, but women, those with disabilities and others. Overt racism that we associate with the 1970s does still disgracefully occur. However, unconscious bias is much more pervasive, potentially more insidious because of the difficulty in identifying it or calling it out. Race, gender or background should be irrelevant when choosing the right person for a role - few now would disagree with this. But organisations and individuals do tend to hire in their image, whether consciously or not. Those who have the most in common with senior managers and decision-makers are inherently at an advantage to get the job. I have to question how much of this bias is truly 'unconscious' and, by terming it 'unconscious', how much it allows us to hide behind it. Whether conscious or unconscious, the result of such bias is racial discrimination, which we cannot and should not accept.

It is not wishful thinking to suggest that we can all live happily ever after as one society without any differences. Because to be integrated into a population means to become for all practical purposes undisguisable from its other members. Something impossible to do when there are marked differences, especially of skin colour, faiths and culture. So, integration is complex, though, over a period, not impossible if we focus on shared values, what unites humanity in a 'civilised' society. Instead of a constant thrum caught from everyday life of why we are different: from snippets of TV and right-wing press reports defining racial difference repeated in a million stories about refugees, poverty, conflicts, that the 'others' with alien habits and looks is less good than the 'self'. Is that why some people have a question mark hovering over them about their loyalty and Britishness? Why do millions of people decide to dislike other millions of people they have never met, even if they had the time? Or is it to do with colour, one of the most accessible markers of difference exploited by politicians. Or is there something secret ingredient in the nation, blood, soil and water in one's place of birth, that makes people accept and hate fellow humans? Does it matter who has power?

Let us look at the culture of intimidation targeted at a specific group of people. For example, it was not the officials in the Home Office responsible for causing misery for the Windrush families? It was not the officials who sanctioned billboards displaying signs saying "illegal immigrants go home." Home Office officials were not telling porky pies during the 2016 EU referendum with the anti-immigrant UKIP poster. It was not landlords, doctors, and bank clerks who asked to perform immigration checks on their neighbours, which the high court ruled were racially discriminatory. And the government's "right to rent policy" makes people with foreign accents or names easy targets for those with racist tendencies. It is also not unusual for Home Office to place more enormous obstacles for routine UK visitor visas from BAME than the white people because of the hostile Home Office culture towards them put in place by politicians. In each case, the culprit was no other than the politicians themselves, *the most honourable member*, pretending they are acting on behalf of their constituents!

*

*So, we need to ask and look at the underlying factors that why: despite inherent British values of fairness, justice, standing up for the underdog, all sound 'civilised' human values universally aspired by humanity, why do white people go against the grain when someone joins public institutions, like the police, army, judiciary, politics, whereby instead of upholding British scruples get swayed by institutionalised racism. To this extent, the government had to launch a race audit in 2017, and police forces often get accused of racist behaviour.*

To understand institutional racism, we need to speak from a place of facts and reason. What it feels like to be a victim of racism? To do that, politicians, celebrities, those in authority after making racist comments should spend a day with those affected by their subtle racist comments. Live a day in the victim's shoes, a day in the shoes of most BAME people instead of the audacity to claim innocence as use of "colourful language", "satire", or "written by a teenager." We've got to keep looking to be better and learn as much as possible to make an inclusive and diverse society as possible. We've got to move forward from the past colonial mentality of superiority, unconscious bias based on skin colour and faith. We've got to learn from our past mistakes. Do everything we can to make sure it doesn't happen again.

Otherwise, it shows that we are missing the point; we don't understand how complex racism is, especially the part played by some politicians in exploiting it to their advantage. And it will not get tackled by lip service, whether it's appropriate to make gestures pre-match or not, ban players for posting racist social media posts, pull down statues of slave traders, stop fans from booing or more legislation. Whilst I sincerely hope that passing legislation will deter racism, this is by no means a quick fix; otherwise, we wouldn't be talking about it. If anything, like many other half-hearted attempts, it's called passing the buck, looking for scapegoats, somebody else's responsibility.   The law commission's review of hate crime laws should be instrumental in this. To be effective, we need to listen to the difficulties faced by the victims and how costly it's for them to seek justice against those with racist tendencies who know too well they will get away without much repercussion from the victims themselves or the 'establishment'.

Also, what's not going to change attitudes against racism entirely is the suggestion of compulsory education, seminars, a boycott of social media to wipe out vile hate. Even statements from the prime minister that he "supports individuals right to protest by taking the knee to make their feelings known about injustices" and other high profile celebrities condemning racism is not going to irradicate without understanding the origins of why it still happens; despite similar past initiatives? The answer is simple. Instead, we need to look at the role played by the politicians before pointing fingers at others, like sports fans, players, staff or even the ordinary public. Because at the end of the day, it all boils down to the mentality of politicians and executives who can't let go of their colonial superiority hangup. Which sadly gets emulated by sports fans (general public), poisoning race relationships due to what politicians and right-wing groups have instilled in their minds. We need to decompress the politics of denial to restore trust if we want to tackle the racist language. I imagine, as with so much of government policies, it is also media-driven. And if politicians claim that "politics and sports do not mix ", they should look at themselves in the mirror by asking the role they have played over the years when it comes to racism, Islamophobia, antisemitism, illegal wars, poverty........

It's about time we asked different questions instead of the same old questions from the same old hymn book: Is the reason the individual police officer has an ongoing racial bias down to the officer? Or, is it the culture of the political dialogue adopted by the twentieth-century born politicians who can't let go of their old colonial mentality?   And if so, how can we encourage the future politicians born in the twenty-first century not to get influenced by the mindset of last century dinosaurs? At the same time, let's not get on the bandwagon and pour scorn on everything. If we do, we will lose a lot of good values. Human society will end up even worse off in the process, like the rise of nationalism seen across the pond in America, India, Myanmar, Israel, China, Russia, and Saudi Arabia.

We should also not lose sight; we have a far better record of race relations in Britain than in America and European countries. Even better than those ex-colonial countries like India, Pakistan and others from where BAME people have originated. But in Britain, we should be mindful not to sleepwalk down the path of America. Where, despite a generation of Blacks who have more significant opportunities than any previous generation, people still get taught that America offers them little more than trigger-happy cops, bigoted teachers and biased employers. It's incorrect and unhelpful as Dr Martin Luther King and a previous generation of Black leaders understood that Black activists and liberal politicians stress racism to serve personal interests, not because it serves the interests of the Black underclass. Therefore non-white people must play their part in addressing racial disparities, not by constantly blaming the white man or neglecting by playing down the role of non-white activists in promoting racial tensions because doing so will only exacerbate them.

Fifty years after King's death, plenty of people are paying him lip service. Far too few are following his example. Even electing and appointing more Black officials, which has been a significant priority for civil-rights leaders over the past half-century, can't compensate for these cultural deficiencies. Black mayors, police chiefs and school officials have been commonplace since the 1970s in major cities with Black majorities. Racially gerrymandered voting districts have ensured the election of Blacks to Congress. Even the election of a Black president twice failed to close the divide in many key measures. Black-white differences in poverty, homeownership and incomes all grew wider under President Obama.

The social consequences of skin colour are different in every country. Yet nowhere racial politics is more baffling than in America, whereby walking or stopping in some no-go areas or bars, whether white or Black, can lead to total silence, even riots. Although nothing's written down, actually stated or against the law. Not like the blatant form of past apartheid in South Africa. Except for subtle forms of racism thanks to dog-whistle politics happening in the name of democracy, not only in America but also elsewhere. We need to tackle this poison and be extremely worried about it before it gets out of control. Let's hope the path pursued by India stoking hatred between faiths and caste does not end similarly.

In Britain, we are lucky compared to others. Our race and religious related circumstances are different, less complicated. And if we want, we can even make multiculturalism work better, become an envy of the world. Once again, the UK can become Great Britain, lead the way, not as a colonial power but as a Beacon of Hope for humanity. Whereas elsewhere, racial politics is strongly influenced and ingrained by past historical events. For example, in America, Black people have been in large numbers for longer than in the UK, though their integration seems a century behind.

Whereas, in India, not a race issue, but religion, cruelly exploited by Britain during the colonial rule to divide Hindus and Muslims, followed by the partition. Equally, now maliciously abused by the Bharatiya Janata Party (BJP) under the pretext of democracy by prime minister Narendra Modi. Translated into English, BJP means Indian People's Party, which seems in name only and not politically. No different to the religious-based tensions in the Middle East and Northern Ireland, thankfully, in the latter, peace has prevailed and shows nothing is impossible if we try to put our minds to it.

Similarly, there are differences between politics and the detached *Softly, Softly* narrative adopted by the police that we enjoy in Britain. In other countries, the police are the natural enemies for many people, and their politicians are corrupt. They see the police act as oppressive agents promoting the agenda of the evil, dictatorial governments. Yet, we should not be complacent since not all police officers are whiter than white as such. Just like politicians, in the UK, we have our share of rotten apples in the police. Albeit not that prevalent as other countries, but still exists undermining social harmony.

Racism doesn't dissolve itself once it's out of the headlines. Similarly, tokenism is not going to tackle the deep-rooted racism that exists. What those in authority don't care about is the suffering inflicted by dog-whistle politics. It's difficult to describe except by experiencing it: How it affects those at the receiving end to read or hear something like that: How acutely isolating it feels: How deeply hurtful to be judged, not on hard work or achievements or sacrifices, but blamed for something based purely on unsubstantiated assumptions: How undermining of everything, despite getting taught what is right and what is wrong: How unjust to judge me and others like me by one standard and white people by another: How utterly humiliated it feels: How demeaning: How defeating: It is difficult to describe.

Quite often, those in authority give an impression that 'they entered politics to make life better for others' and are most likely to hurt the public. Though not directly by the *respected, honourable members*, however, usually by enticing others to do their dirty work by deploying subtle dog-whistle politics. So as not to be seen as outright racist. These sort of references they make seem innocent without hostility. However, they precisely know who they are aiming at: those from the white middle and working-class backgrounds in public institutions wrestling to reconcile their preconceptions and prejudices of Black and brown people living in their midst. Though many of whom may have never spoken or tried to talk to a Black or brown person. Yet quick to define people purely by their skin colour, where for them a peaceful colour-blind world doesn't exist and seem more focused purely on skin colour?

Life is a long journey about being human amongst human beings. Let's make a concerted effort to take at least a step to cover the distance. After all, isn't it the case politicians have entered politics to make life better for others? So, wouldn't it be better than a constant social and political dominant tendency based on a male authoritarian personality? And perhaps a slight shift towards a twenty-first-century 'civilised' society that encourages equality, not racism, would be a better peaceful way to better ourselves?

Still, looking back at what the past non-white generation had to overcome, full credit to the ethnic parents for not transmitting their anger and bitter experiences to their children. Similarly, the degree to which such emotions have ebbed. What's also remarkable is not the number of non-white and white people from disadvantaged people who have failed to climb the social mobility ladder, but the number who have succeeded against the odds. It shows that if we want, institutional racism and "burning injustices" can be fixed by working together.

# 7.

# TIME FOR A GROWN-UP DEBATE

At times, far too many people, right across the political spectrum, media, respective white and non-white communities, whether affected by racism or not, individually or collectively weaponise race, using it as an exclusive political club or tool to bludgeon their opponents (critics). However, it doesn't mean that the scourge of racism doesn't exist in our society. Of course, it does, and those affected by it are not just making it up.

Yet to blithely accuse someone of racism without actually knowing what's in their heart isn't only politics at its very worst; its humanity at its very worst. To grotesquely weaponise race for partisan political purposes doesn't just diminish Martin Luther King's legacy. It hinders progress. We would all do well to remember that everyone gets dealt a losing hand when people play the race card.

Equally, non-white people should not think they are all 'saints'. They need to speak out against racist government policies directed towards minority groups in their countries of origin when people of the same colour, just like them, get persecuted or prosecuted by belonging to a different faith, even those of the same colour and religion as them but not of the same caste get victimised. Racism is racism. And it needs to be called out with no ifs or buts. Like Martin Luther King said, "we've got to do something about our moral standards. We know that there are many things wrong in the white world, but there are many things wrong in the black world too. We can't keep on blaming the white man." [26]

Racism is painful and a humiliating thing to experience. The key to that pain is isolation. When others protest, offer support, and turn that isolation back on the racists, the pain gets considerably eased. Feeling alone with hurt is far, far worse. Racism can only get resolved in a 'civilised' way, in a grown-up 'civilised' manner, not with hostility between the white people - the 'in tribe'- and the non-white people - the 'other tribe'. Otherwise, it would make those with racist tendencies and those affected by it even more entrenched. Hence the onus should be on every member of the 'civilised society to recognise that racism still exists, albeit not the blatant types of the past but equally worrying the dangerous current varieties of subtle racism occurring under the radar.

And if we are serious, we can tackle racism since nothing is impossible if we put our minds to it. What is required is a concerted effort, determination from all sides of the aisle. Our top priority should be tackling the most prevalent form of racism based on skin colour; in doing so, it will open doors to address other forms of prejudice with minimal effort. Often when we look back, reminisce with the passing of the years, interpreting various historic disjunctures and pains with the healing of time and maturity, we wonder why we are still fighting. Why haven't we learnt from those past wounds as it serves no one? And instead of being forgotten, we would be far better off learning from those abhorrent practices to forge a new future, not along the lines of skin colour but humanity. Especially now that we are in the twenty-first century, living in a globalised world. A world, very susceptible, intertwined in every sense of the word when it comes to tackling disease, economy, education, social media, global warming, migration, wars, poverty......

Despite the importance given to our skin colour to identify people, if a physician did not know the colour of their patient's skin, they would find it virtually impossible to say with confidence by looking at what they see inside our outer body covering. Because of the fact, underneath, we are all the same. A marvel of modest yet complex tissues and organs, working together to form a human body, sharing the same emotions of happiness and sadness, irrespective of where we come from, the faith we belong to or where we decide to live and call our Home. Likewise, unlike most mammals, especially our close primate cousins, human babies are born helpless because their brains are comparatively underdeveloped, a book with relatively blank pages. So, it's up to us. We can narrate a positive or a negative story and teach good or bad values if we want.

Otherwise, if nature wished human babies would arrive in the world with a preconceived advanced cognitive ability like a newly born chimpanzee baby, it would have meant a twenty-one-month pregnancy in humans. Something I don't think would have been popular! Not only mothers would be too keen on the idea. Imagine the economic costs? Whereas the advantages of a shorter pregnancy, relatively helpless childhood with long adulthood gives us an ability unique in the animal world. More importantly. Allowing our emotional feelings and cognitive abilities to develop together outside the mother's womb. So that various available learning tools -'inputs'- for a successful vocational career (the material thing) and cultural (the living in society thing) both crucially vital for the success exist in harmony. Not only that. But it provides us with an exclusive ability to learn about life in the real outside world. Have the opportunity to learn about who we are, make an informed decision on making the best use of the knowledge, solve problems, solve differences, most importantly, come up with pragmatic solutions.

Likewise, considering we are born colour-blind, no one is born prejudiced, necessarily driven by racial or religious hatred. Therefore, our brains are not wired as such to discriminate against one's colour. And if that's what nature wanted or meant it to be, then our brains would have been wired accordingly. Yet, it's not the case. It means that our prejudicial attitudes develop later from the stories and lies we tell ourselves. Myths we promote to build cultures and societies. Which, if we want, those prejudices are ultimately under our control. And if we commit ourselves, spend our thinking time to leave a better legacy fit for the twenty-first century for our children, we can change those outdated fascist, colonialist and imperialist concepts that hinder social harmony. Since we know that underneath our thin skin layers, we are the same, have the same ambitions and shared values. Besides, by learning from past mistakes, we can rid ourselves of past stories and poison with new narratives of Hope. A factual reality, a good starting point for optimism, for our cognitive abilities to develop if we devote our time to unravel real problems facing humanity such as poverty, social inequalities, conflicts, global warming.

It is time we moved away from a culture of suspicion. Stop wondering if people will play fair because of past experiences. Not harbour grudges or anger from the past, such as what was fair and what was not. We need to speak, debate not with anger, jealousy, finger-pointing and suspicion. You did this; you did that. But in a grown-up, mature discussion. Also, once rage takes hold, we have often seen the world narrows, often ending in regrets. It even happens when you do it to someone you love, and once the anger subsides, one feels remorse. If not straight away, but when one reflects on it in the cold light of day. And if some people, whether they are politicians or whoever, like hurting others based on their colour or faith, it is best not to let them. The key to defeating them is not to be offended, not to retaliate, not to be violent, not to take it personally, but to recognise the highly offensive nature of their baseless remarks and propaganda by taking *appropriate* action, reasoning and calling them out.

We could all do with understanding how racism often gets confused with prejudice because both innocent and blatant varieties of prejudice exist right across the spectrum in white and non-white communities. As a result, racism can sometimes often get confused with prejudice and used vice versa. Especially as a retaliatory argument by the white people to condemn the burning hatred some non-white people hold against them. And they are right to say it is unacceptable and insist it's a form of 'reverse racism' because there is no doubt that people of colour harbour prejudice against white people and their own. Therefore, everyone has the potential to be nasty, hurtful or prejudiced against others. But there is a marked difference between racism and prejudice, an unattributed fact that defines racism as prejudice plus power. And although those disadvantaged by racism can undoubtedly be vindictive and prejudiced by supporting their national cricket test teams. However, there simply aren't enough Black, brown or mixed-race people in positions of power to wield racism against white people for it to significantly affect their life chances or careers on the scale it currently operates against them.

The argument is a straightforward one. When discussing racism, those who experience it regularly, the non-white minority, the 'other tribe', feel tired of trying to persuade the 'establishment' run by the white majority, the 'in tribe', that it is a pertinent problem, which should be addressed and tackled urgently in a 'civilised' way. It's because the disenfranchised 'other tribe' feel that when talking about racism, the 'in tribe' fails to understand that this is not a straightforward conversation of equals and fairness on skin colour lines, or Muslims and non-Muslims. But more about having a debate with those who have power and those who don't and become victims of those abusing power, lacking empathy how they feel. It is also about those who have authority, who entered politics to make life better for others, as argued previously, refuse to listen to the *voiceless* since they have little concept of what it means to be on the receiving end. Moreover, it is not about putting a few faces from the 'other tribe in some prominent positions to be seen as doing something or knowing a few of them.

Certain things need to be talked about, discussed in a grown-up way. By not talking doesn't mean it doesn't exist or the problem will go away. Of course, there is a suitable place and time to talk about certain things, whereas some things over a period will not matter or get resolved because time can heal. However, we can no longer ignore specific issues, and if ignored further, it not only gets worse but becomes somebody else's problem. Also, we cannot disregard it forever; it will come to roost and keep on haunting us. Racism and discrimination are two of those things that have got ignored long enough. Just like global warming, we can't keep on ignoring it; if we want to leave a better legacy for our children by just wishing, hoping it will go away. However, it won't unless we do something about it, particularly when we consider ourselves more 'civilised' than others.

It has become a nightmare for those who experience it regularly. For the victims, it has become a constant battle. On the one hand, they get told that we are equal, only to find out that there are some more equal than them because of their colour. Making some wonder that despite trying their best, maybe that is the way of the world, and they have to accept the consequences of racism. While those frustrated after years of peaceful protests and dialogue resort to violence to vent their anger, at times culminating in mass-scale civil unrest and looting. Only to be followed by condemnation from the 'civilised' fortunate ones, that there is no reason to go on the rampage. But try explaining to those on receiving end of racism who have tried to reason but feel no one is listening to them. Politicians are equally quick to condemn, yet they have stopped listening to the *voiceless,* and when they try, they get ignored.

The responsibility always gets placed on non-white people expected to engage and tackle identity or racism issues. Nothing wrong with that. After all, they are the ones who have decided to come over to the white person's country. Except it raises the following question. Shouldn't the 'in tribe' also engage in getting a better understanding? Instead of only acting as visitors to the world the 'other tribe' live in daily. It also raises another interesting question, a further obstacle by making the 'other tribe' more conscious of their conduct and work ethics as they feel under constant scrutiny than their 'in tribe' colleagues. The extent of racial bias faced by non-white people in their daily lives in twenty-first century Britain has been laid bare by studies that show an unprecedented income gulf between people of different ethnicities. [27] Whereas, another landmark study on disparity suggests that Britain's Black professionals are twice as likely to be turned down for a pay increase after negotiation than white people. Racial disparities within the workplaces are often systemic, entrenched and come in from everywhere: education, visibility, hiring processes, mentors, the people around you. Then, if you're lucky enough to make it into these good organisations, you're faced with unconscious bias from hiring managers. The problem is deep-rooted and hard to undo since we repeat the same mistakes despite knowing it exists. [28]

These studies reveal stark evidence of everyday racial bias in Britain. It indicates it is down to the 'other tribe' to come to terms with the prejudice by being better model citizens, model neighbours and model workers. And after, against all odds, not putting a foot wrong, still have to prove to those who discriminate against them that they too can be good at their jobs, and in some cases even better if given half a chance to compete on a level playing field. For the 'other tribe', such a daily existence has become a constant battle to change the discriminator's mindset not to get singled out or labelled as 'non-white immigrants are all the same'. In contrast, the white people are not engaged with identity to prove an iota of their Britishness or job credentials. Instead, free to engage in a power game with a different type of politics with a full range of opportunities to succeed to the highest echelons in science, engineering, arts, history, economy, public office, society, religion, charity and media. At the same time, look busy, playing crucially important roles, getting on with shaping the world during G7, saving humanity, when most of the ills faced by the white and non-white disadvantaged people are down to their failures. Whereas Black and Asian people are kept too busy by being told to shape themselves, stop having a 'chip on their shoulder' while stopped and searched the most by the police.

In twenty-first century Britain, race and identity should not be about painting one side as the enemy or victims. One would think we had come a long way from the colonial past when it mattered that one race had to be a dominant race over the other. But now it should be more about common identity that being British is about the future together based on our shared values. It shouldn't be about being white, black or brown, but more about zero tolerance towards racism. And vice versa, it should also be about empathising with those white working-class who sit, fearful, wondering why the world has changed so rapidly around them, and feel that no one is listening to their concerns. Therefore, collectively we should feel great anger at the statistical data that show an unlevel playing field for low-income families. At the same time, we should also be appalled by an increase in food banks, a rise in child poverty, a surge in suicide rates, constant battles faced by disabled people and working-class children let down by the British school system due to general unfairness.

In Britain, the integration between races has improved from what it used to be. Compared to America, where segregation between races is still deep and stubbornly rigid, here in Britain, we prefer integration, not segregation. Similarly, compared to recent Black Lives Matter protests and civil unrests in America, surveys of the British young people, white and non-white, show declining racial prejudice. The new millennial generation who look past skin colour gives Hope for the future that we all have similar aspirations; though, we must not let lose sight of progress instead keep trying to improve our lives until we die. However, it may have been too late for the parents of the first-generation immigrants. Still, it has shifted for their children who wants to join the sophisticated class, where the colour of your skin is not more important than what you can offer, put your mind to and the content of your character. Also, Britain isn't America. It's different because racial discrimination may not be as blatant as in America, yet sadly it has become more subtle in Britain these days. And if we care to examine closely, the myriad of challenges we face quickly become apparent.

Unlike America, Britain is quieter. Less expressively violent. Less "I have a Dream" type speeches of Dr Martin Luther King, yet more dog-whistle politics and scaremongering tabloid newspaper headlines. In Britain, except for a rare moment like the 1968 "Rivers of Blood" by Enoch Powell, we have our own set of delicately refined instincts regarding identity, prejudice and racial hatred. So, Britain does have challenges that can only be discovered and addressed with a more pragmatic approach. That internal chatter and debate, present in so many, need to come out and become an external one, a national conversation, not Chinese whispers, culture wars, curtain-twitching behaviour, suspicious of each other. But by relearning how to see people as fellow human beings, whether it be the 'in tribe' or the 'other tribe'.

It is because the vast majority of people, of whatever colour and faith, prefer to be left in peace to get on with their lives, work towards a better future, the chance to live in hope, love and laugh, unhindered by racial hatred. Otherwise, the positive gains and sacrifices we have made can quickly revert to our bygone age's peculiarities of race and prejudice. We can see the effects on various immigrant communities facing structural inequalities up and down the country. Here too, politics must change, become more open about the underlying causes of the "burning injustices" with a less divisive populist political agenda with racist undertones recently embarked upon by political leaders with self-serving egos during elections and referendums.

However, let's not forget two things. Integration should be a two-way process. How often do we see non-white people get rebutted despite making genuine efforts to assimilate on top of tolerating a range of racist names, even monkey noises, when representing the England national football team? Whereas white people are known not to have a perfect record of mixing. Whether in Britain or when they settle or visit non-white people's countries, they are known to set up gymkhanas and social clubs for exclusive use, with admission protocols serving as barriers to deter undesirable elements from becoming members. Even subtle obstacles like etiquette or dress code are put in place to prevent not only non-white people but also white working-class and disabled people from joining. To this extent, Comic Relief decided to stop sending white celebrities like Ed Sheeran and Stacey Dooley to Africa following "white saviour" criticism as it gave that sort of impression to the under privilege. The world does not need any more white-saviours approach. Therefore we need to engage more, listen to folks we agree with and those we don't.

Similarly, we should embark on a real sense of self-reflection to look inwards on specific issues like racism and consider ways to increase representation to amplify non-white voices and diversity. We need to ask ourselves what else we can do to learn and how we can progress further. Ask ourselves, what would Britain have been like if no one had pushed for change, if non-white and white people had stuck with where we were, say a few decades ago. Would Britain, or for that matter, other countries, have a greater or lesser problem with discrimination? If the spontaneous answer is more significant, then there is great hope for the future. Although some cynics amongst us will say send them 'back home'. Yet then these are the same ones who will miss them because who will do those low-paid jobs while simultaneously also miss the immense contribution made by the non-white people in all walks of life. We should not succumb to the cynics but work even harder to make more progress in our mission to combat racism.

Individual contact, empathy helps build relations, gives a better perspective of the reality of what it feels like to be in the shoes of the 'other tribe'. A little less patronising behaviour like who are you to tell me and "if you feel so strong about local and national issues, you're at liberty to stand for elections or join a protest group" uttered by my constituent MP. Such attitude leads to closed, more stereotyping, defensive attitudes of suspicion and further alienation. In comparison, a bit more understanding, openness, and inclusive debate at the grassroots will lead to a more inclusive conversational educational atmosphere to explore where the little rays of Hope live to address racism and structural inequalities faced by the disadvantaged. By being honest with ourselves, we can understand whether does prejudice lie in all of us? And if it does, does that mean we can understand the other side a little better? It gives an entirely different perspective if the roles of the *voiceless* and those with power - the 'establishment'- were reversed not in an aggressive way like that seen during elections and referendums by inciting racial hatred to get elected.

By recognising that all sides in this debate can get affected will also prevent the 'other tribe' from getting blinkered and stop them from believing they are always the injured party. The innocent victims of the atrocities inflicted by the white people, a blame game, going round in circles fanning the flames of mistrust and suspicion even more. Likewise, at times' political correctness' has also prevented tackling the root causes.

The reluctance to discuss these things does play a factor. It leads to a situation whereby many police officers and other professionals feel almost the best thing to do is try and avoid it for fear of being criticised. We probably have all got ourselves into a bit of state about this. The difficulty in the police service is that the whole matter is being closed down because we are all afraid of discussing any of it, in case we say the wrong thing, that is not healthy. So at the same time, we need to be cautious. We do not end up with a culture of why have you stopped me...you were speeding...no you stopped me because I'm this or that...why have you stopped me...you were carrying a knife...no you stopped me because I'm Black...why have you stopped me...because you just mugged some old lady...no you stopped me because I'm BAME...why didn't you stop that man, he has just robbed a bank... what's the point, he's Black...See where this is going?

Racial violence in Britain has become the subject of intense scrutiny since the public inquiry in 1999 into the murder of Black teenager Stephen Lawrence. Most high-profile hate crime cases have focused on young Blacks, like Damilola Taylor, Anthony Walker, who was murdered with an axe at a Liverpool bus stop by white youths. Yet, these official figures do not give the complete picture of racially motivated murders in the UK. It reveals the situation to be much more complex because white people also get murdered, stabbed, beaten, robbed, and set on fire due to the racially aggravated murders and attacks carried out by non-white people. However, the report also suggested that white people are more likely than a non-white person to report a crime such as a street robbery by a Black or Asian person as a racial incident. [29]

Although collectively, as a percentage of the national population, the proportion of racist murders, attacks and abuse of Black and Asian people are disproportionately high compared to the white people. Even larger if expressed as a percentage of the ethnic minority population. However, we need to be careful not to go down that path because those with a divisive populist political agenda can twist the data to their advantage. They would be correct to say the number of white people murdered, attacked and abused by non-white was much higher if calculated as a percentage of the ethnic populace. Even politicise to further target specific groups by looking at the data as a percentage of population based on colour and faith to make further racially-biased points.

Whatever happens, we should not let those with evil political and religious agendas get us diverted by statistics. However, without any doubt, there should be zero tolerance, no excuse for racist behaviour by people of any colour whatsoever. Also, we must call them out after all the victims grew up and lived in the same society as the rest of us. Any racist murder, crime or act of racism is a failure of us all. Every murder is equally horrific, tragic, a soul-numbing experience for the rest of the life of the victim's family and friends. So, collectively, it should be our responsibility. Not only that of politician's and the enforcement authorities since they often face difficulty raising the issue of racial attacks on white victims for the fear that far-right extremists will exploit such data to stir up racial tensions. Sadly, at times 'political correctness' stops racism against white people from being tackled or condemned.

If we want, we can overcome barriers with a pragmatic approach and honesty from all sides. Because not only is racially motivated crime wholly despicable, whatever the victim's background, but so is discrimination, structural inequalities and institutional racism. We need to maintain balance, a nuance, by making sure not to tip the balance too much towards 'political correctness' but at the same time make sure not to discard lightly under the banner of ' political correctness' has gone mad. I'm a proud British of East African Indian origin and a Muslim – a man of colour; however, it does not mean I uphold lesser standards than a white person due to my gender and ethnicity. But then, we all have to play our part constructively.

So, at this point, we could all throw our arms up in the air and accept we're all prejudiced, racist deep down, so what's the point of trying to debate? But that's not the point I am making here. I'm saying our lives are becoming more controlled by myths and narratives, some good, some bad, deliberately manipulated to cause division to maintain hierarchies to benefit the 'establishment'. I am not disputing that this is not something new since it has been going on from the beginning of time. However, what I am saying is that we are now living in the twenty-first century and claim we have more 'civilised values' better than our hunter-gatherer ancestors. And we have learnt lessons from the vile acts from the dark moments in our history, what apartheid, slavery, racism, ethnic cleansing, genocide and illegal wars have done.

In fact, we do not have to look that far back to witness and experience the scars of twentieth-century atrocities which are happening right now. So, why not start an inclusive, open debate on a positive note to sort out millions of pieces of virtuous and destructive misinformation that our brain receives every day. We all have skeletons, big and small. None of us is above the problem or innocent as such. By processing prejudgments, discarding the useless negative ones, wrong stereotype indoctrination that non-white people are lazy and primitive. Instead, focus on developing the positive attributes further from what we have already achieved by working together.

So, first, both sides need to start a conversation with what we agree to help tackle what we disagree with, the people we seek to change and find those with whom we share similar goals. Accepting one's flaws by admitting them since no one is perfect is far more likely to yield movement on both sides than everybody shouting insults from the top of the hill at each other since few listen when yelled at and looked down upon by others. Do I mean sitting around on chairs and talking to each other? Yes, that's what I exactly mean, especially at the local community grassroots level. Not by being fearful of each other in ever-increasing circles of decreasing understanding by blaming one another and demanding more.

All the evidence suggests that barriers get broken when we stop to talk, and it puts us in touch with people we wouldn't usually meet. By sharing experiences, we can often overcome fears and suspicion and find that more unites us than divides us. The question is, why would people bother. When they feel nobody has a moment in their busy lives to listen. At times even think it has nothing to do with them as we have regulatory bodies like the Equality and Human Rights Commission (EHRC) to do it for us. True, we have all that plus findings of costly public inquiries to learn from, including decades of government legislation, policies and pledges. Yet it seems they have been ineffective, a ticking-box exercise by an army of pen-pushers, which has got us nowhere. Not the way, we the public, would like to make progress.

Otherwise, by now, we would have tackled racism with no need for worldwide Black Lives Protests civil protests we witnessed in summer 2020. Those protests took place because racism still exists, however hard we try to fudge the issue. And passing laws is a sticking plaster, a face-saving exercise, burying our heads causing more resentment, further alienation. It's because one group feels let down, believing the other group is 'handled with kid gloves' and vice versa, a no-win situation. Also, by doing nothing, the cost of inaction becomes too great. If we like, we can put up with racism, even ignore it. Even hope the problem will disappear or resolve itself. It will not; equally, it is not somebody else's problem but our collective responsibility. So, let's talk. Often doing simple things is more effective than costly complex initiatives.

At times civil protests may seem an attractive option. However, as we often see these days, they tend to turn into civil riots and looting, whatever the intention is. However frustrated it may seem or be, an aggressive approach does not resolve underlying issues. Instead of tackling concerns, it causes increasing tensions, more agony. Whereas to the victims of racism, who feel ignored for so long, more grown-up debates become a futile exercise, no point wasting more time. But I think a more civilised approach would be to have an honest dialogue with good people to bury the evil of racism forever without political point-scoring because the consequences of racism are far-reaching, adverse and detrimental. Costly to police, and instead of moving forward creates more hatred towards each other.

By having an open, honest debate, we can look at it from another viewpoint. See, the affected party could be you, anybody's husband, anybody's father, anybody's brother, anybody's work colleague or anybody's friend. It helps to connect better with the other side by focusing on shared values that transcend race, ethnicity, culture, a vision to point out to the other side how wrong they are by blaming others. Such an approach would be far more productive than stoking tensions with US and THEM attitude. Rather than encouraging people to lead lives in a parallel universe, living in isolation within the comfort of their own culture and thus find it even harder to overcome prejudice, not only their own but any prejudice they may face. Because at the end of the day, whether we like it or not, people suffer a similar fate at some stage in life irrespective of skin colour and faith. Loneliness is one such example of prejudice affecting both the young and the old. With an increase in mantle health, Alzheimer and Dementia illnesses, would it not be better to embrace new initiatives to maximise genuine understanding, contact and acquaintances to nurture a sense of equality. A sense of togetherness in social status as part of the same team to help avoid artificial racial or mental barriers.

 Non-white people, apart from their mother tongue, should also make it a top priority to learn to speak and read in English. It will help widen horizons and serve well to foster a sense of belonging by keeping in contact with the broader community. Also, help minimise white people's ill feelings that they receive preferential treatment and government grants to enjoy everything from Diwali light festivities, Notting Hill carnival to council and NHS leaflets in every language spoken in the world. Equally, what the white people cannot understand is: why non-white people can still claim that they are the victims of racial discrimination despite the protection of the legislation. Not only that, but they have changed the inner cities, changed the country's schools, changed the language, changed public institutions, taken up jobs and council estates that belonged to the white people. Not only that. But as guests to this country, they have undermined traditional British values, introduced crime, terror and strange habits that white people do not understand. So, how can they be the victims of racism? We, therefore, need to understand such mindsets, differences, suspicions amongst white and non-white people alike to make further progress.

*

Children are refreshingly non-judgmental and open-minded. We know the uncluttered innocent minds of the young tend more towards idealism, a sense that can get lost, become cynical with age. When growing up, the young don't see race and identity as a significant problem for getting along or even falling out whether in their age groups or not. So, if we can build the foundation at a young age, making friendships with people who are not like them in colour and age will help ease tensions as grown-ups; they will be more open-minded. At the same time, prevent mixing negative stereotyped assumptions and myths about non-white people in early years based on different skin colours and cultures. Focusing more early on our fundamental shared values, which are the same, will help us realise that race and faith should not be a reason to exclude someone or consider them as inferior human beings on those grounds.

Similarly, joining adventurous outdoor activities like the Duke of Edinburgh Award, scouting, girl guide and sports, a programme of localised community activities will help instil a sense of civic duty at an early age. Socially minded group activities like cleaning parks and communal allotments apart from bringing the old and young together will also uplift deprived areas, yielding results residents can benefit from and develop a bond of belonging to a community. We also need to find ways to engage both young and old to participate actively in politics, including public duty in a unique way to harness both talents. The elderly have the benefit of the experience of what they have seen, how things have gone wrong for them in the past, whereas the young are showing interest and vigour in their future and that of the planet, which should be encouraged more. It would also help alleviate some of the blight of modern society, such as loneliness, mental health, anti-social behaviour, social mobility, and social harmony.

Likewise, it's better to talk than write letters to people in the public eye because writing letters can often become a futile mind-boggling wasteful exercise. For a start, no one has time to read them anyway. Unless if you are someone very influential or a celebrity, it's most likely, you will never hear anything back, and if you are lucky, it will be a long-winded reply without addressing the actual issue. Instead of feeling dejected that no one wants to hear what you say, seething with rage, angry with frustrations, it would be more productive to start discussing the effects of poverty, loneliness, and homelessness locally. Communication and contact is a two-way street with both sides coming together to know each other better. The earlier we start that process in our lives, the easier it becomes to address the complex issues later. Only by engaging and understanding we can allay our fears towards each other.

Moreover, what we need to do first is to start asking ourselves some soul-searching questions. How will it affect your consciousness? By asking whether it is righteous not to give someone a job or promote them because of their race? And if people should be arrested more often because of their skin colour? Likewise, whether it is fair ethnic students should be given lower grades at school? Whether it is correct to stigmatise all the followers of one particular faith as terrorists due to the actions of a few? If so, why not stigmatise followers of other religions because of the actions of their members?

By asking reasonable questions and answering rationally, we will not only find out what it feels like to be at the receiving end but find solutions to resolve racism. Also, white people will be correct to argue injustices have been going on from the onset of time, including in the victim's countries of origin. However, it doesn't mean we shouldn't try, and two wrongs do not necessarily make it right. More importantly, it's inappropriate behaviour, not morally upright if we (the white people) prefer to call ourselves 'civilised' gentlemen and ladies. And if we do consider ourselves enlightened, then it is hypocritical because white people do not behave like savages, since this is what makes US, the 'in tribe' different from THEM, the 'other tribe', the uncivilised lot.

In reality, what does get us somewhere by stepping back is a sense of looking at what is right. A journey towards general social harmony and happiness. A multicultural country with people of all faiths, colours and cultures living together. In doing so, appreciate what we have and build a nation at ease with itself, a Beacon of Hope, a shining example for other countries to witness what can get achieved by focusing on shared values. An equal society is better. Not only for the poor but also for the wealthy because happiness is better for everyone, not only wealth wise but also health-wise, to deal with the modern ills of loneliness leading to higher levels of anxiety and depression. At times sharing differences of opinions and grief eases tension. Having your say relieves pain, prepares a person to be less hostile to others.

Simple, informal exchanges at the local level can raise awareness of the white majority of the obstacles faced by the ethnic minority group. It gives an understanding of the common grounds of differences and shared values. Induces a balanced viewpoint, lessens anger towards each other and feels shameful to hold prejudicial exaggerated beliefs based on skin colour. Realising how difficult lives have generally become will increase guilt, and being challenged will make white people open to change. Help adopt a more accommodating stance.

On the other hand, a stance of exaggerated prejudicial beliefs becomes a significant barrier with adverse effects if the minority feels a target of a constant barrage of attack from the white majority. More likely to withdraw into the comfort zone area into a shell of isolation, which has recently become a visible reality for some Muslim communities in Britain. For them, Britain can seem a hostile terrain, a place of constant reminder to account for themselves. Whereas sitting down exchanging ideas often leads to finding pragmatic solutions, when listening to each other's concerns, we realise that talking will achieve a lot more than not talking.

Right from birth, humans rely on social contact and interaction. Putting aside cultural and racial differences, coming together should, therefore, be a natural thing for people who want to build a better community, an infrastructure of amenities whether as babies, children, grown-ups, teachers, the employed, the unemployed, the abled, the disabled, the old. Each one, a tiny shoot of Hope, linked together to build something more substantial to leave a better legacy for the future generation.

We can only achieve this through better contact and communication, not by separation, leading isolated lives, especially in a multicultural Britain. It doesn't mean giving up one's own culture. We can do both. By recognising that underneath our skins, we are the same, and skin colour is an environmental thing, like in British winters and summers, we all go paler or darker. Also, by admitting that white people who settle, work abroad or even when on holiday in foreign countries are no different. More often than not, renowned for gravitating towards their fellow nationals, leading separate lives, practising their own culture, even supporting their national cricket or football teams without any hindrance. Many white people also find it hard to integrate. But even when their command of the local language improves, the language barrier is no longer an issue, yet still, socialise only with other emigrants. Anglo pubs, sports clubs and social groups can be a home away from home for them, and they might get through the week without saying more than a word or two in the local language. So, why it becomes a big issue when non-white people do it? Not everyone is prepared to make an effort. However, white and non-white should be encouraged because it's worth it as there's so much to gain through integration.

Let's be realistic. One thing is for sure. It's most unlikely that the dream of those groups portraying 'Go Home' banners will become a reality. We are where we are due to the failings of the immigration policies enacted by our politicians. I am not saying we should embark on open-door immigration. If anything, I have never advocated for one. But what we can't do is alter facts and reality. The truth is that most immigrants have come to Britain by right as British subjects. Others came as nationals of Commonwealth, ex-colonial countries, and have since acquired British citizenship. They have worked hard, paid taxes, played a significant role in nation-building after WWII, while many of their ancestors even fought and made sacrifices for Britain. Their grandchildren and children are now second and third generation British, and just like their parents, Britain is their home.

So, where they will go! Therefore, it is in the interest of all to come together, forget our differences based on race and religion, join together to build a better, stronger future for our children. We owe it to them even more now. We have squandered resources, accrued outstanding national debt, nearly two trillion pounds of it, which will rise even more post-Covid-19. While the twentieth-century generation will enjoy their retirement on good pensions and creature comforts, the millennials will have to clear their mess. Provided they are lucky to get a job, they will have to work hard to pay the debt for the rest of their lives. Let alone afford to buy a home of their own.

So, it would be far better to start with a more profound sense of more genuine association based on recognising each other's potential, respecting one another at an early age. In that case, I believe the gain will be even more noteworthy if we regard each other as part of the same cricket team, batting for Britain. Not one based on the cricket test mentioned before devised by Norman Tebbit segregating people based on race. Also, education at school and home can be crucial since children don't have the same hang-ups about race until they get older. Quality education should provide a holistic outlook to life within the context of contemporary knowledge for career prospects and mutual respect. Education is the only thing which will help. At the same time, not to expect changes to happen instantly, tomorrow, next year or for years. Yet, it's the answer. Of course, the politicians will not be interested. Like anything, they want a quick fix that will work before the next election. To hand out sweeteners to woo voters. Even if it means it doesn't work and costs more. If only they would invest wisely in education. A balanced mind will not only tackle racism but give Hope, help the individual and the wider community.

*

Fairness and justice are quintessential British values, qualities if rigidly adhered to, can make societies function even better, more equitably both at home and abroad. Yet it's also a diffused, confused concept, powerful changeable words whose interpretation is often challenging to legislate, administer and monitor. We all remember saying 'It's not fair' in many varied situations from a young age. Though, in the world, we inhabit not knowing a more profound sense of what it means. With the standard familiar adult response received from teachers and parents that 'life's not fair' to harden and prepare the young'uns for the unpredictable life's journey, they will face. It's a word so vague, inconsistent without a definitive legal basis. Expensive to seek justice resulting in losers and winners.

Also, an appeal to fairness is difficult to enforce with groups of people who may already feel the world to be unfair against them. Especially when the losers believe the winners have no concept and real-life experience of what pain means to live in a country under a constant spotlight. Where the colour of your skin, or if you are Muslim, can keep you back in education, work and family life. Where losers are more likely to be poor, more likely to be unemployed, more likely to be stopped and searched, more likely to end in prison despite playing a part to rebuild Britain. So when people talk about fairness, whose fairness is being talked about by the white people makes the non-white people wonder?

It would be great if we could tackle the ills of racism or eliminate systematic prejudice. However, one thing is for sure we cannot achieve it by passing laws, initiatives, seminars and conferences only. And if it were possible, we would not still be talking about it after decades to do better than the previous generation. Because empathy and coming together means all sides in this debate had moved towards each other. If we had, we would not now and again get a reminder of the past practices of racism revealing its ugly head as it did in the Summer of 2020 in America, which led to Black Lives Matter protests worldwide. Only to be followed by more public inquiries, a clamour to learn more lessons only to be forgotten.

It would even be more comforting if we were always on the right road map whereby all sides in this debate had progressed by moving towards each other. However, as long as racism exists, we need to keep trying, not by using the same failed methods of the past but pragmatic ones. Like, face to face approach by looking into each other's eyes. Not a bureaucratic process that produces thick documents, only to sit on shelves across the country to gather dust that no one remembers the main findings. Namely, the victim's cries of help should have been listened to early, not ignored. Conducting public inquiries may seem like the victim's families have achieved a degree of justice. But apart from tightening disciplinary procedures, punishing culprits for misconduct and unreserved apologies for the victim's family, the reports are meaningless if we keep repeating mistakes and politicians not learning lessons from public inquiries after pledging to do so. Leaving a feeling have we not been here before.

What are we to make of the findings of all public inquiries held to date? We know those racist incidents, or for that matter, other public disasters, are not one-offs and cannot be eliminated for good. Yet what we do know is that the common theme in most cases is that the cries of help of the victims, if listened to early, not fobbed off, the incident could have been averted and suffering or loss of lives minimised. Also, if tensions are left unchecked, simmering in all corners of Britain can soon get magnified, twisted into something more violent if there is no narrative of Hope or self-regulation holding it back at the local and national level. We need to ask who sets the limits or no limits when people embark on their journeys towards a racist murder or attack? Is it the people close to them? Or the communities in which they grew up? Or the lack of opportunities to know someone from a different race to realise that apart from one's skin colour, people are not dissimilar from me? Or they are just violent criminals? Or maybe, even a combination of some or all of these factors.

Whatever it may be. There is no excuse to take somebody else's life, cause harm to others living in the same society. Racial hatred or murder, whether it's that of a non-white or white person, is a failure of us all. Every death, every knife crime deserves a proper investigation. No matter what you think about the victim. We must try regardless of how hard it is to persuade witnesses to come forward. Although it is essential to recognise that all sides, albeit non-white people, are affected more by racism, it is best not to get bogged down by the numbers game and Home Office data. Because statistics, however useful a tool it may be, can be manipulated depending on whatever message we would like to portray to win or lose the argument. While at the same time missing the broader picture. Something politicians do so frequently to avoid answering when it comes to addressing the underlying causes of racism. Though what is clear without any doubt is that racial violence and discrimination is with us. The failure of the institution is a recurrent theme. And we need a more pragmatic inclusive debate to weed out the evils of racism. Like, find answers to questions such as. What is the bigger picture that leaves parts of the society discriminated against based on skin colour? What divides us? What leads to a sense of nervousness and tension in some sections of our society?

Similarly, it's too easy to play the blame game, blaming others. Also, too easy to blame a singular event. It's equally easy to make it somebody else's responsibility, like the equality commission to solve matters relating to discrimination and racism by putting in mechanisms to monitor or even ignore it. So that the government, the opposition, society, the rest of us, who lead busy lifestyles, can get on with our lives in the comfort of our homes, ivory tower offices and economic security. All it takes for evil to flourish is for the good people to ignore individual responsibility by being too busy doing something else or too rich, relaxed in one's comfort zone to worry with an I'm alright Jack attitude. For too long, we have been tinkering around the edges. Kicking the can down the road as somebody else's problem, and if we continue doing so, it will continue flaring up.

Even the Covid-19 pandemic failed to dampen the feelings of those affected by the appalling acts of racism to participate in civil protests in Britain and elsewhere because they felt that no one listens and years of reasoning with the 'establishment' has got them nowhere. However frustrated it may seem, or it may be, an aggressive approach does not resolve the underlying issue, except it causes more tension and suffering. To the victims of racism, holding a grown-up debate may seem a futile exercise, something they have tried to do for so long and now feel there is no point in wasting more time. But I think a more appropriate approach would be to win the hearts and minds of the good people, the white people leading everyday lives by having a grown-up dialogue to bury the evil of racism once and for all.

The critical point I'm trying to make here is not to play one group against another based on skin colour. It is more to do with an element of recognition that, unlike America's war over race, culture war and social class plays a more significant role than skin colour in causing racism in British communities. It's because discrimination affects both white and non-people, albeit the latter more due to their skin colour. Even if a white person has not experienced class-based discrimination, we need to tackle it without 'compartmentalising' to understand their underlying racist tendencies or resentment towards people of Black and Asian origins. Hence, it's essential to look at the broader concept of defining discrimination, not one based on skin colour.

Neatly summing up or categorising racism may make it easy to be against it; however, it adopts a relaxed or a *déjà vu* stance as somebody else's problem than admit discrepancies existing at the grassroots level. Therefore to root out racism, it's vital to consider all types of prejudices. Since it's natural for a white person to be wary when presented with a set of cultural behaviour outside one's own experience, the experience of your peer groups, and the understanding of what you imagine or want to accept as a community. Or perhaps, that wariness (fear) relating to the 'other tribe' comes from your personality; you are someone who deals with prejudice based on other people's subtle or blatant influences and indoctrination on you, the stories that they tell you about the 'other tribe'.

So, what is the answer? I believe quality education should focus not only on improving career prospects with degrees coming out of one's ears from well-known institutions. But conversational education of the type starting from home to open one's mind to see humanity as a whole to breakdown barriers, not in isolation based on skin colour, faith and culture such as 'I'm alright Jack', only calling it out when it affects you. Because one of the pillars upon which racism sits, namely prejudice, is something easy to associate with to build a group aversion from what an individual may have perceived as a threat based on personal experience at work or neighbourhood reinforced by someone with a similar view. Also, disliking the 'other tribe' as one whole entity with fellow dis-likers gives 'allies', provides cover in a way that an individual dislike doesn't. A comfort blanket, further reinforced when taken in conjunction with sections of biased press reports, social media posts, political discourse that too many immigrants are coming, uncontrolled into Britain. Immigrants who are dirty, rude, lazy and putting pressure on public services.

These stereotyping tendencies to become 'allies' based on stories people hear from others make them feel panicky towards immigrants. As the world becomes noisier with information, we increasingly lean on stereotypes to function. Prejudice thus becomes a tool of navigation. Even though many white people may have never met or known a non-white person properly, in their neighbourhoods, let alone far-flung parts of Britain, who conveniently forget. That the immigrant they hate so much may have saved their lives in the NHS, stocked food in shops, provided care without whom some of the public services they rely upon daily may not function! Therefore instead of reality, such false mentality becomes prejudices experienced by the many deliberately built on factual misinformation talked by the few that leads to racism which is closely allied though not the same, but the latter then follows the former.

Perhaps, now is also an opportune time to re-visit the mantra of Education, Education, Education? Not with a view to flood universities with student population but more to do with the quality, not the quantity of education, a mishmash culture of meaningless performance tables and targets mentioned previously comparing pupils from advantaged and disadvantaged families. Instead, ask why white British and other white non-British children from low-income homes are the lowest-performing at primary schools and worsening as they progress through secondary schools? Whereas several ethnic minority groups, mainly those of Indian origin, outperform white British pupils. The difference is even starker for those on free school meals. Asian and mixed-race children now outperform white pupils, and only Black pupils are doing worse than them. In comparison, a white working-class boy on free school meals is less likely to achieve standard five or more A-C grades at GCSE level than all other pupils. [30]

In the past, lower education attainment levels did not matter. They were less noticeable and not necessary. Because the white working class could find easy well-paid jobs in the local factory and coal mines, but that easy access after leaving school with poor grades or even by not attending school has now long gone. However, echoes of that good life remain in the minds of those left behind, as seen during the Brexit debate, their resentment exploited by the opportunist political leadership with a populist agenda of patriotism. In addition, white pupils still tend to see achieving a university qualification as less critical than children from ethnic minority groups. Since the advent of student fees, white pupils are even more reluctant now to attend universities.

By venting resentment and anger on ethnic immigrants, making a game of winners and losers based on racial hatred will not solve the problem. Not doing anything will only worsen it, more so after Covid-19 when many livelihoods have already disappeared, with unemployment predicted to rise significantly. I hope we don't end up pitting groups and communities against each other. It is a structural issue that existed before Covid-19, affecting both the white working-class and ethnic minority groups. They both have little access to power, although the more impoverished ethnic minorities have even less. Yet both have become pawns in the political power game played by the 'establishment'. As a result, people's attention gets distracted. And sometimes, people seem to get so busy engaged in racial hatred inflicting tensions towards each other, especially on social media hiding behind a screen. They forget that the targets are elsewhere, and people need to come together as an influential force to make those who have taken them for granted listen.

The groups often portrayed as enemies by becoming allies can become a potent force to get heard by the' establishment'. For a start, there is clear evidence that children from some ethnic minority groups on free school meals outperform children from a similar background. So, wouldn't it be nice for once politicians swallowed their pride and took the trouble of finding out what those minority groups are doing right? How about, instead of waiting for politicians who are busy with their self-serving interests to fulfil, ethnic minorities and white working-class people came together to find solutions to where they find themselves? An excellent place to start would be to find out what ethnic minority parents are doing right for their children's education? Helping each other will gradually break racial barriers and improve an education system that lets down those who need most as a stepping stone to a better future. Such an initiative will also help address the national skill shortage problem and needs of post-Brexit Britain, creating wealth via a prosperous economy and employment. Nobody can go back and start a new beginning. But if we want, we can start today and make a new ending.

Traditionally, the British are reasonable, rational and intelligent people, with an overwhelming tendency to lean towards equality, freedom of speech, mutual respect for other's culture, faith and beliefs, rising to challenges. Not afraid to stand up for the underdog, whether it be fighting fascism whereby millions of innocent Commonwealth citizens in Britain and abroad gave their lives. Or coming to aid those in need of support by donating generously, breaking records every year, contributing even more to well-known charities like Oxfam, Children in Need, Comic Relief, Sports Aid, and many other small ones. No different from the shared values of immigrants from various parts of the Commonwealth. That is why when asked to come to help rebuild Britain after WWII, they answered the call making Britain their home. As British citizens, they too believe in the quintessential British values towards the common cause of fairness, freedom of speech, mutual respect for other's culture, faith and beliefs. Similarly, immigrants are also thinkers and rational beings, not prone to irrational reactions with alien habits prone to superstitions as portrayed by some sections of society and the press.

Therefore, before it's too late, I firmly believe that the more we talk openly about immigration and racism, the better we will overcome resentment creeping up in all directions, which require policies that manifest fairness. Many think that this is not the time or the place for the debate. If we cannot talk about it now, then when. Also, the way to control immigration is not through more draconian laws biased against non-white people; usually pledged by politicians to woo voters by blaming immigrants for shortages in hospital beds, schools, housing, and neighbourhoods changed beyond recognition. However, if politicians were honest about it, it has more to do with their past fifty years of immigration, housing, welfare, education policy failures.

I further believe social cohesion and racism can be tackled pragmatically through quality education and social mobility by addressing social inequalities instead of entirely by top-down state action and more laws. Because most white people, friends of non-white people like me and others who mean a lot to us are not racist, despite whatever ills the equalities campaigners can throw at their door by generalising all white people are the same. Therefore, it is crucial for the likeminded, white and non-white people to work together, so there is zero tolerance towards racism. Otherwise, it will only encourage more dog-whistles from politicians with speeches like Enoch Powell's 1968 "Rivers of Blood", inciting racial prejudice and hatred towards immigrants, capitalising on the resentment of the white people from deprived areas who feel let down due to structural inequalities.

Engaging in a grown-up debate will soon become apparent to the white people that not all non-white people are welfare spongers and do not respond like savages. It will alleviate many stereotype misinformation deliberately purported by the 'establishment' and wrongly held by the white people. It will help them quickly realise that immigrants can also respond similarly in a 'civilised' manner, and their core values are no different. More importantly, a person's most valuable asset is not a brain loaded with knowledge but a heart full of love with an open ear to listen. We need an open-minded debate on the subject, not a resurrection of previous generations' mistakes that went wrong. We need to look closely at some of the practices taking place under the disguise of democracy, such as ethnic cleansing, genocides, illegal wars, apartheid and structural inequalities, which are no different to those past abhorrent events.

There is a tendency to think racism in our societies will lessen over time, that attitudes and outcomes will inevitably improve. This belief endures despite frequent sobering evidence of deeply entrenched racial inequalities in Britain. How many more lessons do we all need to learn? Lessons we already know yet remain unimplemented because of a half-hearted approach. Indeed, it will soon be thirty years since the racist murder of teenager Stephen Lawrence, an event that led, after six years of campaigning, to a public inquiry that deemed the UK's most prominent police authority guilty of institutional racism. Many more have followed ever since.

However, while legislating against discrimination is vital, it persists, not lessened. We need to ask why? Are we missing something obvious? It seems we are. So, what is missing is grassroots understanding of the underlying problems, which we will never tackle by sitting in the ivory tower with more expensive public inquiries at a cost to the taxpayer to learn more lessons!  If we want to tackle racism, let's engage more pragmatically by listening to those trying to speak on the subject without motives, who may have some simple solutions to offer.

We all need to come together and debate in a twenty-first-century style 'civilised' manner, make friends in the truest sense, and leave behind a better legacy for the wellbeing of future generations. Anger breeds anger. Hate breed's hate. Also, best not to believe everything one hears or reads, propaganda purported by the press, on social media and politicians with a right-wing extremist agenda about the' other tribe', whether that person is a Muslim, Christian, Hindu, Jewish, Buddhist and even those of no faiths or non-believers.

Instead, let's focus on what we have a lot in common: Hope, aspirations, education, justice, beliefs and the Commonwealth. Irrespective of skin colour and different cultures, we have similar shared values and needs: food, a roof over the head, a job, and a better future for the family. Even the religious doctrines of the major faiths are united in giving the same message: Love thy Neighbour; loyalty to the land of domicile; seek knowledge and education from all corners of the world. I feel optimistic because Britain is the best place to live in the world with an excellent multiculturalism track record, which we can make even better use of based on our shared British values.

# 8.

# TWISTED DEMOCRACY

Some things frustrated voters always demand of politicians: be more honest; be more pragmatic; be more principled; be less ideological; be more accountable; have a vision; sound less angry; talk about values; talk about bread-and-butter issues; admit when wrong; don't remain in denial; don't avoid answering questions; don't make empty pledges. To the voters, this sort of sheer dereliction of duty seems staggering.

Many voters can not understand why politicians quickly blame others when they get caught out with improper behaviour. Even claim as David Cameron did when he was found out over Grensill saga "I think I'm a victim of spellcheck here." No different to Boris Johnson casually discarding his use of racist name-calling as "colourful language."

The government's mantra of collective responsibility means no individual accountability, a blame culture of passing the buck. Is it any wonder Priti Patel, when asked on Andrew Marr's show on 23 May 2021, believes ministers - including herself – "breaking codes and things of that nature" isn't important because they're doing "difficult jobs?" The public perceives the politicians are constantly changing the laws, so they cannot be held accountable for incompetence. Such a mindset is a betrayal of trust, undermines credibility, and is the main missing element in politics.

It seems genuinely incredible that politicians who permanently tell ordinary people that they need to take personal responsibility seriously are often appalling at doing it themselves. Yet, much of the politics they now conduct is in a context of post-truth; not only lying is tolerated, but the very idea of verifiable truth is deemed elusive, lost in a fog of deliberately confected doubt and confusion.

I have always believed trust is one of the essential words among the millions of words expended in our lifetime. A word closely interlinked with honesty has played a crucial role. Shaping lives from birth till death to help disseminate the truth, build relationships, and forge ahead in life in a humane 'civilised' manner. Trust also helps create a mutual bond of loyalty, develop understanding, and expect those entrusted with it will put your well-being before their own. Trust takes years to build, seconds to shatter and forever to rebuild. So, it's vitally important for those with powers to act on behalf of others to honour that trust bestowed upon them.

From an early age, we place immense trust in parents extending to others to widen horizons in our quest for knowledge to better our lives. The word has a strong resonance, primarily when spoken or written by eminent politicians, professionals and religious people. But recently, people's trust has been taken for granted. It has become a norm for politicians to advocate bold sentiments: "the will of the people" is sacrosanct; they entered politics "to make life better for others." On the one hand very eager to be in charge and enjoy perks, yet when they get caught out, they abandon the sinking ship, leaving a disenchanted public to clear up the mess and pay for their mistakes.

Western politicians themselves are busy undermining the very democratic processes that brought them to power. In America, Donald Trump got elected as president with wholesale attacks on institutions and 'civilised' values that have made America the leader of the free world, including a 'free press'. Although some Americans have come to realise his deception, many see him as a saviour. Only time will tell who is right. Whatever the outcome, Trump has done immense damage to American democracy and credibility. What's worrying, he has found new ways to conduct information warfare against open societies. Freedoms that we have taken for granted. He has legitimised disinformation, populism, polarised opinions and intimidation. By stigmatising the parts of the free press as 'fake news', he has undermined trust, denied voters access to the facts.

Trumpian style autocratic tendencies are now hard at work, his tactics unashamedly and eagerly emulated worldwide in Brazil, Hungary, India, Israel, Poland and Turkey. Bad people are rubbing their hands with glee. Big mistakes affecting humanity are being made right under our eyes. Will we wake up before it's too late? It all seems legal, taking place under the pretext of democracy, which saw off fascism, communism, and most forms of dictatorship in the last century. How can America and the coalition of Western countries be taken seriously by Russia, China, Saudi Arabia, North Korea, Myanmar and others when they misbehave. Will they listen to 'civilised' people in the west telling them how to conduct themselves when Trump and others disguised under the banner of democracy behave otherwise?

Just because it happens elsewhere or has happened before doesn't mean it should be allowed to happen. We should not think that it won't happen to us since we are more 'civilised' to know that two wrongs don't make a right than behave just like them. We should not be complacent. In Britain, there is also a growing concern of both disinformation warfare and funding for Brexit and party donations originating in Russia, evidence which the government has not been keen to publish. [31] It is time too for journalists and pundits to move on. Start a critical self-assessment of the political events and commentary of the past years. What we got right and what we have got wrong to hold politicians accountable. So we do not sleepwalk it since its well-known politicians feed tasty morsels to favoured journalists who haplessly dance to their tunes for a trade-off in perks, like a seat on the plane for foreign state visits and honours. While time after time, the press failing to scrutinise politicians and their clan of 'advisers' who have let down businesses and the public with their inability to plan; their abject failure to take tough decisions early enough for people to prepare for the consequences.

Likewise, we should not be arrogant to think that we are going through a temporary phase. And that we have proper "checks and balances", not only in British but also in American democracy, too strong to be toppled by one 'strongman' - or any other type of divisive argument, steeped in national chauvinism and international ignorance. Sure, there is no doubt that Britain's current political culture and institutions are a unique combination of norms and rules, as is the case for every country. However, we can see how easily they can get manipulated from recent skulduggery witnessed in Britain. We should be mindful that whether simply applying the American style of politics, insights and tactics are appropriate in contemporary Britain. In other words, we have to assess legitimacy and morality. And not force propaganda. By heavily relying on twenty-first-century technology and social media platforms to influence politics into rigid frames of the last century world of old-fashioned politics, which has had its fair share of dark moments carried out in the name of democracy. Does this mean that it cannot happen in Britain? Of course, it can.

Donald Trump has already shown what can get done on Twitter in full view of everyone! That has now become truer in the age of populism, which often disdains governmental competence as a trait associated with a hated bureaucratic elite. Trump slashed and burned his way through institutional Washington and its accumulated expertise; his supporters cheered him on as he did it. Encouraging cohorts like Boris Johnson, Narendra Modi, Benjamin Netanyahu, Viktor Orban and others unashamedly to copy, knowing it works to get elected and stay in power. Never mind when and if the truth comes out eventually because it will be too late; they will be long gone regardless of how badly they governed the country or told lies to stay in power for self-serving interests and greed.

What is so insincere is why politicians in the west see the behaviour of others as 'uncivilised' when their behaviour is no different? Why did 'civilised' politicians remain silent when Donald Trump audaciously baptised countries as 'banana' republics when his behaviour was identical, if not worse? Why inciting violence by a defeated American president to hang to power any different from a military coup? Why did ex-President George Bush fail to speak up against Trump's rhetoric inciting violence? Is it because Bush knows something about the illegitimate forcible overthrow of governments that he, as American president, oversaw in the Middle East? Is it because of his guilt during invasions of Iraq and Afghanistan demanding the overthrow of those countries governments that Bush didn't speak? Why are claims of voter fraud by *loser* Trump without evidence of fraud dissimilar from wasting court and police time by the public?

What is also so insincere is that: Why when Donald Trump says "fight," his ardent supporters claim it's "freedom of speech," he was speaking figuratively, it's not inflammatory; whereas when others protest, they are terrorists, radicalised or woke? A study has found that American voters believe there is a link between elected officials' use of heated or aggressive rhetoric and the possibility of violence against people and minority groups. There is broad agreement that officials should avoid this type of language. About eight in ten (78%) say that elected officials using heated or aggressive language to talk about specific people or groups makes violence against those people or groups more likely; far fewer (21%) say this type of language does not cause violence more likely. [32] We've already visited in previous chapters the filthy secret of hiding behind dog whistles by crowd-pleasing snake oiled politicians with the help of the 'free press' in their quest for power. Whereby, they emptily indulge misapprehensions, deceptions, or worse, seeking to realise them crudely, with little concern for the damage they do. But what we have not explored is how these have been reimagined in various subtle forms to create a divisive society in the name of democracy over recent years. Is it any wonder why there is a rise in anti-social behaviour and racist language when 'civilised' political leaders themselves use inflammatory language?

What is equally hypocritical is why chants of "God bless America" by the mob during Capitol Hill riots are not considered terrorist acts, just like Muslim bigots who shout *"Allahu Akbar,"* meaning God is Great in Arabic? Why the whole race and Christian faith do not get tarnished as terrorists, whereas Muslims are? Why is the orderly transfer of power in American democracy marred by violent scenes on Capitol Hill not an act of barbarism? Why five dead, explosive devices and pipe bombs found after Trump "supporters" clashed with police on Capitol Hill, the beacon of democracy, is not a terrorist act? Why does Trump "supporter's" armed assault on Capitol Hill validates violence as equating to a democratic political debate? Why politicians, advisors and those in authority who all claim their main aim is to serve public duty do not speak out when injustices and corrupt practices occur while in office yet only do so afterwards or abandon a sinking ship after a major public disaster?

What is even more duplicitous is that: What the world witnessed on Capitol Hill was not an attempted coup by a motley band of cranks from Haiti, and African countries Donald Trump calls "Shithole." Or, for that matter, by Muslim terrorists shouting *"Allahu Akbar."* We must call it what it was: an attempted coup by the 'civilised' people following orders of the 'civilised' president of America behaving in an 'uncivilised' barbaric manner. This behaviour is an embarrassing low, at par with utterly unacceptable behaviour, an affront to democracy everywhere, not a very good example of 'civilised' values and democracy for others to follow other than hypocrisy. It gives no right to occupy moral high ground, point fingers that such behaviour is more associated with the violent transfer of power that happens in the more volatile nations around the world. While at the same time, turn a blind eye when it happens in 'civilised' democracy like America!

If that was not enough, as the stunning events unfolded on Capitol Hill, blatant hypocrisy was on display when the 'civilised' public could draw comparisons between the police response to the insurrection and the brutal attacks on Black Lives Matter protesters. The contrasting police response to Black Lives Matter vs Trump mob. Whereby, the Capitol Hill police showed respect and restraint for violent, anti-democratic violent protestors and, on the other hand, showed fierce resistance to peaceful Black Lives Matter protests in the summer of 2020. It raises concerns if this is an example of a culture of anti-Black racism in policing, the stark difference in law enforcement approach to the Capitol coup versus the response to George Floyd's killing. What if the Capital Hill mob were Black? Would the response have been different?

Thankfully, elections in the UK have never resulted in appalling incidents seen in America. Not so far. It may not be violent in this country. Yet no one should be in any doubt about early signs of political chicanery. Because it is no secret that Boris Johnson was an even more devoted follower of Trump. He condemned the "whinge-o-rama" after his election in 2016, declared we should "pay tribute" to his achievements, and told US diplomats, Trump was "making America great again." [33] To the extent said Trump deserved to win a Nobel Peace Prize. Johnson, of course, has learnt a great deal from his mentor. The government's attacks on the media, judiciary and civil service, purge of backbench Tory MPs and prorogation of parliament were tactics lifted directly from Trump's book of etiquettes in democracy. While at the same time, Johnson basked in the president's love of Brexit too and appeared to relish Trump's designation of him as "Britain's Trump." The Tory party were not just complicit but partly responsible for Trump's obscenity.

The saying what America does Britain follows in due course. Let's hope the populist divisive politics engraved more by Donald Trump does not head our way. We have seen signs of it creeping into our politics during Brexit referendum and 2019 elections. Donald Trump's popularity should be a wake-up call for the political class to restore trust in democracy. They should speak out when things are not right. Stop kowtowing along tribal party-political lines. Politicians often tell us that American elections are a big test for democracy. But we have also seen what one nasty person like Donal Trump in the name of democracy is capable of doing. Not a good example for others whom we want to convert to embrace democracy. Or on those on whom we try to proclaim our 'civilised' values, making one wonder what those are. Hopefully not greed, hypocrisy, lies, deceit!

Hence, what we cannot afford in the twenty-first century is to take today's democracy practised by twentieth-century politicians for granted that they have millennials' best interests at heart. It may be so. But equally, democracy is more than just casting votes once every few years during elections. Which regrettably, many voters don't even bother to exercise their rights despite believing Western democracy is the best political system. Additionally, lack of accountability amongst politicians has further led to an increase in disillusioned voters. At the same time, democracy in Britain has never been perfect; however, recently, it has been weakened further due to gerrymandering and cronyism. Resulting in the disenchanted public placing trust in the judicial institutions and not politicians, as seen by the rise in legal challenges not only during the Brexit debate but subsequently due to the corrupt and fragile undemocratic practices deployed by politicians.

*

Following an initial wave of condemnation, Republicans concerns appear to be waning and warming towards Trump, fully aware that his supporters are poised to punish anyone who displays disloyalty. With that in mind, party leaders are working to keep Trump in the fold as they focus on their careers. Because of this, a growing number of Republicans backed away from impeaching the former president Trump: despite initial widespread condemnation from members of his party for being responsible for much of the blame for inciting the deadly Capitol Hill attacks killing five people. Why? Because they are scared of losing their seats in the 2022 mid-term elections, that's why, not bothered about justice, truth, trust or democracy. What a bunch of hypocrites? How can America preach to others to behave in a 'civilised' way? With Trump's exit, the party is split, between those Republicans wanting to move on and those elected by emulating him or seeking his support. By being with him, not against him. The primaries are going to be where tensions will get tested. Like those evangelicals at a church rally who worship Trump because they believe he has been sent to them by God.

The Grand Old Party (GOP) may face an uncertain future with Trump's exit but not him. Trump won't be going away. His pincer attack on two fronts just beginning will see to that. Trump will make sure GOP primary voters will remember the betrayal. Not only those five Republican senators but any wavers who supported or thought about a second impeachment trial better start bracing for primary challengers in 2022. There is no doubt Donald Trump will remember that impeachment vote and capitalise on the betrayal. Even if Trump doesn't actively campaign against sitting Republicans, his supporters' loyalty to him could still define GOP primaries. Trump will have his loyal challengers contesting in the primaries. Likewise, his legacy will continue with the political aspirations of his daughter, son-in-law and son in the 2024 or future American presidential elections.

The Trump takeover of the party of Abraham Lincoln makes a family succession more likely than not because the party doesn't care about any of the issues that used to drive the party. Now it's all about Trump, and Trump only cares about himself. In that sense, Trump remains in power, not in constitutional limbo, neither convicted and removed nor cleared, but controlling power by putting his cronies in the position of power. Trump will have his people in the House of Representatives, Senate and GOP grassroots well before the 2024 Presidential election to pave the way, if not for him, then one for his children. Trump's legacy will define American democracy. That

Beacon of Hope and liberty called America, that self-described beacon of democracy, that supposed shining city on Capitol Hill. Now a laughing stock on the world stage. No matter the consequences on democracy, except Trump will be at peace, his dynasty will continue one way or another. No different to what Boris Johnson said during the 2019 elections of 630 Tory candidates, "MPs will do what they are told to do." Instead of relying on their judgment and the voter's needs, instead will serve as Boris Johnson's mouthpiece.

In the UK, we are equally prone to the same impulses of the high-octane events of the Capitol Hill invasion by the thugs. And to think it cannot happen is to remain in denial by claiming there is a difference in degree as the British "keep a stiff upper lip" to stay resolute and unemotional when faced with adversity means all the difference in the world. The reality is British politics is also polarised. Not that we will see the storming of Westminster or anything like the 1605 Gunpowder Plot, but it's easy to see the similarities because of the 'special relationship'; Britain follows in the footsteps of America. No different when it comes to British and American politics; after all, they tend to be kissing cousins: what happens there usually ends up happening here. We, too, have a consensus corrupted by social media, the right-wing and left-wing groups - with all manner of angry, fractured communities and right-wing media loudly insisting their own 'facts'. Our democracy has also been scarred by violence, in particular the murder of Jo Cox MP by a far-right nationalist. Another MP, Rosie Cooper, escaped murder planned by a neo-Nazi who got sentenced to life in prison, a minimum of twenty years. And most recently, the senseless murder of Sir David Amess on 15 October 2021, a veteran parliamentarian who commanded immense respect and affection not only from cross-party colleagues but the public as well.

The reality is that, even though the public didn't storm our parliament, British MPs were jostled and abused on their way to work by hardcore supporters from both sides of the divisive, hostile Brexit debate after the 2016 EU referendum. Britain's culture war is so potent that we have our mobs grappling with politics, responding to the dog whistles of our politicians. We have respectable sections in the media and honourable government members who pump out conspiratorial theories about woke. At the same time, the elite preaches against mask-wearing and lockdowns during the Covid pandemic as violations of civil liberties. When far-right and far-left extremism spills out onto the streets, claiming lives, attacking democracies, it's a result of a million compounded complicities and complacencies.

Trump and Brexit are responses to a political system that's imploding. Democracy that's in urgent need of a radical redesign to wrest it from the liars. I don't blame people for voting for Trump or Brexit: these are responses to a twisted, distrusted democracy. Elections captured: by money, lobbyists and the media; policy convergence among the major parties, crushing authentic choice; hollowing out of parliaments and other political institutions and the transfer of powers to unaccountable bodies: these are a perfect formula for disenfranchisement and disillusion. The global rise of demagogues and outright liars suggests that a system nominally built on consent and voter participation is imploding.

Sadly, we are beginning to see a greater degree of shenanigans and acts of cronyism in British democracy. In 2019, to get elected, Boris Johnson, just like Donald Trump, stopped at nothing. Even if it meant breaking the laws of the land, tell porky pies. Together with the right-wing press, Mr Johnson led the nation into a constitutional crisis to woo voters with a populist agenda, pedalling insulting and divisive statements, like "people versus parliament" and "enemies of the people." Such selfish behaviour of pitting one group against another only serves to cause more resentment, further alienation. It encourages the public to emulate such behaviour. Whatever the political belief, one should set a good example for others to follow and make a difference. But to do that, politics needs to open up more to the ordinary public, to reflect empathy of real-life issues and the "burning injustices." And not just speech-making, then go back on what they said after being elected, becoming confined to self-serving egos and party interests. The proroguing of parliament in 2019 by Mr Johnson and deceitful slogans like 'enemy of the people' in right-wing newspapers only serves to undermine democracy.

How can we preach non-democratically elected dictators to behave in a 'civilised' manner? Why would China listen to Britain over its expulsion of four Hong Kong politicians? The likes of Donald Trump and Boris Johnson are no different from Narendra Modi, Jair Bolsonaro, Benjamin Netanyahu, Aung San Suu Kyi and others. They all behave as 'legalised dictators' and charlatans under the umbrella of democracy in their quest to grab political power. And, if allowed to go unchecked, sow their seeds to produce the next generation like them to fulfil their brand of divisive politics. The current trend proves that they are making progress by inciting hatred with a populist political agenda; this is precisely why it is vital to learn the correct lessons from the past. It is up to us, especially the next generation (millennials), to learn history's past lessons, making sure to exercise their democratic right.

India is one country that often gets mentioned, thrown around many times as the "world's largest democracy" when discussing democracy. However, it's becoming increasingly difficult to overlook India's fast-declining democratic standards under Narendra Modi, who thinks it means 'legalised oppression'. Like the daily assaults on civil liberties during farmer's protests and threats to India's Muslim minority. In

India, hate speech is legitimised and rife, whereby peaceful dissent gets criminalised, freedom of the press faces new constraints, jails are filling up with political prisoners and peaceful dissenters as the servile judiciary turns a blind eye to the injustices. At the same time, while this is happening, the west and Britain remain silent not to jeopardise prospective post-Brexit trade deals with India!

Tyrant Modi's hate-filled campaign to de-Islamify India is nothing new. The west knows fully well Modi has already presided over the deaths of more than two thousand dead, including the blood of three Britons of Indian origin during the 2002 anti-Muslim riots in Gujarat. Suppose it doesn't matter much as they were not white! Incidentally, Mr Miodi had faced a travel ban imposed by the US and UK. But now, Mr Modi appears to want nothing less than the destruction of the Islamic monuments in India and is hell-bent on the obliteration of the 200 million Indian Muslims by making it difficult for them. Let us not forget that he has already forcibly taken away Indian citizenship from many millions of Indian Muslims and rendered them stateless. A blatant crime committed by Mr Modi even though India is a signatory to the UN declaration of human rights, whereby citizenship is a central tenet. Instead, the UN and the west have remained silent, don't care, while all this is happening in India under their noses by Mr Modi's ideologically driven, hate-filled agenda. Do they not care what happens in India? But how can Britain and America even dare condemn Narendra Modi, or China and others, when the track of the record of its political leaders with a populist-nationalist agenda is no different to theirs!

India has now slipped two more places to 53rd in the Economist Intelligence Unit's Democracy Index—from 27th place in 2014. Sweden's V-Dem Institute currently lists India among the top ten countries most quickly becoming autocracies, on the verge of losing its status as a democracy due to the severely shrinking space for the media, civil society and political opposition. [34] Therefore, for America and the moral west alliance of democracies to work effectively against China, Russia, Myanmar, Saudi Arabia, Afghanistan, Iraq, Iran, *et al.*, it is vitally important to adhere to consistent standards. Pressing these countries to embrace western democracy while turning a blind eye against gross violations by allies like India does not look good that the 'civilised' Free World is serious about human rights. When under Modi, increasingly undisguised tyranny of shocking acts of religious and caste intolerance violating human rights are also occurring in India in the name of democracy which is no different from the appalling actions of oppression in those countries we are quick to condemn!

*

Despite being a *loser* during the 2020 US presidential election, Donald Trump tried everything in his power to maintain control of the White House doing what Trump knows best: how to cling to power, how to divide people, how to protect himself after leaving the White House, as he could face prison time because of pending legal investigations and civil suits. That risk of prosecution looming over him made Trump tighten his iron grip on the presidency. Surrounded by political and legal advisers sharing similar values, he kept himself busy replacing senior Pentagon officials with loyalists and pardoning cronies to protect himself instead of tackling Covid-19 to save American lives and livelihoods. Trump even shored up his influence by awarding Narendra Modi the prestigious US military decoration Legion of Merit as insurance to help secure his future business interests in India. The politics of it stinks; the path chosen by the most powerful country sets an awful example, gravely undermining trust in democracy.

How can America preach rogue nations to embrace democracy? When the doling out of amnesty by the ex- American presidents, a privilege aggressively deployed by Donald Trump is no different to corruption. It's an abuse of power, overriding courts, juries and prosecutors, wiping away convictions and sentences to a group of his cronies just weeks before his presidential term ended. Applying his standard of justice for his allies shows how politicians are rotten and corrupt to the core. It makes a mockery of democracy and justice in the full glare of the public. Is it any wonder the people have lost trust in politicians? How can the public be blamed for doing the same?

If anything, the act of pardon doesn't make those recipients not guilty. Instead, it proves they are guilty to the teeth and will continue with their criminal activities as loose cannons. Such corrupt use of the presidential pardon is an affront to justice. It lets off criminals unpunished. Donald Trump is not the only American president to abuse the privilege and lose the trust of people. No former presidents, Republican or Democrat, have spent time in prison or jail, including Richard Nixon in 1974 received a pardon from President Gerald Ford after resigning in disgrace from the presidency for obstruction of justice despite the abuse of power in the Watergate scandal. Also, Bill Clinton didn't face criminal charges, although the House of Representatives voted to impeach him in 1998 on one charge of perjury and another for obstruction of justice.

This kind of attitude is music to those big corporations paying slave wages or destroying the environment want to hear. It just serves to amplify the so-called differences between the haves and have nots because the political parties are paying no attention since ultimately they report to the same corporate handlers and wealthy donors within the same corrupted system. There is nothing wrong with being extremely rich and very successful, especially when somebody has worked hard for it. But the wealthy need to remember that excessive greed does not help those at the other end of the scale relying on zero-hour contracts and food banks. Also, it is morally wrong when the rich try their best to resist taxation of their wealth and profits. Such greed means starving the government of much-needed revenues to invest in public services, decaying infrastructure and repayment of the national debt.

Such mindset and the winner-take-all voting system, and the lawlessness of campaign financing perfectly suits those at the top. The ruling class do not want a wide array of options for voters; just two, same genes, different features. As the right-wing has become more and more extreme, Democrats and Labour suddenly look like the party of the people. But they're not. They play within the same apparatus as the Republicans and Conservatives. They are, as the cynical saying goes, the lesser of two evils. What's happening in America and Britain is no different in India, Kenya, Myanmar, the Middle East, Israel and other ex-colonial countries. Over there, we also witness people of one colour getting weaponised by access to the levers of power, the strength to do something with a slow trickle of prejudice because of the links and networks needed to build an 'establishment'. The majority position - democratic or not - with a political agenda inflicting suffering on the 'other group' because of race, faith or tribe, can only be described as racist. It is no different when they accuse ex-white colonialist nations like Britain of playing the 'divide and rule' game when they ruled India, Kenya....

Politicians never truly own what they say in their speeches as their own opinion. After claiming the mantle of being a rare breed politician only concerned with the future, an altruist of sorts to make life better for others, a patriot first, who didn't seek this cause but instead had it thrust upon by others. They then go on to profess where they stand only to hide later behind the opinions of others, and quick to point out what they say or write in their handsomely paid newspaper column's reflects conversation of their constituents and the wider public, namely the silent majority. Therefore, it is time the public regained democracy by dumping politicians with self-serving egos and party interests so that the electorate get what they voted for, not a government that thinks it has the right to impose its will on all.

Another helpful ploy politicians often use is that what they say reflects views of ordinary people from outside the Westminster village politics, which colleagues fail to understand. They deploy tactics like 'I feel your pain because I'm one of you' to rouse and connect with the audience to gain credibility. It conveys legitimacy giving an impression of an 'honest' politician who will solve their problems by listening to the people, especially on immigration, Brexit, sounding like they're acting on behalf of the general public. In a way, it is a cowardly way of stoking racial hatred, an US and a

THEM attitude, to get elected without taking responsibility for the consequences. Apart from enhancing their political cause further, they also cherry-pick facts and figures to support arguments with posters and catchy slogans. Reminding how quickly the white population and their towns will become overrun by hordes of non-white people with peculiar cultural habits, especially those of Muslim faith. And how the decent white people will find it hard to get jobs and face shortages in public services.

*

There is no doubt that trust in politics is at an all-time historical low. It is also correct politics is a dirty game. As Harold Wilson said, "A week is a long time in politics," therefore, politicians are more worried about media headlines and spin to satisfy the appetite of 24-hour TV news channels. Accordingly, focus more on short term announcements knowing too well will soon be forgotten as the media moves onto the next breaking story. Also, the politicians do not have the stomach to do it as it involves commitment. They know they only have to pass the time, look busy doing something, suck up tax payer's hard-earned money with empty pledges, as they may not be around in five years. So best to use their time lining up their pockets planning for a comfortable retirement on gold plated pensions funded by the taxpayer and lucrative posts acting as consultants advising businesses on how best to lobby and fool government ministers just like they behaved when in office.

Politicians are also good at shaking hands and waving pieces of paper after meetings in alleged triumph. Without telling how much taxpayer's money has the government wasted, and at the behest of British businesses, at times on a false no-deal scenario invented during Brexit or Covid-19 strategy solely for political theatre? Even if it meant making pledges that may or can not be honoured and whether it incites racial hatred or not. Such deceitful lies have led to a large part of the disenfranchised population looking for comfort as they feel ignored, rejected, appalled by the present situation in the oldest democracy in the world. Who knows where it will end unless we somehow pull ourselves back from the brink, find a way to rekindle trust in democracy and constitutional principles we once held so dearly?

Trust in capitalism is equally waning. The ideological victory battle of democracy and capitalism over socialism has coincided with widespread voter dissatisfaction. When asked to choose between the capitalist system they live under and the socialist system, which they don't, voters prefer socialist policies. It is because state-funded public services like the NHS, welfare, housing, and education look a better working model towards a fairer good for the people. In contrast, capitalism gets associated with greed, tax evasion, corruption, unequal wealth distribution and exploitation of people. It is now an opportune time for democracy and capitalism to evolve further to keep pace with people's optimism to be a part of the democratic process that reflects real-life issues. Not an unaccountable patronising political system dictated by few individuals or groups with financial, media and legal power who lobby politicians to influence policy-making.

Democracy and capitalism, as a brand, seems to have passed its sale by date, not fit for twenty-first century needs. Both reveal reputational crises. Cracks appearing which people find difficult to stomach, especially when they see abuse of power by the 'establishment' played out daily in front of them on TV screens in living rooms and not held accountable for policy failures. At the same politicians who are failing people use social discord to their advantage with a divisive political agenda based on nationalism to hang onto power to cover their failings. As a result, we see a rise in patriotism because large parts of the indigenous population worldwide are looking at short term benefits and any political party or a leader who offers a quick fix. It doesn't matter as long as a political leader provides a change, whether they deliver or not, provided it's not more of the same. It doesn't matter for the politicians, as long they get elected to continue milking the system using whatever means at their disposal.

Politics has now become the age of populist patriotism. A right ding-dong, here today, gone tomorrow. It is a mad scramble for votes on short-term policies to entice voters irrespective of medium-term and long-term consequences on the country's future while feathering their nests. After all, they will not be affected as they will be long gone for others to deal with the mess. The growing anger gets targeted at those now in power. The same crowd who managed to sneak back with more pledges or the new one who managed to win on a better mix of promises. While at the same time, both parties know full well that they would most likely fail to deliver their pledges. And the cycle will get repeated, as has been the case over the last few decades. At the same time, the public seldom sees politicians on the front line since they usually lead well secluded protected life in their Westminster village with a high cordon of security and layers of bureaucracy placed around them. The only time to be seen on TV screens blaming each other, shouting at one another, setting a bad example to the public during PMQs. Same with the rich who also live in well-protected mansions and resorts.

So now, feeling frustrated, the impatient disenfranchised voters pick on the refugee placed in social housing - of which there is an extreme shortage since no one has explained why as a country under international law we helped enact, which they signed to are obliged to do so. Anger also gets targeted at immigrants, the people of different skin colour and faith, who have made Britain their home, paid their taxes, worked hard against all odds to build a better future. When asked in surveys after surveys, is it any wonder that 50% of people think there will be more racism against only 20% who said less? Since 1983, only once the British Social Attitudes Survey found those saying less outnumbered the more group. While over 40% of people in Britain agree that some ethnic groups are 'born less hard-working', with one in five agreeing some ethnic groups are 'born less intelligent.' [35] Similarly, levels of prejudice have been shown to increase towards the ethnic people after the recession following the 2008 financial crisis and subsequent austerity measures imposed by the coalition government since 2010. Bearing in mind, the immigrants were not responsible. But as usual, they are made scapegoats by the politicians to pay the price for their mistakes. Just like Muslims become easy targets of racial hatred following Islamophobic drivel from politicians.

*

Whether at the local or national level, every political, social and economic failure means less contact, less tolerance, a rise in prejudice with worse cultural and prosperity outcomes. The debate on discrimination affects not only the immigrant population but also the white working-class. Because since the 1980s, local white communities still feel the pain due to the industrial decline and social change, and the scars are still visible on the landscape left behind by the destruction of bread-and-butter manufacturing industries. And however much we try to reason, it is not the fault of the immigrants for economic and social ruin but that of politicians who are responsible for those policy failures; it seems to get lost during the debate in the age of populist-nationalist politics. Despite even when history shows the crucial role immigrants have played in the making of Great Britain. It does not alter the debate for those who feel let down who do not see it as politicians' fault because of being led to believe that it is the fault of the immigrants. Like we saw it exploited during the Brexit debate with eye-catching slogans "take back control." We can only wait and see what happens? Let's hope the future generation does not have to suffer and pay for the mistakes of the twentieth-century-born politicians.

During the Covid pandemic, when Britain needed strong leadership to make critical policy decisions instead, we ended with the highest rate of excess deaths in Europe and worst-hit economic growth. The Conservative government purged of political talent by Boris Johnson was late to apply a national lockdown and didn't know whether to keep the economy open or protect the NHS, instead wrecked both. The government then faced a severe further dilemma during the final stages of the Covid pandemic. Now one would have thought the pandemic would inhibit populism when people's lives are at stake. But not so because old habits die hard, especially amongst seasoned right-wing politicians. On the other side of the argument, large majorities, the public, top medical experts and scientists favoured a second lockdown without any delays to minimise unnecessary loss of lives and demands on the NHS.

Whereas the rebel right-wing Tory MPs railed against the threats to prosperity and civil liberties.

When it suits, the government of the day are very good at blaming the opposition for "playing politics" and vice versa even though the government had overseen the worst coronavirus excess death toll in Europe. Rather than wanting to plan meticulously, act and prepare for the possible worst-case scenarios for each conceivable wave of the virus instead, politicians trumpeted a constant false hope for the sake of having a chipper story to tell. Of course, there will always be last-minute, rushed things that have to happen in a global pandemic. How can it be that, on the one hand, politicians ignore the advice given by scientists and medical experts, then comes out of the blocks bragging that the government is following scientific advice and how prepared it was. However, it was not the case when the government ended up delaying lockdown measures?

People can accept reality, but it is the faffing that's more painful when the government fails to be honest with the public. Like when it ruined people's plans to see their family over Christmas by failing to give clear lockdown instructions over the festive period. Likewise, when it failed to shut down borders on time to prevent the Indian Covid variant from spreading. Nothing during Covid-19 can convince the public when the government forgot to think of workers like critical care nurses, police officers, firefighters. No wonder shift, hospitality and public sector workers felt let down when rules changed last minute. The government was not proactive or prepared after making a hash of it – as it has done with care homes, exam results, the Test and Trace system, and the feeding of hungry kids. So how can the Government claim that it had not made any mistakes? This defensive attitude was summed up by Priti Patel on 22 December 2020 when she audaciously declared on BBC 4 todays' programme: "The government has consistently throughout this year been ahead of the curve in terms protective measures with regards to coronavirus. "

And just like many colleagues, including Boris Johnson, Nadhim Zahawi uttered on Andrew Marr's on 30 May 2021 the famous mantra of "hindsight is a wonderful thing" when asked about how the government had failed thousands of people in care last year. And continued to utter the same pledge made over the months by him and Boris Johnson, "I hear you, and we will learn those lessons," and "we're going to have an inquiry into what went wrong in the pandemic." What beggar's belief, despite the government recognising the urgent need for an inquiry, why delay it until May 2022 with a lame excuse not to divert valuable government time away from dealing with the pandemic and economic consequences. Bearing in mind the billions government has already squandered, not only during the pandemic but also during Brexit no-deal fiasco and many other policy U-turns that has diverted valuable government time and money! But when it suits, the government can commission a quick investigation in the middle of the Covid pandemic like the Cred inquiry mentioned previously.

It also took the Covid-19 pandemic for the newly elected Conservative MPs representing northern seats to realise the social inequalities faced by the poor. And warned Boris Johnson to make good his election-time promises to "level up" while conveniently forgetting that the same party has been in government for a decade, who have neglected those same poor. After decimating the NHS and public services for around a decade, it's no surprise that Covid-19 stretched public services beyond their limits. The catastrophic effect of Covid-19 is the final nail, weighing heavily on almost all parts of society.

Likewise, when we needed to get our democracy, social services, education and health back on track, MPs were busy playing partisan politics for self-serving interests. More and more Tory rebels were clamouring to defeat its own government on overseas aid cuts, including the former prime minister Theresa May backing a government U-turn to reverse its policy on foreign aid. [36] However, what the government ministers were worried most about was not the foreign aid rebellion about helping the poor. But the reason was more to do with that the measure to cut the foreign aid budget was extremely popular with the Tory base. As one frustrated government figure put it: "If we can't get this through, what can we cut?" Sadly, such attitudes highlight how government makes policy decisions in the name of democracy at the expense of others! Although it's refreshing to see politicians speak out, which is healthy for democracy, it shouldn't be about when it suits them. Bearing in mind, many have often kept quiet and colluded to approve draconian austerity cuts. Like those to public services, free school meal vouchers, hostile Home Office environment, imposing the famous 'bed-room tax' and so forth, the adverse effects of those still affecting disadvantaged people today, not forgetting some were chief architects of those policies.

Instead, what would be more helpful if the Tory rebel MPs spent their energy finding answers to why the recipient nations are poor? How long will Britain continue providing foreign aid? What needs doing not to make the poor rely on charity? What good is history if we don't learn from the past not to repeat the same mistakes? The bottom line is that Britain's role in the UN, World Bank and International Monetary Fund (IMF) needs revisiting. It should not stifle the growth of poorer nations so that the west can thrive, not forgetting the ongoing purge of natural resources from Third World nations that continues today. Just like it happened during the colonial era, but now under the pretext of deploying various 'civilised' financial institutions and mechanisms, such as the IMF, the World Bank and China, that still control their destiny.

Now wouldn't that be more purposeful if Britain led the way by stopping the sale of arms to regimes committing acts of apartheid, genocide, human rights abuses? That way, it will not only save innocent lives but cut UK's foreign aid budget completely, help improve UK's reputation in the world by leaving a better legacy and restore trust in democracy at the same time. A strategy with multiple benefits, not one of destruction selling arms to the poorer nations followed by foreign aid. At the same time, wouldn't that be wonderful if the Tory rebel MPs focused more on that and become Tory heroes, those who stood for humanity at home and abroad!

What beggar's belief that on the one hand Britain, like America, supply arms to regimes engaged in wars inflicting civilian atrocities and casualties. On the other hand, as "white saviours" of humanity send foreign aid to rebuild those broken societies Britain has helped destroy in places like Yemen, Gaza.... The irony being the foreign aid given by Britain, America or, for that matter, by others is a fraction of the money spent by those countries waging inhumane atrocities by purchasing weapons from Britain, America and others. Another flipside to the " white saviours" gesture is that it makes those receiving foreign aid feel subjugated, helpless at the mercy of Britain and others. At the same time, those donating foreign aid are the twentieth-century politicians born with colonial mentality with an unconscious bias of superiority over others.

Similarly, the new Covid-19 research group of Tory rebels voted against their government's lockdown restrictions on the grounds it's an infringement of "civil liberties and fundamental human rights." Bearing in mind as members of the ERG had claimed that the EU undermined British sovereignty. Nigel Farage was equally appalled, and as usual, jumped on the bandwagon to announce the launch of an anti-lockdown party. Politicians stop at nothing to further their cause even when people's lives are at stake. Teressa May also joined the Tory rebels during the parliamentary national lockdown debate on 2 November 2020 and abstained by not supporting the government. How can she justify her stance? Because when it came to the "civil rights and fundamental human rights" of British ethnic immigrants and the Windrush generation, as Home Secretary, she resorted to draconian immigration laws, followed by illegal deportations due to the hostile Home Office environment.

There is nothing wrong with this boisterous stuff from Tory rebel MPs, whether it's to do with the foreign aid, civil liberties or lack of investment in the northern seats. After all, this is what democracy should be about, serving public duty? Except they forget that the main reason the most vulnerable are still facing hardships is the direct result of past short-term-knee-jerk cost-saving penny-wise, pound-foolish policies, which have come to roost. And raises the following questions: Why did the same

Conservative MPs not rebel before? Why did they not vote against the punitive government legislation on welfare reforms, bedroom tax, austerity and draconian immigration laws? What about the "civil rights and fundamental human rights" of British citizens from ethnic backgrounds? What about the liberty of those they are now denying by imposing theirs?

Same names keep coming up who have victimised ethnic minorities in their famous "Go Home" posters and well-paid articles in newspapers inciting hatred. Same names who voted for austerity cuts and against free school meals for children from poorer households. They are now joining forces to question "liberty and civil-rights" violations during the Covid-19 national lockdown! Shouldn't politics be about governance for the benefit of the people, not party loyalty or self-serving political egos? Opposition politicians are no different.

Equally, Boris Johnson could not stand up against the Tory rebel MPs because of his own track record in such matters. He is no different to them and Nigel Farage. They are all opportunist politicians with egos and greed. Likewise, there is no doubt, Boris Johnson would have railed long ago against the government in his handsomely paid Daily Telegraph newspaper column attacking others if he was not the prime minister. His corrupt faith spreads like rust through his administration. What goes around comes around. Just like he has done to others throughout his political carrier, such behaviour undermines public trust, wrecks public policy. Count how many times the government during the pandemic told us we faced a choice between protecting the health and the economy when we actually saved neither that effectively.

The real reason some prime ministers do a good job is that they have a strong team behind them. Boris Johnson fired all the strength in the Conservative party because he was not good at guiding them; others left on their own accord since they saw through him. As a result, the country has ended up governed by a greedy B-list cabinet chosen for membership of the Brexit cult, not for competence who are essentially floundering without a 'leader'. Boris Johnson is merely a poser, which doesn't help, yet the coup has successfully deprived the Tory Party of talent, allowing him to reign in comfort for a few years. Likewise, when will the opposition Labour Party and the Trade Unions think about the people and the country instead of scoring political points as more important than our nation's welfare?

Down the centuries, Britain has generally been lucky in its prime ministers and opposition leaders in times of crisis. In calmer periods, it may not matter much who is nominally in charge of the country. However, during the last couple of decades of frequent disasters like illegal wars, financial crisis, Brexit and Covid-19, Britain has been led by the political leadership of such poor and wavering judgement that it is difficult to find a figure of comparable incompetence in British history. It's difficult to decide who is/was the worst prime minister to have kept the plebs in the illusion that they have their best interests at heart? The reality is that they are not political leaders but managers with self-serving egos; here today, gone tomorrow.

Greed and unaccountability also continued unabated during the Covid-19 pandemic when the country was facing unprecedented times. Instead of the government protecting taxpayers' money by undertaking open and competitive tendering, contracts ended up in the bulging pockets of cronies of corrupt politicians. Especially when the purpose of procurement law is to ensure the public interest gets served first. So, contracts should go to those ablest to deliver, significant at times of crisis when stakes are high. However, that didn't hold back greedy politicians to line up their pockets. As details have emerged of school-meal contracts given to Tory party donors, alongside scandalous evidence of the resultant food parcels, it's noticeable that those same voices have remarkably little to say about where taxpayers' money goes. In another investigation, *The Sunday Times* reported that the government had awarded £1.5bn to companies linked to the Conservative party during the coronavirus pandemic. [22]

To the general public, cosy deals strike as absolutely a shocking indictment of a shambolic, corrupt government. However, like the bankers of the 2008 financial crash, they'll undoubtedly get away with it. Completely wrong but utterly inevitable because of the relaxed self-serving attitude adopted by those in power. Today's economy masquerades as a free market. If anything, it's a rent-extraction machine for cronies. The pandemic unexpectedly dispersed the smokescreen. Voters view the government procurement process as corrupt when cronies of politicians get handed billions in Covid contracts.

Similarly, the UK and other countries opted for the locked-down world, favouring politicians over voters while providing preferential NHS hospital admissions for the privileged when they caught Covid. It also favoured the rich over the poor and the white-collar middle class over the shop assistant, waiter, small business owner, manual labourer or anyone less worthy. At the same time, if you are young, the risk of losing your job may be more frightening than the risk of catching a virus that probably may not harm you. Hence you can find rational or at least understandable reasons to rally with those who pretend there is no need to take emergency measures.

A competent government would buy you off or ease such concerns with an efficient working Test and Trace system that could track and isolate infected people and allow the rest to earn a living. Perhaps worst of all - and incredibly - none of the countries with world-class experts have proactively put forward an effective medium-term plan to stimulate growth and how to manage this avalanche of debt. Other than leaving the mess created by politicians and their 'experts' born in the last century for the twenty-first century born generation, who have had no say in the matter!

*

One of the first things we get taught about liberal democracy is that the structure of a healthy political system has separate branches with distinct responsibilities and the right checks and balances to prevent the concentration and abuse of power. Yet, in recent years, one of the many difficult lessons for liberals has been the belated realisation that accountability requires more than institutional structures. A functioning democracy *also* depends on a balance of power between the government and an ecosystem of independent actors who can publicly hold the state to account – including a formal political opposition and media organisations remain neutral, not affiliated with the government or beholden to its financial backers.

The real question should be how have politicians, 'experts', and commentators been allowed to get away with wallowing in their delusions of grandeur for so long? Erica Newland, who worked as a legal counsel in the Justice Department from 2016-2018, has said: she and her colleagues were "complicit" in supporting an "anti-democratic leader", Donald Trump. [37] Because of which, sadly, as we saw despite legal expertise of hers and others, their talents ended up having the opposite effect, making policies such as the 2017 ban on Muslim-majority countries that got overturned by the courts. Regrettably, like all 'advisers', she or her colleagues did nothing at the time; they didn't resign. Only to admit later in 2020, she would have served the country better if she had spoken earlier and quit immediately after the president assumed office. Not some two years after leaving her position, and Trump had lost the presidential election. Such hypocrisy is nothing new. How often have we heard the same story before? Except raises the question of whether these 'experts' are worth the money they get paid?

Justice in America is at an inflexion point. Among the most contentious issues are race and policing. Whereby what justice looks like depends on who is on the receiving end, which raises several questions. What can be made of the state of the American justice system when police and the communities they serve are at odds? What can communities do to keep people out of prison and help incarcerated transitions, drop-outs back into society? Bearing in mind, America takes pride as a beacon, symbolising democracy, justice and freedom. It may be so, though it raises profound doubts that despite the democratic rights, the law enforcement, the legal community, the academia, the advocacy and the media, mistrust and polarisation run rampant and threaten to divide a fractured society further. It is an apt metaphor that nothing will work if the heart is not in the right place and the proper determination to achieve the desired goals despite all the checks and balances.

Perhaps the lessons we can learn from the recent summer incidents of 2020 in the middle of a Covid-19 pandemic, and the presidential election are? While America may be a land of opportunity, a land of laws, a land of legal experts and justice, yet would still reduce a person to the colour of their skin and find them unworthy. Even in the twenty-first century 'civilised' America with all law enforcement mechanisms against racial discrimination, it does not matter. Whether a Black person is a visitor from a majority African nation, just the Black colour of the person in America means they have to negotiate for their humanity with a system that constantly alienates, erases and punishes them. In a Black majority country, disappearing into the crowd can save one's life.

However, in America, being Black is always like having a target on the back for being Black, and lead a white police officer to kneel on a Black person's neck and eventually kill, like what happened to George Floyd. It is not the purpose of this book to record injustices that have taken place except to illustrate we can have as many anti-discrimination laws as we like, but it makes no difference at the end of the day. And politicians should not think laws can fix everything because they do not know what it feels like to be at the receiving end. Many of them didn't grow up with some of these civil rights issues. So, at times the understanding is not there with problems like police brutality, racially profiled for stop and search, discrimination at the workplace; that's why we still end up discussing the same things non-white people have experienced over the years.

Similarly, in Britain, we have our fair share of advisers, 'experts' called SpAds, equally good at absolving responsibilities by blaming others when things go pear-shaped! What good is to be surrounded by highly paid 'experts' advising government when the advice given is not good and legally challengeable. At the same time, the taxpayer pays the cost of legal challenges and the victims suffer the consequences. Civil rights watchdog the Equality and Human Rights Commission (EHRC) found failures to observe existing government policies contributed to the Windrush scandal. Whereby, the Home Office "effectively ignored" equality laws when it drew up controversial 'hostile environment' policies to crack down on illegal migrants. Instead, it ended, causing profound problems for entirely legal migrants from the Windrush generation, who arrived in Britain from the Caribbean between the late 1940s and the 1970s. [17]

No different to the admissions by Dominic Cummings in his seven-hour castigation of Boris Johnson and his government during a parliamentary select committee on 26 May 2021. Except Cummings conveniently forgot to admit his involvement in promoting lies and deceit when he was at the heart of the government as the most senior adviser to Boris Johnson, including the part he (Cummings) played not only in the Brexit debate but to get Johnson elected in 2019. So, where was he when the country needed him? It shows how low politicians and their 'experts' will stoop to in their quest for power! Considering what Cummings described in his testimony was not only the government failing in its duty but the failure of the very checks and balances. The absence or weakness of those oppositional forces to curb the excesses of power have not gone unnoticed by the general public.

The reader will recall what Cummings revealed about the early stages of the pandemic in 2020 was not new to the many in the country. After all, they are the ones who faced the consequences of those failures in real life. Regrettably, it also highlighted that those occasional political disasters are not caused simply by a lack of knowledge or inadequate information. But it also shows how terrible governments can sometimes survive. And indeed thrive, even though their faults are visibly evident to the public. It's not because the public doesn't care about the "truth", but they are helpless to do anything until the next election, by which time it will be too late and forgotten.

The "truth" about any government is itself a narrative, not merely a set of facts. In public discourse, the argument over "truth" must be made consistently and persuasively to stick and make sense. To do that, we need effective opposition, and regrettably, there isn't any at the moment. Conservatives and certain sections of the media have seen to that. The Lib Dem's integrity has been in tatters in their quest for power in exchange for a few ministerial posts since going into coalition in 2010 with the Conservatives. In the process, the Lib Dems not only inflicted severe hardship on the living standards of the disadvantaged by colluding with the Conservative's punitive austerity cuts to public services but ended up getting the blame for it.

Whereas infighting within the Labour Party, together with a lack of political leadership, failures of past policy initiatives, cleverly exploited by the Conservative party and the right-wing press, means that the Labour Party will remain in opposition for the next decade or so. Despite the fact, the Conservative party has been in power most of the time but seems to get away by blaming Labour for everything. It's because, despite skirmishes with certain sections of the media, every blow landed by way of hard-hitting investigative journalism into government failures has been undercut by the influential right-wing media coverage fawning over with as gossipy language. In the process, it undermines the gravity of the seriousness while giving an impression of a media that is doing its job in the country's interest though, in reality, is primarily for their self-serving interests.

Over the decades, regardless of costly mistakes and wastage of taxpayer money, Covid-19 or not, politicians, SpAds and civil servants continue to lift salaries and build gold plated pensions. Many continue to milk the system, further costing the taxpayer when they end up in the House of Lords and receive Knighthoods for helping political leaders in their skulduggery despite their legacy that they sold out the ordinary British people betraying their trust in them. Not to be left out, Boris Johnson hands out peerages to his brother, political friends, cricketers and donors who supported him over divisive issues says something is drastically gone wrong in politics. It does not instil trust amongst ordinary people when politicians lecture the public that they too can achieve great success by aspiring to anything they want to in life; the world is their oyster only to find out otherwise. What sort of message are we sending when we face particular challenges where our world cries out for political leadership and ways of inhabiting life that draws us together rather than tears us apart?

Likewise, the public has witnessed politicians who have led the country to wars, austerity, Brexit and much more claiming to be sound policies only for the public to find out later that they are cheats, liars, adulterers, greedy, irresponsible individuals. Some who can't even manage to keep their own families together! It seems the future of this country is in the hands of many disturbed individuals who have enough family problems on their plates - how can people possibly expect them to focus on their responsibilities half of the time with so many distractions around them! It seems the country is paying the price for being governed by a group of entitled, arrogant Etonians and Oxbridge yahoos. And when they get caught after the initial media frenzy has quietened down, done and dusted, they fade away to their country piles don't even wonder what the poor people are doing today.

I'm in my 70s; if I peg out tomorrow, I could still say I had a good life. Many older people like me should worry about our grandchildren, and I think most of us do. To most, the choice in the 2019 general election between Boris Johnson and Jeremy Corbyn was hopeless; our voting system is at a breaking point. I guess we won't fall for the slogans and wickedness in ideology much longer. These negative things and self-serving egos have bred politicians who do not have ordinary people's interests at heart.

It's hard to find a trustworthy politician of whatever flavour because absolutely no one in politics is fit for the purpose these days, and it's a misconception to think they have people's interests at heart. It looks we are moving out of being a Democratic

State where the government makes decisions on our behalf into a State whereby the government tell us what to do. Regardless of any democratic process that is supposed to be present. In other words, known as 'legalised' dictatorship under the pretext of democracy which, together with a weak opposition and a biased press, means a 'government' free to do what it fancies without being held responsible for failures.

But history tells us that electors will tolerate liars and buffoons only for so long. Eventually, the worm will turn, and it will not be a pretty sight when that happens. There are already vital signs that public respect for politicians is at an all-time low. What will happen if that contempt declines even further? And if they don't want to find out, they need to get their act in order, weed out the corruptible, self-serving hypocrites from their ranks and get on with the job they were elected to do.

*

In the 2021 local election, a Conservative candidate confided he was worried I was going to win because he didn't get much help from the party during his campaign. Due to the belief within the party hierarchy that Knaphill is a safe Tory seat, and he, with his Pakistani Muslim background, will be guaranteed support of some 400 local Knaphill Pakistanis whether he engages with them or not. He was equally concerned; it would prevent him from becoming the Mayor of Woking with repercussions on his family's status and reputation as "kingmakers" in the community. He then went on to say I should not have contested the elections, but I reminded him I have stood against your fellow party colleagues in the past. I thought it was patronising to take voters for granted and use them as pawns. And I pointed out it should not be about Muslims and non-Muslims, Pakistanis and non-Pakistanis, US and THEM, and I am surprised that you accept this thinking within the Conservative party hierarchy. I further reminded him that for me, it's about ALL residents, not who they are or what faith they belong to, because politics should be about serving public duty, not dividing people for self-serving interests. And what is required most is party leadership that brings communities together, not hate that stirs up division amongst people.

I reasoned with him that as a Conservative, he should resist not encourage such mentality within his party that just because he is a Pakistani Muslim, Muslims will vote for him. It's not helpful since it gives a wrong impression that politicians can take Muslims for granted. I urged him not to succumb to such a divide and rule political agenda as it is not healthy for democracy. As a Muslim, I find it an abhorrent practice, an insult to my faith Islam which nowadays gets judged by the hypocritical behaviour of Muslims, who don't speak to put the record straight, which then leads to

Islamophobia. Just like it's an insult to judge British values by the hypocrisy of a few politicians or individuals with unconscious bias with racist undertones of twentieth-century colonial mentality.

During the election campaign, I discussed the neglected local issues with the electorate. I also discussed my views on conservatism, capitalism, and socialism. I mentioned that I believe the principles of free-market (capitalism) are something we practice; we live all the time, no different to the survival of the fittest animal instinct we all possess, practice and take for granted happening around us. But as an animal species, we also live in a society, and like other species, we depend on each other's kindness for communities to function efficiently. Therefore, it's essential to understand the good aspects of socialism by focusing on what humanity can do to tackle inhumanity for those affected by social injustice and lack of opportunities.

Yet regrettably, in reality, both capitalism and socialism seem not to be working. It makes no real sense of politics when we see socialism stifles inventiveness, ingenuity, competition and others treated as more equal. In contrast, capitalism presents two severe problems: pollution and greed, resulting in hugely unacceptable levels of inequality. And by taking the good bits, by leaving out the bad bits, we can have the best of both worlds.

Whereas conservatism, in my view, is about not taking things for granted that the world owes me a living. It's more about family values, hard work, putting food on the table, a roof over the head, aspiring to do best to give our children better opportunities, respect laws, and so forth. At the same time, socialism means benevolence to invest in peoples' future by putting something back individually and collectively as a state into the society, so the disadvantaged also have the right tools, a level playing field to succeed in life, and not by denying them opportunities. What's hypocritical about both and not fair is one rule for the rich, those with powerful connections in the right places and another rule for the disadvantaged without connections.

And when challenged on the doorsteps by the loyal Conservative party supporters during my election campaigns, I reasoned with them I am a staunch conservative with a 'small-c' who believes in conservatism, which I think is quite a widespread view among the electorate. Because like others, I also believe in working hard, respect laws, and pay taxes to leave a better legacy for future generations. But regrettably not the sort of conservatism practised by Boris Johnson and his government that promotes greed, cronyism, sleaze, nepotism, misogyny and more. Now whether you agree with me or not, these are not conservative values; it's an insult to conservatism, audacity on the part of Johnson to claim otherwise. I won the argument on most occasions except a handful of instances when one voter told me to get off the premises, a few were not interested in politics, and two slammed the door.

To me, the job of politics should be to clear up dirt and reduce inequality with a well-designed targeted investment in public services that unblock barriers to connectivity and help fulfil individual aspirations for society's good. The way to do that would be to make sure that from a very early age, we all have access to top-class quality health and education better than those in the best private schools and hospitals so that there is no need for their existence since there would be no demand for it. As I have mentioned previously, quality education and health are the wealth of the individual and that of the nation. It achieves the aspirations of an individual and, on broader aspects, helps society address racism, radicalisation, anti-social behaviour, loneliness, and other scourges in our multicultural Britain.

*

What next? We can continue with the blame game individually or collectively for short-term gains. Nations blaming nations, politicians blaming politicians, people blaming people, faiths blaming faiths, north blaming south, rich blaming poor, and tinker at the edges. I believe a good place to start would be to ask why specific sectors of society still feel second-class. To do that, politicians need to show a greater understanding of the real-life issues not just by sitting in the ivory tower listening only to the so-called 'experts', but through the network of close, evolving personal relationships at the community and grassroots level. To achieve that, voter's need to exercise their democratic right with a huge turnout during local and general elections, so they are not taken for granted by politicians along party lines.

More importantly, irrespective of whether the messenger is telling the truth or not, it all boils down to trust, trust and nothing but trust. And trust in the 'establishment' is something in short supply that also has a knock-on effect on the people. We witness similar political shenanigans at the local level from councillors playing games at the expense of the rate-payer for self-serving interests and egos. Instead of serving public duty for which they get elected, they vote or abstain against motions brought in front of them on party lines. Whatever the political belief, one can make a substantial difference. And politics needs to open up more to ordinary people to reflect empathy of real-life issues and "burning injustices" of life, not just rhetoric. But sadly, modern-day politics is so confined to self-serving party interests that a job of an MP or a local councillor is no longer a voice for the people. Instead, it has become one of fear, of de-selection or missing out on a plum position by not towing the party line, resulting in compromising political convictions and an unwillingness to support issues relevant to national and local interests.

Pundits often say that the Conservative party and the right-wing press are good at deliberately stoking divisions. What's perhaps less acknowledged is that they do so mainly by inventing them: those who campaign for more inclusive policies become "the woke mob" and "the looney left"; those who want students to learn about the darker parts of Britain's history become "people who hate Britain;" judges and politicians who want to follow basic parliamentary procedures become "enemies of the people," "saboteurs," and "traitors," etcetera. In every case, they claim that the future of the nation is at stake. Yet not so if we look at what has followed after such exaggerations, isn't any particular political agenda other than stoke animosity by waging battles primarily for self-serving egos. The persistence of this culture war narrative based on exaggerations gives an image of an irreconcilable rift at the heart of British society.

However, this image of an irreconcilably divided nation is just that, an image because few people know or seem bothered by what culture war or "wokeness" even means. A spate of polls in the red wall, northern constituencies won by the Tory party in 2019, plus based on personal experience during the 2021 local election campaign, is largely inconsistent with the rest of the country, indicating we are not as divided as many would have us believe. I don't think the voters are half as divided over Brexit as people think. So many of the problems we've created in this country are because we sit in rooms, having artificial conversations about people rather than with them. If we look around, we will see communities working together, all sorts of that going on around locally, every single one and group doing their best to serve humanity in whatever way we can.

The cynicism and bad faith that motivates much of the culture war should warn us against one of the dominant tendencies within the vast literature on our polarised times: to blame evolutionary biology and an inherent 'tribalist' instinct we all share. Which our brains know we need our groups to survive. Though by conjuring up a primordial past as the source of our divisions, we lose sight of all the contemporary forces and strategies deliberately designed to inflame, even exaggerate, our differences. And political leaders like Johnson, Trump, Modi, Netanyahu, Bolsonaro, Orban, Farage, the prominent architects of this dreary divide and conquer approach are very good at causing resentfulness, are also its chief beneficiaries. And as history shows can lead to fascism, world wars, apartheid and persecution of minorities based on race, creed and faith. Not that it's not happening now because it is already taking place in some parts of the world?

Politics has worryingly sunk to an all-time low by having it so good to never so corrupt and vile today. It shouldn't be about people joining this or that protest group or political party. It should be more about making politicians accountable for their actions to restore trust, not make a mockery of our democratic process and public institutions. Our politicians have led the nation into a constitutional crisis, committed to breaking the laws of the land and lying to woo voters with a 'populist agenda' pedalling insulting and divisive statements.

Such selfish behaviour pitting groups against each other causes resentment, and alienation which encourages the public to emulate such behaviour in real life. It is true lying amongst politicians is nothing new. It has been going since records began except not to such consistency that some politicians believe making laws makes them above the law, and lying is an accepted requirement. It is a shame; on the one hand, the 'establishment' tells the public law enforcement forms the centrepiece of government policies, yet they will pick and choose what laws to respect. The world must be laughing at us, professing to be a great democracy then ignoring the laws or international treaties signed by the government passed by the mother of Parliaments.

Similarly, in America and Brazil, denial of the health crisis by Donald Trump and Jair Bolsonaro during the Covid-19 pandemic was profitable rhetoric that played to their right-wing audience. They complained that wearing masks was a loss of liberty as the state's repressive apparatus and believed that the government has no right to tell what drugs we can and cannot enjoy. They hate the indignity of being forced to accept the same restrictions as everyone else. It offends their core belief that the fittest will survive while the unfit must take their chances. Demagogues are known to fuel anxieties with lies. If you don't support Brexit, 80 million Turks could come to Britain. If you don't vote for Donald Trump, Black Lives Matter will move into white suburbs. If you don't repatriate immigrants, public services will get overrun. They offer a strongman who can assuage voters' anxiety with straightforward solutions like "Get Brexit Done" or "Make America Great Again", never mind the consequences.

At present, the public perceives bad behaviour, insulting sections of society or greed gets rewarded when politicians openly advocate breaking the law, so the people also feel why they should respect the law. We have to ask what examples are we setting in our public institutions to promote social and moral fabric. It is crucial politicians are good role models for the young and old to emulate. Anti-social behaviour has become a scourge that cannot be tackled entirely by more police officers or laws. For a start, we need to nurture positive relationships, mutual respect, empathy and trust. It is fashionable for opportunist politicians to demand stricter laws to curtail the rise in anti-social behaviour instead of pro-active solutions and a deeper understanding of real-life problems.

What Covid-19 has done, not produce anxiety but reality, the fear of death? Politicians have long equated patriotism with the armed forces. Yet you can't shoot a virus. Strongmen like Trump, Farage, Johnson, Modi, Netanyahu and others, find themselves redundant against the power of nature because the public trusts the medical and scientific keyworkers more, and not them. Those on the frontlines against Covid-19 aren't conscripts, mercenaries or enlisted men; they are our doctors, nurses, pharmacists, teachers, careworkers, store clerks, utility workers, small-business owners and employees. Let's hope we learn the lessons of what nationalism and humanity mean.

# 9.

# STRUCTURAL
# INEQUALITIES

Pages and pages of well-documented evidence
gathered over the years from costly public
inquiries after each public disaster make a lengthy
miserable read of missed opportunities, bad
practice, incompetence, corrupt attitudes, and
arrogance. Lessons not learnt, findings
brushed under the carpet, victims' pleas for
help ignored, and if heard on time could
have avoided the disaster.

Politicians forget that disadvantaged households
are tired every day of the week to make ends meet
on low wages, lesser opportunities, and austerity.
Despite pledges, successive governments have
failed to tackle structural inequalities. At the
same time, the victims in their daily
struggles still push the boulder uphill and,
unlike normal folks, cannot aspire towards
a better future on a level playing field.

The most striking findings of the many costly public inquiries since the 1980s,
including the ongoing one into Grenfell, has a common theme. Life for the
victims feels asymmetrical, without Hope, however much we try to see within
it, in the stories we tell of it. It's ragged, endlessly frustrating - the same old story. The
victims, white, non-white or both, feel belittled and unwanted by public agencies,

especially when their pleas for help get ignored. Such arrogance is demeaning, short-sighted, mean-spirited, singly not fair because if heard on time by the 'establishment' instead of contempt and lip service, suffering and loss of human lives could be averted or, in most cases, minimised consequences.

Here's why the victims feel ignored despite a common theme emerging from past inquiries affecting the lives of people which have found: that children from more impoverished homes and those with disabilities do less well in school; that people from poverty-stricken homes and those with disabilities do less well in employment; that fewer men and women from council estates fill executive posts in public offices and leading businesses; that fewer students from low-income families go to Oxbridge, that poor people are less healthy, rely on food banks, school vouchers or die early, that the political class lack empathy until a disaster happens. Only to get forgotten again until the next one!

And to cap it, every specific inquiry into people from Black, Asian or Muslim background have highlighted that because of institutional racism, they face handicaps many folds more than their white peers from more impoverished homes. Discrimination which they often have to tackle on their own amongst a sea of white faces. Some of whom still harbouring that slight 'old chap' attitudes of past colonial mentality, public schools and memberships of exclusive clubs, who think it gives them the touch of entitlement and superiority over those who can not recite from memory the new edition of Oxford English Dictionary.

Is it any wonder people from poorer white or non-white households feel ignored by the politicians? The victims cannot understand what precisely is the problem with the 'establishment'? Not knowing what's going on in their lives is one thing. But not listening to them is unforgivable until a disaster happens; causing suffering and loss of lives is pure contempt. Not learning lessons from past inquiries is beyond belief. The public is getting tired of hearing politicians say 'never again' after each disaster, only to see it happen elsewhere. How many more lessons do politicians need to learn?

It will be no different when the much-promised public inquiry into handling the Covid -19 pandemic announced by the government gets underway in May 2022, which will be too late for the innocent victims. Other than the colossal cost to the taxpayer in legal fees, the findings will have the same tell signs as those revealed previously. Namely, not listening to the low-paid public sector key workers risking their lives in the frontline. Equally, the thick report on the Grenfell inquiry findings will be least surprising when published!

It's an added insult that structural inequalities still exist, particularly after all these years. Primarily when politicians of all political persuasions have described past public inquiry findings to be watershed moments. With politicians clamouring from roof-tops that never again it should be allowed to happen. Only to forget, shout again from even higher roof-tops after another public inquiry, condemning everyone except themselves. We have had Windrush; even a race audit has failed to address the "burning injustices." Despite knowing long before the recent Runnymede Report in October 2020, structural and health care inequalities affected Black and Asian people more than the white people [17,19], so it should have been least surprising that the death rate in these groups would be higher during Covid-19. The time for learning lessons from the many public inquiries held to date has long passed. It is time to implement the common findings from those inquiries.

To the people, it feels like déjà vu, another reminder of have we not been here before, with the same rhetoric from the politicians to do better, to be better and never to allow it to happen again with an unwavering determination towards change and a level playing field. Public inquiry reports since the 1981 Scarman Report into the horrific events in Brixton have all exposed structural inequalities affecting not only the non-white but also white working-class people. The constant drip of more inquiries into discrimination against non-white people has followed since, including calls of help from white people from disadvantaged backgrounds, which got exposed during the 2016 Brexit debate. All these public inquiries show that we have defined the geography of difference and defined power. Those who have it and those who will never have it, however hard they try. It's because some people get treated as more equal than others, despite being told otherwise by political and religious leaders.

*

Improbable coincidences do occur. It is not unusual to link the basic mentality of those in authority when treating non-white people as inferior even if that person happens to be far better qualified, whether in education, sports, politics, religion or any other profession. Such is often the reality of the situation faced by the many leading everyday lives, a constant battle to get heard or access public and private services. The handicap worsens depending on how many boxes on the disadvantaged background scale the individual ticks, namely language barrier, attire, religion, sex, neighbourhood, income.

As seen during Covid-19, those needing help tend to miss out most from a lack of knowledge of the workings of the welfare benefits and entitlements? The government's argument against holiday food vouchers was that there are adequate avenues for those affected to claim additional support may well be true but completely misses the point. Because even when benefits have been available, the need to seek help from food banks for low-income people has continued to rise. The reality is that even easily accessible benefits often go unclaimed due to one significant obstacle; the utmost difficulty faced by those in need is accessing services when raising an official complaint or seeking justice. Like the tax system, those with wealth can exploit legal loopholes most and even claim personal expenses. In contrast, those mortals without much know-how or professional help accept the word of the inland revenue officials.

Additionally, those in need of help have to rely on the benevolence of charities and people to do it for them. The onus is always placed on the victim to pursue their rights when routine NHS appointments are not honoured, conditions misdiagnosed, or patient notes wrongly recorded.   Even if there is a public disaster or loss of lives with a call for a public inquiry, such an inquiry will take years to get to the truth; by then, it will be too late. However, why should it become a constant battle for ordinary people, white and non-white alike, to go through extra loops, public inquiries and complaint procedures to fight for their fundamental rights to get heard? And when they do complain, they get ignored. There would be no need if the 'right channels' did their civic duty diligently. As it is, people have enough daily pressures to attend; that is why they elect politicians who should not pass the buck but act on their behalf!

Bureaucracy with layers of a chain of command without direct contact has also not helped address structural inequalities. Mistrust has crystallised because those in need feel ignored by the layers of enhanced status put in place by the famous British 'buffer' between the officer class - the 'establishment'- and the 'lesser' folks. The poorest and most disadvantaged feel their pleas for help falling on deaf ears until a severe disaster occurs when it's too late. It raises the question as to why they feel left out or treated as second-class. Is it because they lack the tools or the confidence to stand up to those who treat them as inferior subjects? Whether it be the public or private sector expected to serve them? Is it because those in authority know fully well, they will get away with it as it's less likely the victims will complain? And if they do, they will get nowhere because they lack the know-how to do it and lack the stamina to endure the ordeal of raising a complaint. In addition, when lodged, complaints often get ignored with a long-drawn-out bureaucratic process to wear out the individual. And by the time a decision gets made, it'll be too late, or the complainant has given up. Also, by then, the culprits have got off scot-free without addressing the victim's concerns. Similar complaints made to Public Health Ombudsman or seeking help from Parliamentary Health Select Committee also becomes a lost cause, one of endurance. To the victim, complaint procedures seem like window dressing exercises to give the impression real-life concerns of ordinary people are being listened to by those in authority. Is it any wonder people from disadvantaged backgrounds get inadequate health, housing and social care?

Likewise, after a convincing celebrity style TV launch of campaign initiatives and research projects by the do-gooders to help the victims address racism and other injustices. One would think the do-gooders will have the courtesy to reply after asking the public to get in touch. Sadly, it's not that easy as it sounds to contact the do-gooders, be it politicians, celebrities, TV presenters or news reporters, because bureaucracy reigns supreme. Also, it's essentially down to the lack of convictions on the do-gooders part since such gimmicks are more for their self-serving interests. Even contacting the broadcaster, be it BBC, ITV, or government agencies, does not become any easier. The 'establishment' should take the trouble to find out for themselves what happens when the public tries to contact by phone or sends an email to help them understand why the public feels disillusioned. Until they abandon these double standards, how can there be a proper understanding of the difficulties faced by the disadvantaged, be it white or non-white people?

Hopefully, most of the readers will never expect to face and get plunged into this dilemma. Whereas those who may do, perhaps, will not fret, accept, or even tolerate being treated as a second-class citizen. While some of you, due to time constraints and language barriers, will not be that bothered to stand up for your rights. Whereas perhaps some are quite capable of resolving the matter after a long-drawn battle with the 'establishment' of the wrongdoing. But the one thing I have learnt from personal experience and many public inquiry findings, that injustices don't discriminate, whether you are white or non-white - even if you are from a disadvantaged background or not, albeit less if you are rich. But even then, anyone can get reeled in, wealthy or not. Anyone can be wrongly accused, convicted as evident by an increase in public inquiries into police conduct. And if you are, you want the system to work. When it doesn't, the consequences can be unthinkable. Sharing stories will help us understand how broken the justice system is, the barriers faced by those who need to be heard, supported, and why we should urgently start listening properly to the *voiceless* before it's too late.

I have experienced a similar attitude in my dealings with the Home Office, NHS, or any official business involving the private or public sector. It does not get easy. At times it becomes a constant battle to stand up for one's rights, with the individual having to face a barrage of bureaucracy, especially if the person comes from a disadvantaged social background. The likelihood of being treated as a second-class citizen increases if that person is non-white of immigrant origin, less fluent in English. No different from the experiences of many others, the only difference being I have stood up for my rights, whereas many others would give up because of lack of time or can't be bothered pursuing justice. Also, getting my first book stocked by the two local libraries at no cost to the taxpayer required a colossal effort. Even my constituent MP found it acceptable, comfortable to tell me not to waste his time when I felt I had to draw his attention to pressing real-life issues.

Now there will be those who will jump on the bandwagon, claiming they have not encountered barriers in private or public life, and even proclaim that I may have an inferiority complex. They are entitled to their opinion, but all I can say is that it may not have been their experience. However, we need to have an honest, inclusive debate if we want to tackle structural inequalities. Ask the victims to come forward and be surprised how many have been affected or felt there is no point in challenging because the 'establishment' will ignore them anyway.

Whatever one's opinion, the fact remains that inequities exist in all aspects of life, including healthcare for the disadvantaged, with complaints overlooked were also identified independently even during the Covid-19 pandemic. Experts noted that many people of colour who worked in essential services were more likely to contract the virus. Especially those low-paying jobs were more likely to be linked to a higher prevalence of underlying structural inequalities. What makes it appalling is that the 'establishment' also ignored ethnic physicians when they raised concerns relating to risk assessments and the lack of PPE. When they complained, they got the standard excuse, don't comment on a specific case as all forms of discrimination are taken very seriously. And every allegation is thoroughly investigated so that lessons are learnt because the NHS is committed to serving everyone. Yet the irony being the victims who complained were professional doctors and consultants who disagreed; they felt their concerns had fallen on deaf ears.

Wonder why it has taken a pandemic for politicians to realise the consequences of social injustice, economy, education and psychological damage on the poorer sectors of the society. Real-life handicaps have existed long before, and Covid-19 lockdowns just made it worse for the disadvantaged poor. I am pleased the report by the Runnymede Trust has cleared the myth that during Covid-19, the reason deaths amongst BAME were disproportionate and over-represented with severe illnesses is not because of "genetic" or "physiological" differences as claimed by the government but due to structural inequalities.[19] Such misrepresentation and misconception of facts are the main reasons for failure to address the "burning injustices" faced by both white and non-white people in their everyday lives. Sadly, costly public inquiries have come and gone, followed by more pledges without tackling the root causes. Not only that, but it also provides ammunition to those with extreme right-wing political agendas to demean people on racial grounds with unfounded comments based on "genetic" and "physiological" make-up.

Structural inequalities still exist all around us: poverty, mental strain, racism, sexism, bullying based on sexual orientation, homelessness, social exclusion due to disability or age, to name just a handful. Too often, the system fails those that need protection. Something somewhere has gone wrong. I think it's traceable to the failure of the 'establishment' - the professionals, do-gooder celebrities – as well as us (the *voiceless*) to properly engage with one another about what is good or bad about the way the 'establishment' delivers fairness which has led to dissonance in public's faith of the system. The lack of openness by not directly engaging with those affected has often obstructed the quest to discover the truth of the matter. Freedom is when you embrace your power to choose your response, letting go of the constant need to fight for your right.

*

Too many children start from a disadvantaged position in their journey towards good mental health, and circumstances beyond their control hinder many in their adult lives. We all have mental health problems, and we all have experienced them at some stage in our life, whatever our background. But regrettably, the risks of mental ill-health are not equally distributed. Those who face the most significant disadvantages in life also face the greatest danger to their mental health. This unequal distribution of risk to our mental health is what we call mental health inequalities. For centuries, mental ill-health has been overlooked, misunderstood, stigmatised, and inappropriately treated as a taboo for a long time. Although much of it is changing, misunderstanding and stigma are not yet things of the past. As a society, we may have made some progress. However, we have a long way to go before the extent of mental health problems is comprehensively understood, recognised and responded to on time for our individual and collective wellbeing.

Another irony of Covid-19 was it made the government rightly concerned to ponder long over school closures since it posed higher risks with long-term consequences hard to make up. The potential learning loss with vast implications for lower socio-economic groups will widen inequality and reduce social mobility. In addition, losing the childcare provided by schools has broader adverse effects on parents' work and family life of those on low incomes. Despite all these negatives, the government decided were not enough to outweigh the extreme risks to public health of increased possibility of Covid transmission by keeping schools open, highlighting that the government understands the importance of education even though forced to keep schools closed. Since they realise the importance of education, wouldn't it have been more appropriate and beneficial to have a similar attitude before the pandemic to prevent the children from poorer households from being left behind?

Unfortunately, if there is no significant remedial action, lost learning will translate into more reduced productivity, lower incomes, lower tax revenues, higher inequality and potentially expensive social ills. The lack of urgency or national debate on how to address this problem is deeply worrying. The necessary responses are likely to be complex, intricate and expensive. Yet, the risks of spending too much time or resources on this issue are far smaller than the risks of spending too little, letting lower skills and wider inequalities take root for generations to come. The inescapable conclusion is that lost learning represents a substantial long-term risk to future prosperity, the public finances, the future path of inequality and general wellbeing.

Studies show that during national lockdowns, the school closures apart from a loss of face-to-face instructional time had significant adverse effects on students' educational outcomes and mental wellbeing. It's not surprising all students lose out when schools close. However, what's most discerning in a country like Britain with the fifth-largest economy when the impact was far more significant for some than others due to structural inequalities. Huge disparities such as the digital divide for children without laptops from poor households made it even more difficult for schools to compensate through the provision of online teaching or how much parents could compensate through home-schooling. [38]

The closure of public parks and amenities also meant that the children spent more time indoors with fewer recreation activities. The evidence found marked inequalities along the lines of family income or type of schooling. The best way of ensuring fairness in the future is that lesser education standards and facilities do not further disadvantage pupils from low-income families. It is crucial that the learning lost by students during the pandemic, which got exposed due to structural inequalities, is accounted for because all our children, from rich or poor households, deserve better and nothing less.

The studies further highlighted that nearly three quarters (74%) of private school pupils benefited from full school days. In contrast, almost twice the proportion of state school pupils (38%), a quarter of pupils had no formal schooling or tutoring at all. Also, children from higher-income households were more likely to have had online classes provided by their schools, spent much more time on home learning, and had access to resources such as their own study space at home. Children whose parents were out of work or on low income were much less likely to have additional resources such as computers, apps and tutors. We must support our young people in schools and homes to receive the best possible remote education. Young people growing up in struggling towns should now be encouraged even more by teachers and parents that there are no barriers to education, to go to top universities or into specific well-paid jobs if they worked hard.

It took the pandemic for the 54 Tory MPs (mentioned earlier) from northern seats to realise the consequences of social injustice, economy, education and psychological damage on the poorer sectors of the society, the apparent social inequalities regularly faced by the *voiceless*. Something they could have done much earlier if they had cared to listen to the disadvantaged. However, they forget that it's prevalent due to the decades of neglect on their part and a failure of Labour politicians who are no different whether in opposition or government. When it suits, the government of the day is very good at blaming the opposition of 'playing politics' and vice versa. In other words, politicians, generally speaking, are quick to absolve their responsibility by blaming others and passing the buck. Equally, MPs are quick to adopt a 'moral' high ground when it suits them, not when it affects the *voiceless*. For example, Tory MPs, including the same 54, voted against the motion to extend free school vouchers outside the term time during Covid-19 lockdown measures during the debate on it. It was left to Marcus Rashford to fight on behalf of England's most impoverished families forcing Boris Johnson into a humbling U-turn.

We need to ask: Why do serious real-life issues go unnoticed or ignored by politicians in the twenty-first century in Britain? Why do we have to wait for public disasters like the pandemic to expose the worsening effects of structural inequalities affecting the poor? And why they have got neglected for decades by successive governments and MPs from across the political spectrum? It's about time we heed the warnings. Learn the lessons from the costly public inquiries to ensure public sector professionals - from politicians, GPs, teachers to social workers, benefit staff and probation members- are held more accountable when they ignore concerns. It's also strange when charities get millions of pounds of funding, yet the poor don't get provided real practical help when they require it. Where does all the money go? Perhaps charity groups need to invest where needed most, less on things like marketing and salaries - at the same time asked to prove what actual practical, helpful services they are providing to keep their funding. Some urgent review/investigation should look into this multi-million-pound industry.

Regrettably, when the British people needed a government that was committed to defeating the Covid-19 pandemic that has blighted people's lives, livelihood and education, the rebel Tory MPs were playing politics, fighting amongst themselves; like ferrets! Whereby, rebel Tory MPs were more concerned the government had adopted a strategy devoid of any commitment to "civil liberty." They were more worried; there was no clarification or guarantee when the government would restore our most basic freedoms and never take them away again. At the same time, claiming people were telling the rebel MPs, they are losing faith in the party leadership as they are not standing up for people's fundamental civil rights. The Tory rebels succeeded in arguing vehemently against their own government's lockdown measures because of their impact on civil liberties and basic human rights. Now wouldn't it have been nice if these same MPs had also stood up for the children from impoverished families over the school meal voucher fiasco? So much so when it comes to the people's civil liberties and fundamental human rights of people from poorer households facing structural inequalities daily!

Covid-19 has opened a pandora's box. Exposed structural inequalities with politicians often heard saying we are facing "unprecedented times." No doubt about that. But what they forget the effects of Covid-19 have worsened due to decades of neglect and short-term knee-jerk cost-saving policies at times based on a pennywise pound-foolish attitude. Therefore, when the nation faced "unprecedented times," we were unprepared and got caught out. And the government ended up wasting billions of pounds, squandering more than that saved during a decade of austerity. The cuts to emergency planning contingencies being one area whereby outdated PPE cost many lives, and the government wasted billions paying the middlemen. Some were cronies of theirs who got lucrative contracts to secure supplies costing significantly more. Many items were faulty, not fit for purpose with the consequences felt by the key workers in low paid jobs in the frontline saving lives and caring for others. [22]

If we'd been healthier, better educated and better paid at the start of the pandemic, we would have done much better. Mainly if the gap between the most and least deprived weren't as big, then we would have found it easier to weather the severe consequences of the Covid-19 pandemic. What Covid-19 has done is to make the burgeoning economic and mental impacts that existed long before even worse. It is now an opportune moment for Britain to reimagine how to tackle structural inequalities. An excellent place to start will be honest politics to restore trust, and politicians should place constituents first, before their self-serving party interests. Doing so will revive the true British spirit of endeavour and enterprise seen during and after WWII when the country worked towards the common goal.

*

According to Joseph Rowntree Foundation, it expects poverty levels in the UK to double in the wake of the pandemic. An estimated two million families, including a million children, are likely to struggle, unable to afford to feed themselves, stay warm, or keep clean as the recession deepens. [39] A whole generation of more destitute children will never recover from the "cruel blow" Covid-19 has dealt low-income families unless the government urgently draws up a plan to help them get back on their feet. While at the same time, it has inflicted added burden on our children and grandchildren to pay off the enormous two trillion-pound national debt and rising, squandered by the unaccountable 'establishment'. A debt the millennials will have to pay with no guarantee of their future or let alone whether they can afford to own homes. On top of that, address global warming, migration crisis and terrorism, the direct consequences of illegal wars and tensions the twentieth century born politicians have created in certain parts of the world.

What the wealthy and the politicians conveniently forget is that poverty is relative. One can say a lot against and very little in its favour. It also depends on the scale, duration, or regularity one has fallen victim to poverty. There are inevitably times when respectable affluent members of the public have also fallen on hard times in one form or another for short periods. When parents have gone without food, eaten less, homes repossessed or faced evictions, and even walked to save on bus fares so as not to deprive their children. However, we can never compare hunger with those who face extreme hardships regularly. When someone does not know where their next meal will come from is absolute poverty. Whereby have to rely daily on food banks and charity over a long period for the rest of their life. It is also true that people appear to befriend you when you are wealthy, yet precious few will do the same if you are impoverished. If wealth can be a magnet, poverty can be a repellent.

Yet, poverty can also often bring out remarkable heroism, daily feats of survival amongst those faced with such adversities inflicted upon them during conflicts, pandemics or natural disasters. Similarly, what hunger feels can only be understood by someone if they have experienced it when you don't know where your next meal will come from next time. Likewise, those sitting in the ivory tower will not understand what meal vouchers mean to those in need of them. It took a twenty-three old Marcus Rashford. He was born just three years before the start of the century, stepped up to the task to give hope to the new generation. Whereby, he drew on his own experience as a child growing up in poverty, which most twentieth-century born politicians will never understand what poverty felt like regularly. Just like the millennial, Greta Thunberg is getting geared up to tackle the problems the millennial generation will have to put right because of the mistakes and lack of empathy from the dinosaur thinking out of touch twentieth-century politicians.

And quite rightly, Marcus Rashford has become a national hero for demanding a response to child poverty. Sadly, he gets abused racially for good deeds, making one wonder about the mentality of those inflicting it. However, he has remained undeterred to articulate his own lived reality of what hunger felt as a child – one of the many, not the only symptoms of child poverty. But the uncomfortable truth is that a U-turn will not address child hunger for good. Because, as Covid-19 struck, the

UK was already facing an epidemic, a child poverty crisis. There are 600,000 more children in poverty today than back in 2012. [40] It has risen for perfectly understandable reasons. The majority of 72% of children are from working families who can no longer make ends meet. They are not the welfare spongers but the victims of structural inequalities. Therefore, it gets us nowhere near finding solutions to child poverty without addressing the underlying root causes. Bearing in mind those children growing up in poverty, as parents, they will find it even harder to raise their own children.

There is nothing wrong with being very successful and enormously wealthy when somebody has worked hard for it. However, why do the extremely rich wait to perform charitable acts until they have amassed vast wealth? It doesn't mean that wealthy entrepreneurs should abandon sound business principles and not enjoy the luxuries of life because money does help one get noticed. Since there is no substitute for wealth, but it should be more about business ethics, how they made those profits in the first place. Likewise, there is a limit to excessive greed at the expense of others. For instance, if profits were ploughed back by paying workers a decent wage for their labour, workers would not have to rely on food banks and welfare benefits. It would also help if the wealthy paid their fair share of tax needed for public services instead of hiring expensive lawyers and accountants to exploit loopholes to avoid paying tax by investing in tax-free havens.

Incidentally, the costly professional fees are then written-off against the tycoon's tax returns as expenses. The public who pays tax (PAYE) at source is dealt a triple whammy by the wealthy. They pay low wages to their workforce, avoid tax, and add insult by re-claiming accounting expenses incurred to avoid paying their full share of tax. Charitable acts are also tax-exempt, resulting in further loss of tax revenue for the government to spend on public services, an additional whammy for the public to endure. Now wouldn't it be better if everyone paid tax equally, instead of having complex systems for the wealthy to exploit and then act as philanthropists, saviours of the disadvantaged and the poor? Charitable acts by the very rich are like handing back some of the money taken out of the public purse. So, why have loopholes in the first place to encourage tax avoidance? The government is at fault, not those exploiting the laws. Moreover, if the government spends resources wisely, there would be less need for charitable acts.

No one can deny that the achievements of the wealthy and celebrities require great sacrifices, hard work and visionary decision taking. Yet when reading biographies of the famously rich, political leaders, celebrities, including those of eminent people in science and sports, it soon transpires that most of them have had some help. What is also most noticeable when reading the biography of the famous forensically albeit not openly admitted is that they have received direct or indirect support. Such as financial, guidance, contacts, from one if not a few individuals, and in some cases even motivated or spurned onto the right path by someone's benevolence. It is vitally important to appreciate and show humility that success needs luck, apart from hard work, sacrifices, and suffering. It also helps if one is in the right place at the right time, with essential skills to take advantage of opportunities when they come along. Therefore, the wealthy must help the poor and the needy in their upliftment by building health, education, social care and welfare amenities, like that practised by philanthropists Cadbury, Joseph Rowntree and others like them over the years.

*

One of the most critical public health measures implemented to combat Covid-19 was when the government advised whole populations to remain in their homes for extended periods other than to collect essential supplies, care for others or exercise during national lockdown measures. Although the lockdown and the partial closure of the economy and social activities were crucial to slow the pandemic to save lives, there is no doubt that the dramatic short term impact on the economy will last well into the future. It is a well-recognised fact that poverty has important implications for both mental wellbeing and physical health. In general, many adults are feeling uncertain, worried about their future. Such anxieties are not only felt by those in jobs but, in particular, amongst unemployed adults, with primary concerns being around financial security. Equally, working parents are finding it challenging to balance the needs of their children coupled with the demands of employment. Not only them but so do parents of children with neurodevelopmental disorders requiring special educational needs could also do with more support to cope with changes in their children's behaviour, who are experiencing higher stress levels because of school closures during the lockdown.

Among many things, what is worth remembering is that the challenges brought on by Covid-19 have just exacerbated existing structural inequalities and unfairness faced over the decades by people from poorer households. It has demonstrated that problematic gaps in the social safety net can quickly become catastrophic when the system comes under pressure. It forced people to think about their homes, jobs, health, education, and welfare in new ways, highlighting structural inequalities in housing and repercussions on broader aspects of life. Even among people that have homes, the lockdown experience varied dramatically. Therefore, what Covid-19 has done is provide an opportunity to rethink the direction of our social policies over the longer term.

Similarly, larger homes allow more space for storage, work (if working from home), exercise or solitude, spacious gardens and more storage space for food and essential supplies – which meant less frequent shopping visits during the lockdown. In contrast, poor-quality housing means more time exposed to damp or other unhealthy conditions, cramped quarters, frequent trips to shops to replenish supplies. Likewise, a lack of a garden or additional outside space has immense physical and mental health consequences on the young and old alike. Equally, homeless people faced an even greater risk, exposing them to close contact with other people due to the lack of homeless shelters.

Children are an often-forgotten group regarding discussions around housing, perhaps given their perceived detachment from housing issues. Yet, housing is central to children's health and wellbeing, which school closures highlighted the widening educational handicaps was partly due to housing inequalities. And, the subsequent detrimental effects of poor housing were exposed during the lockdowns when homes became new learning environments since not all children live in homes with space, privacy, and quietness to do schoolwork. Which meant many spent more time in poor-quality homes exposed to higher health risks, with parents trying to meet housing costs at a time of great financial uncertainty. Such pressures led to changes in parental behaviour, strained family relationships with consequences on their physical and mental health. Loneliness played a key risk factor of lockdown for the mental health and wellbeing of children and young people.

*

Sadly, structural inequalities do not exist during childhood only but continue well into adulthood. A higher proportion of Black and Asian people usually tend to work in lower-paid sectors despite being more likely to have a degree, under-employed, and overqualified in their job. A problem more prevalent among ethnic minorities than it is among whites. However, because of Covid-19, now white people are also directly being affected. They are also taking jobs well outside their comfort zone, making it even more difficult for ethnic people due to the shortage of jobs in lower-paid sectors, leading to higher unemployment levels among non-white people. It will widen the structural inequality gap even further, making it even worse for their children.

Amid concerns that the poorest receive the worst healthcare and have the most insecure jobs, the focus on in-work poverty requires urgent attention. With most people in poverty now living in working households, the terms of the debate have shifted somewhat over recent years. Single-parent families have been the worst affected by the trend of wages falling behind living costs. Yet, while understanding the specifics of life in the working poor is hugely (and increasingly) important, we shouldn't put all of our poverty-reduction eggs in one basket. Also, worklessness remains an issue. One that increasingly affects some groups more than others. By not recognising the urgency, we will continue to ignore the pressing needs of large swathes of the British population. It actively damages our ability to tackle pervasive economic and social challenges - like poverty.

Consider housing, for example. Relative housing costs are significantly higher for renters than for homeowners, placing the former group at a much higher risk of poverty. In 2016, for instance, mortgagors typically had housing cost-to-income ratios of around 12%. While those in social housing faced around 30%, and private renters recorded rates of almost 35%. The study conducted by the Resolution Foundation concluded that when measuring poverty on an after housing costs basis, raised the poverty rate for all low-income earners, with a marked effect on the non-white people. [41] Primarily driven by the higher prevalence of renting in these populations as reflected by homeownership rate for Black families at 24% is less than half the UK average of 53%. Likewise, rates are also low for Bangladeshi and Pakistani (34 %) and Chinese (35%) groups. In contrast, for white families is higher than average at 56%.

Below-average homeownership rates, low wages, and educational attainment levels among most ethnic minority groups go a long way to explain differences in the prevalence of poverty. Efforts to boost homeownership rates and lower the housing costs associated with renting – should be part of the mainstream goals for anyone interested in tackling structural inequalities. It will be highly beneficial to both non-white and other disadvantaged groups. Equally, many examples of Council housing estates built after WWII were shining examples as the largest and finest in Europe across the country, now ghettos in urgent need of repairs. Regrettably, over time, many such areas have become only notable for their desperation. Gleaming projects are brought low by a lack of money and a lack of will by successive governments. At the same time, attracting political praise and attention of those only interested in serving the interest of people who went out to vote for them. In comparison, inner cities, high streets and Council housing are allowed to deteriorate, becoming ghost towns.

Such places have become home to many ethnic immigrants just before them was home to Irish and Jews migrants - vast blocks of flats with water dripping down the walls, mould growing in corners. With neglect come crime, drugs, gangs and hopelessness, plus a slim chance for the second-generation children of immigrants to get out of poverty as they see the hollowness on their parents' faces. Who themselves still witness similar past disparities in housing, jobs, NHS appointments, constantly a battle to prove their worth and stand up for their rights? Worried they aren't wanted here, looked upon with suspicion, many becoming victims of the 1981 Nationality Act. And subsequent draconian immigration laws directed towards them by the very politician Teressa May standing on the steps of Downing Street pledging to tackle "burning injustices" who had before played her part with vans with "Go Home" signs driving around in their neighbourhoods. Such hypocrisy doesn't instil Hope.

*

Statements stereotyping sectors of the community has also not helped. If a tiny minority of BAME commit crime, claim welfare benefits, show reluctance to the Covid vaccine, it doesn't merit generalisations that "they are all the same." Doing so makes BAME feel like second-class citizens when many do decent days of hard work to earn a living. Not drawn a penny on welfare benefits or don't even know how to claim benefits and are eager to have the Covid vaccine, not vaccine-hesitant as portrayed in the media. Just like when some politicians get found out of racist, antisemitic, or Islamophobic behaviour within their political parties doesn't mean "they are all the same," and the BAME don't rush to generalise that they are. While politicians quickly refer to their own as few "bad apples" who will get rooted out, they do not generalise that "they are all the same" as they do to the BAME. Isn't it surprising it rarely happens when it's one of their own involved? And if it does, it's usually after becoming a national scandal like the infamous MPs expenses, sleaze; even then, they went to great lengths that there are only a few "bad apples" or try to change rules through the backdoor. So, shouldn't generalised stereotyping of all BAME also be made unacceptable?

Such divisive statements only serve to turn white against non-white people and vice versa. We need to face reality. That despite those people who work hard all their life, why do they still face structural inequalities? Is it because of the hurdles they have to overcome? If so, what are those hurdles? Are those hurdles peculiar to them? Are there more or fewer than other people face? What happens if they don't get over them? What if the 'establishment' contrives a set of hurdles so high that getting over them is not the point. And surviving becomes being ignored, and no one is listening to them. And also, those in the minority who commit a crime and are jobless need to be heard, not tarnished. I am not saying it should give them an excuse to misbehave. But politicians should try to understand what it feels like to be discriminated by the 'establishment', especially when you can offer so much to put something back into the community instead of taking from it.

It often seems official government statistics for those at the receiving end have been compiled 'on the back of a fag packet', giving false hope to those at the bottom of the social mobility ladder. It is awful, absolutely disgusting, divisive and hurtful trying to make success against odds. It's painful to think that so many fellow human beings did not achieve what they could; no one believed in them, gave them a chance, or invested any time in them. Sadly, it is still happening now in twenty-first century Britain. It should not be allowed to happen in a country with the fifth largest world economy. We can't let many beautiful, talented individuals put by the wayside and forgotten, hoping that the problem will go away and resolve itself by blaming each other. Schools and workplaces can be scary if no one cares, and people fall further into the poverty trap if no one cares. Feel marked with a dead future. Different expectations lead to different outcomes, and groups drift apart; separateness becomes ingrained and affected groups become more distant from the mainstream society.

To the surprise of absolutely no one, job seekers should expect fairness based on merit from employers in the labour market prospects for everyone. However, the trouble is it is not so. When sent set fabricated CVs where the only difference was ethnic background, studies show white candidates were three or more times likely to be asked for an interview. Surveys have also found that non-white people are more likely to get overlooked for a work promotion in a way that felt unfair– more than the proportion of white people. What is striking, non-white people also face such handicaps in public institutions? The least likely of all places where one would expect less racial bias due to the intellectual abilities and liberal attitudes of the 'establishment' would know intelligence has nothing to do with skin colour. Therefore, it is most surprising when the Royal College of Physicians reported that non-white NHS doctors find it harder to get consultant posts than white NHS colleagues who are more likely to be promoted than them. It is no different in other professions. I have mentioned in my first book about my personal experiences of discrimination I faced during my university and employment career. How the authorities ignored me, and such unconscious bias gives legitimacy to established racism within the system.

However, it shouldn't mean that we should pass more laws to bring equality, privileges, and opportunities because such enforcement measures and positive discrimination often have negative impacts. They end up causing more resentment within the white population, giving an impression of bias, favouritism that a non-white person got the job, council house and treated differently, not on merit. Regardless of their ethnicity or social background, every person should get opportunities to fulfil their potential at work. It is achievable. But first, we need to start by changing the political discourse without the US and THEM attitude deliberately aimed to divide people for self-serving egos.

I am not naïve to think that we can eliminate discrimination, yet I am sure we can alleviate differences to make a more inclusive society with the right approach. There is no doubt progress has been made; however, we can make further progress. Not by ignoring, papering over the cracks as someone else's problem will only make it even worse. And in the long run, it leads to civil unrest, which we see popping up everywhere due to unfairness. The supreme function of political leadership and statesmanship: should be to ease what ails a nation, address issues of all its peoples, to ease tensions through deeds, thorough words of wisdom and practical policies to help those affected, suspicious and shocked, not with a bluster of metaphors of divisive politics and lying but with the balm of real Hope.

*

To understand the underlying causes, a good place to start would be to speak to those who feel disadvantaged and squeezed out. Ask why sectors of the society still feel second-class, and as individuals need to prove anew daily, rarely get the benefit of the doubt, and have little margin for error. In straightforward terms living in any country where you are not a majority feels like you are the victim of all the snubs and pains as a minority. Of course, various form of discrimination has indeed been going for centuries. Except the difference is that we have moved on, like to be called 'civilised', made to believe we can all fulfil our dreams if we work hard irrespective of our background. There is nothing wrong with that; after all, there is no such thing as 'free lunch' in this world. And if it is, then somebody else is paying for it. Also, in life, nothing is guaranteed except death and tax unless you are a politician who, after having squandered millions, if not billions, of taxpayer's money on vanity projects, remain unaccountable because it is not their money.

But what is not fair or wrong when a victim feels deprived and believes that they never rose to the highest ranks in public institutions such as the NHS, university and judiciary because of their immigrant background! Now, perhaps their colour, faith, age, sex, whatever handicaps they may have, has nothing to do with their lack of ultimate promotion. Or treated as a second-class citizen, stopped by the police, even more likely get a stiffer sentence in courts or get deported by the Home Office. Or maybe the individual is a bit rude, a bit mediocre, a bit lazy, a bit of the wrong appearance, has a bit of a chip on the shoulder. Or a bit of all these handicaps things that, if you are white, are not necessarily a barrier to promotions.

Whatever excuse we may come up with, that colour doesn't matter, and it's no longer a barrier to success in twenty-first century Britain. Yet it seems somehow it does matter since the government's own data and surveys conducted independently show otherwise that it's a different picture in real life. In the labour market, non-white people, some with university degrees, are over-represented at the lower end - the cleaners, the carers, shop workers, security staff- and underrepresented at the upper end – the managers, the executives, the policy advisers. Ask those with personal real-life experience who have faced that tiring, upwards climb throughout their lives despite even many folds better at the job. Many non-white people wake up daily to arrive at the same position on that same slope despite working twice or even harder. Not only in employment but also treated second-class when accessing public services such as NHS appointments or seeking justice when making a complaint. The exhaustive process they get subjected to wears them down. Giving up in the end or not bothering to pursue it because they know it will make no difference.

Likewise, no one disputes that non-white people are all saints; also, they can be lazy or, at times, not good role models, just like no one can expect all white people to be perfect. But if we examine closely and give credit where it's due, we will find such generalisation is not a universal trait because many people of immigrant backgrounds work hard in all walks of life. Whereby they go the extra mile in their line of duty, working diligently in scientific and challenging fields with colleagues from different cultures and faiths in a language that is not their mother tongue. Britain's history speaks for itself the contribution made by the non-white people. Even during Covid-19, far more BAME people lost lives and non-white NHS doctors, nurses, public sector workers made sacrifices. They suffered disproportionately more because of a lack of equality, a safe space to work, PPE and better testing facilities. Numerous studies have also highlighted that the death rate amongst non-white NHS staff who delivered direct patient care was three times more than white colleagues.

At the same time, we need to be realistic instead of blaming each other with one-sided angry arguments and protests. We need to move away by confining our debate on race to a battle between non-white people, white people and the colonial past because it restricts our ability to find a path towards solutions. Also, amid that chaos, we see white people from disadvantaged backgrounds left behind on the social mobility ladder that needs addressing if we want to live in social harmony. Doing so will open up a possibility to better understand prejudice that is not only related to race. But it is at the heart of the very 'establishment', an instinct against the 'other' be it white or non-white disadvantaged people. We see it in the differing standards of public service at their disposal. Whether it is the NHS, housing, education and social care, what it boils down to in the end is a lack of confidence, awareness that I could be like you. What we need to do is to move away from the culture of empty rhetoric. Ask why serious real-life issues go unnoticed or ignored by politicians until a public disaster like Grenfell, Windrush, school meal vouchers, civil unrest happen?

There is no doubt that there is no substitute to work, to build happiness and wellbeing than not having a job. Repeated studies have found that it is a constant struggle for those on zero-hour contracts and low-paid jobs who find it difficult to put food on the table and rely on food banks and charities for life's essentials despite being in employment. While those affected the most come from disadvantaged backgrounds with structural inequalities. We know economic hardship reduces social capital and reduces self-resilience. The essential ability that is needed to manage the daily challenges we encounter as individuals and as groups. An estimated 22% of all households in Britain are on relative low incomes, whereas 19% on an absolute low income, about 14 and 12.5 million people respectively considered to be just about making ends meet. [42] Of these, as expected, people from some ethnic groups are over-represented, about 65% Bangladeshi, 55% Pakistani, 45% black Africans, 30% black Caribbean, 25% white other whereas 20% are white British. [43] The data speaks for itself, and easy to conclude that low income is an ethnic problem. To an extent, it is true.

However, it will be wrong to ignore another worrying trend. Increasing evidence that the number of British white working-class people is joining a growing social underclass. Disconnected from the mainstream, whose earnings have got outstripped by the rise in living costs. People whose incomes are less now than a decade ago. It is a worrying trend. It is not only because of an ever-increasing social underclass earning less, left behind, not part of the economic success story in a country with a prosperous economy, but also its impact on race relations. We do not need to look that far back. People, especially in the North, voted for Brexit despite all the uncertainties it would bring. As an alternative to the status quo, a direct result of the austerity measures since 2010 and the 1980s pace of de-industrialisation had taken a heavy toll on the white working-class communities - one which they believe the middle-class has often failed to grasp to date.

Also, the shock for the many white working-class people is that they feel forgotten and do not feature in the structural inequalities debate. They see it being more biased and focused on non-white people. It may seem like that but not necessarily true because white people do not face the same obstacles as non-white people. What they face is the lack of mechanisms to deal with systematic issues that discriminate against them. However, this is not to do with their skin colour but is associated more with their white working-class background. So suddenly, they find sitting with non-white people sharing the same table old worn-out table with limited financial resources to correct structural inequalities ignored over the years. And Covid-19 is not going to make it any easier. Therefore the government mustn't forget the ever-growing social under-class of white and non-white folks.

How we respond is exceptionally crucial to prevent people from turning inwards by becoming more protective towards each other belonging to their colour. In the process, they become more isolated from those of the 'other tribe', even allowing an element of prejudice to influence one's thinking as an outlet to blame others for their misfortune. At times, sometimes egged on by the media construing facts dishonestly with offensive, discriminatory, provocative eye-catching slogans to increase sales and profits on the back of others misery. It is also a misapprehension to believe that racial fear, hatred and suspicion towards each other would altogether disappear if it was not for the right-wing press and the politician's lack of will to tackle the handicaps faced by the ever-growing social under-class. Say, for instance, the paranoia towards the politicians is unwarranted. We should believe and rely on them to fix the structural inequalities, then how come after decades of pledges, those in the poverty trap is on the increase with the gap widening between the haves and have nots? Therefore, to some extent, the blame lies at the door of the politicians who have let people down.

Similarly, it is too easy for the comfortable 'I'm alright Jack' brigade to portray that it is the fault of the white and non-white social underclass. To think the problems are of their own making. They are lazy and depend on welfare handouts, and there are several charities they can rely upon to get help from or who will fight on their behalf to get help. No doubt some of these charities are doing a remarkable job under extreme conditions, despite lacking financial resources, doing a good job at times risking their lives. But it is a sticking plaster without tackling the root causes with adverse outcomes because it can lead to greater dependency on handouts with a loss of self-dignity and morale with no escape from the poverty trap. Despite all this help, we need to ask why there is an increase in poverty, homelessness, and food banks, of which there are more off than MacDonald outlets. Is it because we are missing the wood from the trees? Is it because we don't understand the underlying root causes? Is it because we are too distant from them? Is it because we are looking through our microscopes at an old problem often overlooked within the context of twenty-first-century demands?

Living and growing up in areas short on Hope, opportunities extended further by boredom, where unemployment, alcohol and drugs due to decades of neglect as someone else's responsibility would ruin the senses of many, even those with 'I'm alright Jack' attitude. Where blaming others becomes easier if everyone tells you to do that. Millions of youngsters across Britain in low-income households have fallen behind their peers academically due to school closures and pushed deeper into economic hardship due to job losses among parents. Their prospects were very uncertain even before the Covid pandemic.

And what Covid-19 has done is that it has made their plight even worse. It has dealt an additional cruel blow to the white and non-white social underclass, which will affect their life chances more by exposing structural inequalities that were there as an undercurrent for decades. It will live with them throughout life. I'm sure about that.

It won't be a quick fix, but it has to start now. It needs to move from ad-hoc sticking plaster responses to having a coherent determinate plan. It needs to be part of that legacy of "building back better." It needs to move from a concept into a strategy, and the program needs to start with kids. Put the support in place to enable present and future generations to flourish. The pandemic has shone a harsh spotlight on the structural inequalities children have been experiencing for a long time. Let's hope for the first time a lot more people have understood what it means so we can all get a chance to be proud winners, not having to rely on welfare benefits.

# 10.

# "TAKE BACK CONTROL"

Mendacity has become common both on the right and left of the political divide. Whether it's during the Iraq war, austerity, Brexit or a world health pandemic, all that matters to politicians is that if the end justifies the means, then the means can include lying, bluster, not answering straightforward questions. This contempt has gradually eroded the compact workings of established principles, creating the space for showmen to exploit the vacuum. Politicians are now feeding a toxic culture where the very notion of evidence-based truth and accountability is dead. Where one side never believes the other. No one listens anymore. We just yell anger at each other. Who's right and who's wrong.

No one can deny that the "take back control" slogan was brilliant. Yet, it drove a deep wedge between the Brexiters and Remainers. It may have further divided the British people making them more aware of who is on which side of the argument at the heart of British public life. Remainers may continue to maintain the slogan was the biggest delusion, whereas Brexiters will vehemently disagree. One thing is for sure; it's now in the past. Brexit is done and dusted. Only time will tell what the outcome will be.

Though the sad reality is, over the past few years, what is happening is that we have a bunch of very ambitious demagogues who will stop at nothing for self-serving egos. With a belief, there's a quick, easy way to tap into the populist base to gain political power at whatever cost, even if it means the breakdown of people's trust and damage to their livelihoods. The prevailing political atmosphere looks as if the UK has fallen into the hands of lunatics engaged in an astonishing act of national self-harm.

However, politicians are wrong since there is a limit. This issue is more extensive than anyone's ambitions. As Jacques Abbadie said, "You can fool all the people some of the time, and some of the people all the time, but you cannot fool all the people all the time." [44] In this increasingly hostile world, the public will grasp what's at stake and eventually come together. The sensible ordinary people will soon question politicians' motives. Realise it's still not too late to halt an act of folly embarked upon by the politicians over the last few decades.

One thing is for sure. Brexit has changed politics. Whether for better or worse will be down to the people. What the Brexit referendum did was open a pandora's box, as referendums so often do, driven in part by a simple question on the ballot paper, the electorate made full use of and grasped the opportunity to vent their decades of fury built inside them. Frustrated by the sense that the political class had failed them. And this is what the slogan did do so effectively. It didn't just combine a sense of a positive future, albeit never elaborated or defined, except suggest a sense of rightful identity and ownership.

I believe it's this identity and ownership from which the British people can immediately benefit. Literally, "take back control" of how politics is done by holding politicians more accountable for their actions. Not in a destructive way used by the Vote Leave campaign to mobilise the anti-establishment support of voters who felt let down by their politicians. Instead, constructively by restoring trust in democracy and public institutions since there's a growing sense of a broken political system in today's Britain. It's this ineffectiveness that is a significant threat to voter disenchantment. Why do so many think the political system is not working? It's because modern politics is no longer polarised along the 'old fashion' lines with a clear ideological distinction between political parties. Instead, it is more polarised along the lines of politics of hatred, populism and nationalism. It's not just the contemporary political situations that have generated a culture of 'fake news' and mistrust but also the recent developments in the media world. Whereby newspapers, their owners, their editorial staff collude with the politicians to fabricate and smear lies to increase sales without any fear of getting found out.

A look at British politics will highlight the actual source of this breakdown. Although it may seem that politics operates along the 'old fashion' ideological divide along tribal party lines. In reality, it's in name only. Because over the last few decades, instead of the intense ideological battles between Red and Blue, which often proved highly productive in policy terms, delivering the best ideas from both sides. For instance, in the past political parties were deeply sceptical of each other's policies: one side of the political divide pushed hard for balanced fiscal budgets, free markets; while politicians at the other end of the spectrum demanded more borrowing to fund free public services for all and state ownership. Whereas, what we witness now is convergence leaving an enormous vacuum without pragmatic policy initiatives except for politics of appeasement, nationalism, populism and debt, which has resulted in an army of politicians on both sides of the political divide who have run out of ideas opting for an easy option. Adopting a combination of both policies has proved enormously influential without much to choose between for the electorate.

Likewise, today's problem is that too many politicians have come to view public duty as a political career, a gravy train, greed, cronyism: with a lot at stake, a war, where victory is paramount, and compromise is a dirty word. This take-no-prisoners approach threatens to cripple the best-of-both dynamics. Revitalising Britain's culture of democracy is essential where people and country come first, above party and ideology. And even if suppose the political leaders are reluctant to play a prominent role in this effort. Then, in that case, people should "take back control" of politics by voting out those politicians with self-serving egos and party interests since the implications for the nation are so significant, even more so now post Covid-19.

Humanity is crying out for visionary political leadership to stop the endless cycle of atrocities of blaming each other. Not by waiting who will give in first as no one wants to be the first to lay down their weapons because they feel it will leave them in a much weaker bargaining position. And, of course, there has got to be equality, not just arrogance. Otherwise, we will never find peace. Humanity working as one has managed to settle many past conflicts in the last century. Who would have thought disputes like the two World Wars, Vietnam War, Northern Ireland and Bosnia, would get settled even if it meant compromising or accepting defeat for some? Yet they did!

If there is a political will, we can settle conflicts in Kashmir and Palestine like in Northern Ireland, achieved through peaceful negotiations and 'people power', which also brought down the Berlin Wall. Similarly, the break-up of the Soviet Union saw the rise of republics like Russia and others becoming sovereign nations. At the same time, apartheid in South Africa was settled based on logic when commonsense prevailed. All these obstacles got dismantled, showing that these 'uncivilised' acts of segregation can get resolved if we want. All that is required are visionary, iconic leaders like Mikhail Gorbachev and Nelson Mandela, who both saw the reality of the situation in their respective countries.

To stop people, turn inward away from the endless noise and rage of political chicanery will require honest politics. Not regurgitated, pre-packaged ready to pull off the shelves with empty slogans like "New Labour" or "One Nation Conservatism." Here today, gone tomorrow. Instead, what is needed more now than before is politics that addresses real-life concerns people face in their lives to live. We need to tackle how and why we got to this divisive populist politics of fear, racism, civil unrest, this land of warring factions, tribal hatreds that serve sections of communities and not the wider society. It is essential to construct twenty-first-century politics from the best of our traditions because, despite all our differences, we share a lot: common hopes, shared dreams, a bond of fundamental human values.

*

Since time immemorial, there have been three primary indices of power: military prowess, economic wherewithal, and political clout, which is what happened when half the Western World was dragged into the Iraq war over the "weapons of mass destruction" on bogus evidence concocted by the CIA. On arrival, there was nothing except the death of over three million civilians and soldiers. And there is no doubt it will happen again unless people "take back control" of the politics by making sure politicians do not abuse power bestowed on them by the people for self-serving egos and greed.

By not engaging in the democratic process gives the narrative to a select few to control the majority. And therefore, it becomes a democracy in name only, a form of 'legalised dictatorship'. How often have we seen abuse of privilege by those in power? The conventional wisdom of 'don't talk politics' gives political power to those who talk politics. Correspondingly, if most people place themselves into the social contract not to talk politics, it is left to those who speak politics to control the agenda. Add to this that it will often be the case that minority viewpoints will get entrenched. While the views of others, the majority, not publicly permitted to challenge them, will end up with a situation where very few points are up for discussion by very few people with the proper connection to the corridors of power.

In a world where most people are told not to talk about politics or 'don't talk politics', we end up with 'political experts' and career politicians. Elected officials, lobbyists, and their occasional challengers become the ones who control what is essential gets discussed, leading to more and more concentration of power with less and less involvement from the individual citizens. It threatens the very routes of our democracy. If we don't speak up, then who knows the truth? Nobody does except those privileged ones while denying the majority access to the facts, making an unpredictable future for the rest except for the select few able to discuss politics as reflected by the outcome of recent elections and political uncertainties.

Many were shocked, including David Cameron, when the Conservative party won a slight majority in the 2015 general election. To avoid dissent amongst the rebel Tory MPs, he now had to honour the manifesto pledge to hold a referendum on the EU membership offered as a bribe to woo UKIP voters. Something he didn't expect would have to do since it was uncertain he would win. However, he resigned soon after the 2016 EU referendum, leaving the country to clear up his Brexit mess. Additionally, the 2016 EU referendum outcome left many stunned, including the principal architects Boris Johnson and Nigel Farage of the 'Vote Leave' campaign, who couldn't believe they had won.

Similarly, the 2019 general election outcome shocked Boris Johnson, especially by the Tory party's winning margin. In America, many were equally shocked that Donald Trump was elected President in 2016 as the polls didn't predict a likely outcome, considering many media outlets had supported Hillary Clinton in her bid for the presidency. These recent political events show many quiet voters who showed up at the polls existed somewhere below the surface. On the surface, this doesn't seem to be a huge issue. In the end, the voters got the person they desired in office or the result they wanted. However, below the surface looms a deeper problem. It's a disconnection from the truth. Somehow enough people that supported those causes existed. But most people didn't know that. Now that's scary for democracy. Our lawmakers go to work with a distorted view of what we, the people, want. And laws might get passed based on that distorted view. What's more, it's unpredictable how this distortion of the truth will impact outcomes. And to put it right, the electorate has to wait another five years, by which time it can be too late.

For instance, had the campaigns of Vote Remain and Hillary Clinton known about the distortions, we may have had different outcomes today. By not speaking up, as individuals, we are hiding the truth. Elections every few years are not enough to give the feedback our lawmakers need. They need to hear our voices regularly. An informed and engaged population will lead to laws and policies that reflect the people's wishes more accurately. And that's going to be critically important for the reasons I'll get to in a moment to "take back control" of democracy. On top of fixing structural inequalities and challenges post-Covid19, lurking underneath are equally important events that will affect everyone. On the business side, technology is enabling big things to happen. Artificial Intelligence, cryptocurrency, international treaties are at the front and centre in today's political world. Many governments are scared about the power of cryptocurrency. The rise of digital and decentralised currencies takes away one of the core functions of government, creating and maintaining a monetary system.

This loss of power has not gone unnoticed by those in government. And regulations are changing too. More and more governments are getting active in fining technology companies that don't conform to their view of acceptable behaviour. If they get enacted, such policies may mean that, in some cases, we may be moving to a world where we go back to regional and national business versus international as these complex forces interplay. Yet, very few people seem to know or are talking about what is suitable for humanity and the world's future. Without knowledge and conversation, we don't know what we, the people, want. Looming in future is the rise of Artificial Intelligence, which will mean the possibility of monitoring and control as we've never seen before. Many laws today are only partially enforced. For instance, people often break the rules on speeding, jaywalking and spitting on the sidewalk but are rarely caught or fined. Artificial Intelligence will bring with it the potential of enforcing all laws with considerable uniformity. Such a game-changer in law enforcement may have profound societal impacts. There are many other once-in-a-lifetime human historical events happening today that politics will impact. Which means it is even more relevant to talk politics instead of avoiding it.

The regulation of digital currency, the potential of deglobalisation, the monitoring and control of Artificial Intelligence are just three of the many critical issues decided at present. There are many more out there. However, one thing is for sure. The power of these technologies to change global commerce and culture will be significant. The use or non-use of cryptocurrency in the future will impact all of humanity. It will determine how our society develops, decide the balance of power, human interaction and economic progress. Similarly, Artificial Intelligence, with its ability to potentially create and enforce laws raise huge ethical concerns that could impact every man, woman and child alive today. These issues are too big with a significant impact on the future of society. Equally, the politicians need to be aware of what the majority of people are thinking. We need informed discussion leading into the future. And politics needs to adapt to change. Or else. The present crop of twentieth-century born political leaders, some with colonial mentality, is a perfect example of why politics must adapt to serve twenty-first century needs. And it's only the ordinary people who can bring about a change to benefit themselves.

*

Our political system does not represent the actual voter's choice in any election. That's why we either have frequent elections or a see-saw of parties in power even if a government goes a full term. While the civil service has to remain constitutional consistent, remain impartially and independent during government cycles. But regrettably, the civil servants are now undermined by unaccountable politicians and SpAds in their quest for power and pure greed (in it for themselves). Equally, the rot in professional standards in the civil service, just like in politics over the last four decades, has not helped. At the same time, the top civil servants have compromised their neutrality by not questioning the political class about the practicality of some dubious policies enacted by politicians. Which has led to government incompetence; expensive U-turns exacerbated further by weak political opposition culminating in a costly inefficient system of governance with an overall drop in public standards costing the taxpayer. At the same time, the immigrants getting blamed for shortages in school places, NHS, housing, jobs. This grab for power is not going to protect our democratic freedoms or national interests.

While simultaneously, it's not the ordinary public who robs the public purse of billions of pounds, that's politicians and tax dodgers; or buy influence and subvert democracy, that's down to greedy politicians and billionaires. Likewise, ordinary people do not let our public services fall into ruins. That is the fault of politicians with self-serving interests and egos. While concurrently allowing people to go hungry, administer cuts to ALL services, and yet they can find the money for huge payoffs, it seems something has gone very wrong here. Politicians, celebrities, footballers & CEOs are all vastly overpaid whilst the rest of us fight like dogs for the scraps. Not one of their kind saved anyone from the Covid-19 virus because they were too busy saving themselves. Poor NHS workers toiled saving others whilst putting their necks on the line initially got offered a diddly squat 1% pay rise for their efforts! The whole political system is rotten to the core. Like in Lebanon, in 2020, the entire government had to resign since people had enough and wanted change. Now we may think it can't happen in Britain as we are more 'civilised'. But it can, just like nobody ever envisaged riots outside the world's most powerful institutions. Yet, we saw it happen on Capitol Hill in the most robust 'civilised' country in the world endorsed by a democratically elected president himself!

Here in Britain, we should not be amazed or denounce leaders like Trump *et al.* Over here with Boris Johnson and his Conservative government, including the opposition politicians are no different. I don't think they do things any better than Trump other than just like him, look after own interests once in power! It's just an illusion that they will make a difference! Go back for as long as you can remember: people cheered, felt saved when Labour got into power with a landslide majority election win! Then, a few years into their tenure, people start to question things that are happening, going wrong or question politicians for not implementing policies they said they would on the election campaign, etcetera! Then the Tory party starts to make a noise; we'd have done this, we'd have done that, we will do this if we are elected, and much more! People like what they hear; the Tories pull away in the polls. Tories get elected. Then Labour repeats the same process. See where this is going. It's the same everywhere. They are here today, gone tomorrow, the mouthpieces of those with the real power in this world - and I'm sure a lot of people will have an idea who they are. If not, maybe you need to think about computers, currency speculators, Facebook, Google, Amazon, media moguls, or large families with wealth beyond our wildest dreams. These groups meet behind closed doors. All secretly planning what's best for us, well for them really, and cue back to more election pledges followed by more government illusion!

*

When I was growing up, I could not grasp the idea of politics. What democracy meant? Understand why we need countries, borders and why people cannot accept or treat others as fellow human beings. I could also not comprehend how can random people like politicians who were *strangers* to me were the ones who knew what rules were best to abide by in my life. I wasn't able to understand why there were rules that needed to be made anyway and then only for people to say "we live in a free country" when there were rules and orders to be followed? Or why would people say "it's freedom of speech," yet when those who try to speak get ignored anyway? Or when they talk of a fair, level playing field, we are all equal, people can fulfil ambitions, and when those who work hard towards a better life end up finding it's not that straightforward as it may sound?

To add a little bit of a twist to the plot, I'm going to tell you the truth here: I did not grow up to be an Anarchist. Because those around me brought me up to respect people, the laws of the land of domicile and the society so we can live in social harmony, it's a hardly tricky task; it's a formula of success in all walks of life, as well as in one's personal life. Though I still cannot fully comprehend the very concept of politics (which I'm sure even politicians themselves can't wholly explain), I sure have learned since then.

However, most importantly, now that I have learned and am a bit wiser in my old age, I have developed a particular curiosity about politicians, the mysterious decision-making strangers I didn't know in young adulthood. So, the question for the younger generation is, are you brave enough. The world needs you and your input. The 'establishment' needs to know what you are thinking, your wisdom to get things right. Can you help shape the world the right way? Can you help make the future that is right for humanity? Can you commit, so your voice gets heard by those in power on these and other important issues? It starts with you. Get involved today; please don't leave it as late as I did. However, having realised the importance of politics and voting, I am doing my bit because it's never too late.

While growing up in Tanzania, I never had an opportunity to vote when I reached voting age. Politics was something above most young people's brains. Our main ambition was to focus on getting a good education to succeed in life. As far as I can recall, the meaning of politics was not clear, as I had focused more on science subjects from an early age. I never got an opportunity to study politically oriented subjects to generate interest. It was not until 1970, at the age of nineteen, at Dar es Salaam University, I became aware when I met politically-minded students who would discuss communism, capitalism, socialism, and apartheid in South Africa. For me, it was nothing more than just banter, part of university student life. It was a strange, disjointed activity by potentially angry students, which at times felt quite tense, giving me an impression that politics could be dangerous, get people into trouble, and perhaps best for me to keep away, which I did until 2017. However, since settling in Britain, I have always believed in exercising my democratic right to vote. I have also instilled in my children and others not to take this precious freedom for granted.

One thing is for sure that although I grew up not showing much attention to the politics of how people got governed, the result, nevertheless, is the same. Because when we lose sight of justice, it unfastens and floats away, leaving us with a nominal political system, not a democratic system in its truest sense. Also, when we look at various past and recent events, what makes me wonder why they were allowed to happen in the first place? Like most conflicts, I still cannot understand why people let this happen: for example, why nobody had stood up to Adolf Hitler? Why did the Jewish people, the gipsies, the intellectuals, disabled people, and the other innocent people elsewhere not receive loyal support? Now I can understand why. It's because the general public enables it to happen by turning a blinding eye.

Whether it be conflicts, poverty or any other ills, it allows bad people to get used to doing bad things. They become casual about it, and many good people start accepting bad things that happen, as they simply get used to them, passing them off as trivial and inevitable. If we stop supporting and protecting each other, we not only create hell on earth for others; we create hell on earth for ourselves. Sometimes, even our elected representatives will not bother to think of the outcome or lay the groundwork but are quick to run to the nearest TV camera to announce policy initiatives drafted on a crisp packet to vanquish whatever fantasy excites them on the day. These days politics is more about themes that create controversy, only to disappear into the ether without actual policy trace, to reappear again when politicians desperately need a news headline to distract peoples' attraction from reality.

As you approach old age, you find out that there is a lot more to life. And one thing we discover, find satisfying in old age is the advantage to reflect. You appreciate quality things, not quantity though most of all, you have also gained experience of what worked and what didn't. So, when I sat down to write this book and my first one, *Hope and Shared Values: A reality check,* I thought about my childhood in detail for the first time and writing awakened my curiosity. Not only to write an audit of my childhood which is an inevitable part of ageing. But also the real-life difficulties I faced to exercise my democratic right to get heard, which I found how hard it was to do then made to believe otherwise. And over the years, I have realised I am not the only one and decided to speak out for the *voiceless.* Particularly on the subject: Why should we care about politics? Not only the old but why also the young people specifically? The answer is simple: as long as you actively care about politics, your life is in your hands. At least to a certain extent. Of course, we can turn our backs on all things political; in the hope, somebody else will stand up for your opinion. Except where would that get us other than let somebody else decide your future, but then we shouldn't complain if they don't or let you down.

I believe that the moment we start to turn our backs on politics is when we lose power over our lives. In the process end up giving power to others to transform our lives in whatever way they wish. The moment we stop caring about politics is the moment we also lose control of events. It may sound very dramatic, maybe it is, but I want you to understand the sheer significance of this issue: especially for the young people who need to stand up for what they believe. They need to care about politics since it concerns us more than we think. We need to follow elections, vote as soon as we become eligible, and voice our opinions.

The young people have their future and that of the world in their own hands. So they should not take their eyes off politics. Somebody born in the twentieth century, my advice is not to believe the present crop of politicians born in the last century. I don't think they have the interests of the millennials at heart because most of them are still living in the past with a colonial mentality of dividing, compartmentalising people into 'tribes'. Whilst conveniently forgetting how good they have had it, a state-funded education, gold plated pensions, while draining the public purse to the tune of two trillion pounds of the national debt to pay for their failed policies for others. On top of that, their legacy of global warming and job uncertainty.

*

There is no doubt that politics matters, and we cannot live without it. However, the political dialogue has got to change. One way of doing it is voting for a politician committed to serving public duty. Regrettably, there has been an increase in hatred towards them, and venting anger against them will not help because we need public institutions for the effective functioning of our society. However, if we feel that our politicians are failing in their duty, then it is up to the people to "take back control," do something about it. Therefore, the onus is on the people to elect politicians who will serve by listening to the electorates, not those with self-serving egos.

Politics should be about governance for the good of all the people. And as we saw during the pandemic, no one got spared; if global warming remains unchecked, it will be no different. Therefore, it is imperative to recognise we live in an interconnected world. And Britain needs to play an active role. In that case, we must not think that sovereignty means isolationism with more of the same divisive populist politics which sadly has been followed too often in the past few decades. Now is the time to put aside self-serving personal and party interests in the national interest. That's why I must admit I feel a bit more political over the last couple of years. Of course, everybody does because of the populist brand of politics thrust into our faces by divisive leaders like Trump, Modi, Johnson, Netanyahu, Farage, etc. However, politics should not be about north versus south, white vs non-white, this religion vs that religion. Especially when the recent Covid-19 pandemic has shown, borders do not exist and how vulnerable we have become in our twenty-first-century globalised world.

Like the many, I also used to think it was a waste of time to discuss politics or religion. I shunned such confrontations because, for some reason, over time, it has become more and more polite not to discuss politics to the point where people designate 'politics-free areas'. I get it. Politics is a highly personal, highly divisive topic, at times becoming uncomfortable. It can end friendships. Until now, I shared similar sentiments with the majority. Though now I think it is high time we do talk about politics. Not in an aggressive but 'civilised' way. I believe there are fundamental reasons why we should engage. Some of the reasons might not be surprising. However, some definitely will be.

Mine, for example, are based on real-life experiences when I tried to engage in politics with my constituent MP. Who point blankly told me not to contact him except "very, very occasionally." And, when on a separate occasion, he had said, "If you feel so strongly about local or national political issues, you are always at liberty to stand for election yourself or get involved in appropriate charities or pressure groups." It made me realise what an arrogant attitude for my MP to adopt. On the one hand, he is supposed to represent his constituents, and on the other hand, he has the audacity to tell his electorate not to waste his time. It is not appropriate behaviour because it only serves to undermine the main objective of democracy. So is it any wonder the electorate don't bother to vote?

Like the many, I felt disfranchised, *voiceless*, not knowing whom to approach, left to my own devices. I didn't want to join pressure groups and get branded as a trouble maker or a *jihadist* because of being a Muslim. Yet, equally, I believe in exercising my democratic right to get heard through appropriate channels peacefully. That's why we have elections to elect people to represent constituents who the taxpayer pays to perform a civic duty. That experience, together with many others over the last couple of decades, led me to play my part in serving civic duty. I am now of the opinion religion is a choice; I can choose not to follow it if I disagree with the teachings. And when the time comes for me to die, it will be between the Creator and me, whereas my thinking towards politics has changed drastically. I have realised that being disenchanted with politics is not going to help but to the contrary. If we think about it, irrespective of whether I engage directly or not, at least by voting, I'm making my vote count; I have had my say. By not voting, politics will still affect my daily life, not only mine but also everyone's life.

Whether we like it or not, the lawmakers are making political decisions on our behalf, such as what to tax or not, what public services to fund or cut, when to go to war, legal or not, the quality of the air we breathe and much more. So, it's better to vote. As pointed out later, it will become apparent to the reader why a huge voter turnout during elections will make politicians less complacent and not take constituents for granted. Politics is critical in the development and functioning of public life and civic liberties, more now than before due to a lack of trust in politicians and the explosive self-serving populist political agenda embarked upon by them. Today, the world looks like a chaotic place, with conflicts and crises popping up everywhere. Unfortunately, it will get messier if allowed to continue unless more work gets done to stop the juggernaut of greed, deceit, and conflicts inflicting pointless suffering on innocent civilians.

So, here is my admission as to why I decided to enter politics in 2017. At the ripe old age of sixty-six, I decided to stand for election to offer an alternative voice by doing honest politics to restore trust in democracy. I had no epiphany, no singular revelation, no moment of truth to become a politician as such and prefer not to be called one other than a community-led person with a desire to serve public duty. Perhaps it was because of a steady accumulation of thoughts, based on an ever-increasing feeling that the communication I had entered into with cross-party politicians and successive PMs was falling on deaf ears. It seemed that the ever-growing crop of career politicians was getting detached from the public with self-serving interests which are more important to them than their constituent's. Meeting the voters during my election campaigns made me realise why many people felt that politicians do not listen to their concerns. The main reason some people don't bother to vote is that they have lost trust in politicians. But one thing I must confess, I have never been inclined to join any political party or protest group. It is because I believe it is the duty of the learned professionals: teachers, doctors, police and judges, religious and political leaders, as the 'defenders of society', to uphold welfare, moral and social values of society and the nation irrespective of their political or religious beliefs or for that matter their race, sex and creed.

*

Most people see politics as the government and the lawmakers. That's true, but it's a bit more complicated than that. Every law made will impact many. Sometimes the decisions will affect people in a wrong way. Every vote that you make will either break people or make people. For example, if a new law gets enacted in your area, you might want to make sure that you and the people around you know that a new law has come into force so that no one breaks the law without even knowing it. Also, if something dangerous is happening around you or someone you know, you need to be aware of the situation. So, it is imperative to understand what is happening around you.

Another reason to care about politics is to have a say in what will happen. Everyone should have a say in what should happen because we all live side by side with each other, and it would not be fair if someone got left out. Also, each vote makes a difference in the way we live. Therefore, it is always important to share your opinion. The way you vote will affect many people and their everyday life. Finally, it would help if you cared about politics because the decisions people make will affect many lives. For example, if someone wanted to build on the land, it might be suitable for the people who worked in the area, but residents who lived nearby and loved the land and relied on it for water and food might be devastated. Sometimes things that sound like good ideas might be very devastating later. These are just a few reasons why you should care about politics. Politics are fundamental and very complicated.

Some people might not care about politics, but they will regret not voting when something terrible happens. Equally, politicians abstaining from voting is an insult to democracy. Especially when they knock on people's doors during election campaigns, urging them to go and vote. And when they get elected, they go to parliament as an MP. Their job should be to represent constituents, not abstain when communities, irrespective of where they live, suffer from structural inequalities, social injustices, mental well-being, and public health. It is this sort of politics that does not address people's real-life concerns. There are too many chiefs and few Indians.

Usually, female MPs, female political leaders and female professionals show greater concern, empathy relating to human values, environment, upbringing, culture, education, health. Most women seem to be better than men in such matters. They seem less ruthless, more accommodating than men because they think for the good of humanity. With a few exceptions, we also see women are the voice of reason in Westminster, local councils and elsewhere, in contrast to the rowdy, raucous behaviour of their male counterparts observed at Prime Minister's Questions. Also, when men try to be compassionate during a time of sorrow, loss of lives or senseless suffering, a lack of compassion can be seen lurking underneath. Whereas female MPs, during parliamentary or public debates, are more dignified, passionate, dedicated, better role models than their male equivalents, who come across as selfish, troublesome, evil and dishonest. Let's hope more women play a more prominent role in public life.

Tribal party politics and political deceit are among the main reasons for voter disengagement across the board, leading to a declining sense of the efficacy of politics locally and centrally. A feeling that the main political parties are all the same, and all politicians are the same. Namely greedy. It makes no difference who is in power when the public witnessed chaos, a broken Westminster in the middle of a constitutional crisis on the brink of Brexit negotiation disaster with threats of prorogation of parliament. At the same time, Tory and Labour Party imploding with defections from disillusioned MPs rejecting tribal politics. However, it was refreshing to see some MPs perceive what the general public and true democrats have suspected for many years. That self-serving party-political interests, tribal allegiance leads to hostility leading to a rise in nationalism, populism, social unrest, extremism, racism, nimbyism, nepotism and more. The whole thing stinks!

The current situation encourages many MPs to vote along tribal party lines instead of relying on their judgment and constituents' needs. Of course, no one disputes that in a debating chamber, there is strength in numbers. However, if politicians disagreed a little bit more often, instead of just agreeing for the sake of it, they would serve the public better instead of letting a few vocal voices get away dictating the agenda with a bluster of oratory debating skills. The quality of conviction-based politics is on the decline. Most MPs are now passengers on a party ticket, selected not on merit but on the grounds whether prepared to kneel on the party line, follow like a flock of sheep, do what told, not what's right. Like Boris Johnson said during the 2019 election about his 630 Conservative party candidates: "MPs will do what they are told to do", meaning those who didn't vote for his party will get ignored. Labour had similar purge and incriminations following their defeat, rooting out those who failed to sing from the same hymn book.

\*

In 2019, the Tory Party's share of votes was 44%, so 56% did not vote for them. The turnout was 67%, while 33% of the eligible electorate did not vote for any political party. Therefore, a lot of people's views remain unrepresented. However, politicians from big parties will be quick to point out that in a democracy, there are always losers and winners. Yes, no one denies that. But it does not mean we should not look at other options before it gets worse. In a thriving democracy, we need to look at ways to engage voters to increase turnout during general and local elections. It will be good for democracy and bring out the best in our career politicians, as they will realise they can no longer afford to be complacent by taking the voters for granted, by getting elected on low turnouts. A low turnout favours established political parties. It is a major stumbling block for genuine democrat candidates contesting elections with limited resources. Still, when they decide to stand, it shows what they lack in terms of oratory or writing skills and funds; they are not short of conviction and honesty in their determination to serve civic duty. Career politicians have broken the public's trust, and the electorate can reclaim their democratic right with a large turnout during local and general elections.

We need to restore trust in our democracy and hard-fought freedoms if we want to leave a better legacy for our children. Not by divisive tribal politics but by addressing: Why do we need to fix corrupt politics? Why democracy and capitalism have got to evolve to meet twenty-first century needs? Why, more than ever, we should find better ways for voters to know who they elect? Why must we elect politicians who speak with honesty when in opposition and when in government? Why should we elect politicians who stand up for broader society, not masquerade as democrats by towing the party line for self-serving interests? Why it is crucial for the young to vote so that politicians don't take them for granted? How to address low voter turnouts during elections by embracing positive aspects of social media?

The best way for the electorate to "take back control" of democracy in its truest sense is to exercise their hard-fought voting right. A privilege we enjoy because of the millions of lives sacrificed during two world wars and other conflicts. While not forgetting until 1918, women in Britain were not even allowed to vote since they were treated as inferior citizens to men when it came to voting! Huge turnouts at elections are not only good for democracy but also help bring out the best in our politicians. At the same time, low turnouts during elections allow tribal politics to flourish, encouraging complacency and unaccountability amongst 'safe seat' career politicians. Equally, a huge voter turnout also prevents career politicians from relying entirely on their army of party loyalist voters to vote them in. It's, therefore, vital to keep politicians accountable. High voter turnouts will ensure that MPs served not along self-serving tribal political lines but in the interest of all constituents. If they didn't, the 33% who usually do not vote could easily tip the outcome of the election result, which would effectively govern the wider community's interest instead of being taken for granted by their constituent MPs or local councillors. Another vital difference in modern politics is that, unlike in the 'olden' days of tribal politics, the division along party lines in the twenty-first century is not that distinct.

Similarly, in the past, politicians came through ranks at the local level. They served apprenticeships in communities gaining real-life field experiences before progressing to the national level. Unlike career politicians these days with university degrees in politics, philosophy, law, media, economics and the like, followed by 'fast track' political internships and promotions based on loyalty to the 'establishment'. Today, it seems more about egos: claiming expenses, a good salary, greed, power to control others. I'm sure the system's beneficiaries will strongly disagree with this; all I can say, the record speaks for itself; politicians need to find out for themselves by listening more to the feelings of the ordinary people. I believe this can only happen if there is a big change of attitude, a change which can only be brought about by "taking back control"- 'people power' - electing politicians with scruples, a conscience.

The sackings, defections and resignations of MPs seen in 2019 in Tory and Labour parties confirm there is no room for thinkers and intellectuals in both parties. It doesn't serve the electorate well because, in a healthy democracy, openness, consultations, and disclosures are far better and practical in serving public duty. Tribal politics has broken the public's trust in democracy. Surely the Conservative party, as firm believers of 'free market' and competition, should be able to see through the weakness of the party loyalty structures that it stifles talent. Competition is healthy and efficient, just like private businesses as opposed to nationalised ones. But then, the breed of politicians has now changed. No one wants to rock the boat and stop the gravy train. The mindset in British politics needs revisiting before tribal politics becomes a more significant threat, post-Brexit, post-Covid-19. We need to rectify the situation before it drives a wedge between people, communities and social harmony. Pitting one group against another leads to venting anger, hatred on easily identifiable racial targets and the disadvantaged people.

The public often gets reminded that MPs need proper remuneration to attract the best calibre of people to enter politics. As a result, we have seen a massive increase in their salaries and perks. However, it's not entirely true. The main stumbling block to attracting talent is tribal politics and the selection process. Because to get selected, the potential candidates have to be submissive,  more compromising to the demands of the party hierarchy, or face threats of deselection and promotion prospects. We have witnessed politicians elevated to ministerial posts by turning on the charm, kowtowing to please the boss and the skill of how not to answer questions. So, instead of promoting excellence, the 'old' tribal party loyalty stifles intellectual ingenuity and ability; rewards incompetence, as seen by an increase in the number of U-turns and public inquiries. It's a telltale sign of shackled politicians deprived to think for themselves or what is good for their constituents and the country. The collective responsibility means no one can be held responsible; no one has to own up to their mistakes, allowing politicians to blame others and pass the buck. Since being a politician is the easiest thing they have ever done for most of them, and made even easier surrounded by like-minded people who don't question.

Ordinary people have been appalled by the present state of affairs in the oldest democracy in the world. Who knows where it will end? Unless we somehow pull ourselves back from the brink. Find a way to rekindle the respect for democracy and constitutional principles we once held so dearly. Now is an opportune time for democracy and capitalism to evolve further to keep pace with people's twenty-first-century aspirations. Not an unaccountable patronising political system dictated by few individuals or groups with financial, media and legal power influencing politics. The two-hundred-year-old party-political system has not been fit for purpose for the last few decades. We now have a breed of Oxbridge, ex-public schoolboys educated career politicians. It appears that parliament likes it that way so that those in the 'club' can leech thousands in expenses and other fiddles.

Nowadays, it seems it is not about serving people but more about profiteering from them. If we think about it, nothing of substance has been achieved for decades since the formation of the NHS and the social housing building programmes after WWII. If we look closely, the state of both is on its knees, as more gets taken out than put in, which could be cured in an instant by proper investment, political will and belief. But the politicians do not have the stomach to do it as it involves commitment. They know they only have to bumble along, doing nothing, except suck up the taxpayer's hard-earned money with empty pledges, as they could be out in five years.

Time and again, we are beginning to witness the consequences of the first-past-the-post, a system first introduced in 1888 to replace a complex system favouring the wealthy landowners and old-fashioned politicians. Now, it may have worked at the time since people had far more pertinent priorities to worry about than to vote. Also, in 1888, women did not even have the right to vote. Likewise, people did not enjoy many civil rights, so why would they be interested in which political party governs them. But it is different in the twenty-first century. Because people's expectations have changed, not only in terms of aspirations but also their complete outlook, due to travel, human rights, diet, jobs, leisure, and many other things that have changed in the world they live.

For most ordinary people, the division along old party-political allegiance is not as distinct as before. If anything, it's more confusing considering we all have to work, whether rich or poor, we are all working class and homeowners, whether we own a small house or a big mansion, which means many of us are landowners. Society has moved on so much beyond recognition, so has the public's values and priorities have changed drastically, not always necessarily along with wealth or worker's rights. Also, in the past, for most people, education, homeownership, environment, health, leisure and so forth were a lesser priority. It meant political views amongst the privileged were more distinct on those lines, easily reflected and divided along party lines. Whereas, now, the divisions along party lines are not that distinct. There are more affluent, educated, 'upwardly mobile' people enjoying better standards. As a result, we have a population with a range of priorities. People who don't fall into the traditional political categories and the parties have lagged to accommodate them. Conflicting views held within the political parties also do not help, causing further doubts in the public's mind. The electorates have reached a gridlock in democracy and need a pragmatic system to allow the public's real-life concerns to get heard. Not ignored amid chaotic, divisive tribal politics.

Perhaps more interaction at the local level is needed, not only along party lines but more widely, and looking at proportional representation models to enhance public participation in democracy with conviction politics, not self-serving party-political interests. Democracy in its purest form should allow, or at least allow, everyone to speak, be listened to by those elected, not out of reach of those who have elected them. The majority of the electorate should not feel democracy is only for those with hierarchy importance or those who shout and protest the loudest or for the appeasement of party faithful. It is now up to the people to "take back control" with a larger voter turnout during elections to restore trust, Hope and fairness in the truest sense of democracy.

# 11.

# STRONGER
# WORKING TOGETHER

The further that you go from the British shores, the more people are alarmed at witnessing uncertainty and unpredictability in a country they always respected and considered a byword for predictability, a Beacon of Hope for the Commonwealth.

If there are two critical lessons for politicians to learn post-Covid-19 pandemic; it is to realise the vital role of ordinary people irrespective of their creed, class and race and those from the Commonwealth. Secondly, politicians should not ignore problems until the last minute because the lack of investment in public services makes matters worse in the long run, even more expensive to tackle.

Covid-19 is the reality of today's world, and what we learn from it for the "new normal" is up to each one of us. Such as all the things we take for granted, only to miss so badly, only to appreciate when deprived. Also, how we tried to connect using zoom meetings and other technologies, even lighting up streets over festive periods, knocking on neighbours if they needed help because we all felt stranded when our liberties got snatched away from us. How desperate we felt the need to connect is also a reality of today and tomorrow, which many lonely people face. So, let's use the lessons learnt through the rocky paths during Covid-19, whose tomorrow one fails to imagine. Every event in history is a novel scenario, yet no time or tide can defeat human endeavour to navigate this and other capricious times.

The question on people's minds is what will be the long-term consequences of the Covid-19 pandemic? How will it affect us? Of course, no one can for sure say how it will impact the economy, people's lives and their future well-being? That only time will tell. Yet, we know that in a short time, apart from the apparent effects on the economy and health, the pandemic exposed many things we take for granted, don't even think about or care about. How we missed doing simple things in life? How we took the trouble to look after each other? How we witnessed structural inequalities affecting those from the poor households most?

On the brighter side, there are many lessons we have learnt already without holding any expensive public inquiries. And if we learn from those lessons, it will be the best way to repay the sacrifices made by the NHS staff, public sector key workers and the general public who have lost their lives, livelihoods and endured hardships. Not only that, but we will come out more robust than when we entered the pandemic if we start putting into practice the simple things we did right, missed most, how we managed. More notably, not repeat those same old past mistakes. If we did that, the lessons should remind us: How vulnerable we are? How interlinked our human society has become? How dependent on one another we are? How to continue the practice of the ancient sound doctrine 'Love thy Neighbour' to help others? Why should we adhere to social and family values? How we managed and survived the temptations of excessive material possessions during lockdowns when shopping malls, cafes and recreation activities were minimal? One of the most relevant lessons to learn post-Covid-19 is that the world has changed in several ways never imagined before, especially what can happen to us in a short period to our careers, businesses, and lives as the world around got transformed.

There are always moments when something embodies the start of something. For example, during the Black Lives Matter protest in June 2020, we witnessed the powerful image of a Black man carrying a white counter-protester to safety frames Hope from a day of chaos and race-inspired violence in London. Similarly, during the 2017 London Bridge terrorist attack, we saw people helping one another. Even during Covid-19, we observed non-white and white people in the NHS and the public sector working together, risking their lives to help others. Equally proud moments when our non-white Olympic heroes win gold medals lifting the country's spirit just like footballers, cricketers and many others representing British, English, Irish, Scottish and Welsh teams. There is an endless list of present contributions, not forgetting past ones fighting side by side in two world wars for the freedoms we enjoy today.

These acts generate Hope, a belief that we are stronger by working together. In doing so, we can all have a brighter future and a new tomorrow that would soar, become a great power of argument and unmistakable evidence to achieve much more. Instead of misconstruing factual evidence or deploying scaremongering tactics inciting hatred to attack Muslims by pedalling lies in the media against them with the audacity to claim it has nothing to do with Islamophobia and racism. Lies such as Muslims have higher birth rates, and mass migration from Muslim countries will overwhelm the white population. Imposing *sharia* laws in the West, resulting in the best countries in the world like Britain, America, Australia, and European nations becoming another war-torn Middle Eastern country with people at each other's throats leading to violence based on sectarian differences. What is so strikingly hypocritically obvious is that sectarian and caste differences played out amongst Christians, Buddhists, Hindus, Jews, Sikhs or others with even higher birth rates are of no concern to the right-wing media and politicians. So, if it is not Islamophobia, what else could it be?

Equally, according to the mathematical laws, it is impossible to achieve a Muslim majority even if the government manages to keep its pledge to "take back control" of British immigration after Brexit. Because if we take the Office for National Statistics estimated total population of 66,796,807 in mid-2019 Britain, there are about 3.4 m Muslims. It would take generations for Muslims to become a majority, even if they were the only ones allowed to breed! So, on that score, there is nothing to worry about that Muslims will take over Britain or any other 'civilised' country in the West. On closer examination, it shows what lengths lying occurs amongst 'civilised' politicians and media to deceive their citizens or readers into inciting hatred, encouraging them to go against their own religious belief of 'Love thy Neighbour'.

Similarly, it may look like Muslims are at each other's throats along sectarian lines. It may seem within the global geopolitical situation and greed over the control of oil reserves that one *Sunni* majority and one *Shia* majority country want to dominate the region with Western interference making it more war-torn in the name of democracy. Yet on closer examination, these sectarian differences didn't exist before the 1980 Iran-Iraq war. When the West, led by America, switched sides to support Iraq after the overthrow of the Shah of Iran. Or, for that matter, before the 2003 illegal Iraq war once again led by America with support of Western coalition forces, including Britain. Before this, *Shias* and *Sunnis* lived, worked and prayed together, even got married without any qualms. They still do as can be seen annually during the *Hajj* pilgrimage, where millions congregate as one, even dressed alike with one purpose only, as Muslims to follow their faith.

Let's be honest. There will not be a Muslim or, for that matter, another faith majority in Britain or any other 'civilised' country in the West, India, China, Myanmar or elsewhere than its own religion in the majority. Because in the eyes of God, if people of whatever faith or no religion are so despicable, why would have God created them? What matters most is to respect fellow humans' lives, as they also have similar aspirations for a better life. Suppose we believe in that, then what right have we to discriminate or inflict suffering on defenceless people based on faith, race, class, sex, or/and nation. Likewise, the test of divine power in any religion, including Islam, is more about respecting and getting along with others. Let's not make it worse by encouraging racism under the pretext of nationalism and politics of populism. If we look around, give credit where it is due, we will see some fantastic British and other Western nationality Muslim doctors, nurses, teachers, engineers, scientists, accountants, politicians, and authors in all fields serving humanity. Similarly, during the Covid-19 pandemic, Muslims, just like many others, have been at the forefront, risking their own lives to help others. A shining example of what patriotism is all about; innate pride in what the country does and stands for.

How can we forget an immigrant success story in a country where a debate about the willingness of German citizens with Turkish roots to integrate into public life has never been far from the headlines for the last decade. The credit to develop the Covid-19 vaccine was due to the pioneering role of the husband-and-wife team of Professors Uğur Şahin and Özlem Türeci. The children of long-maligned 'guest workers' from Turkey. You can say the man and woman who saved the world, lives of people of all faiths and those of no faith. Just like those decorated Muslim soldiers during the two world wars who gave their lives to fight injustices, something those trying to divide us dare do except being the first to hide in their protective bunkers. In contrast, Muslims will continue doing their share of valuable work in every Western country without being at each other's throats or thinking of just breeding children to become a majority, whether in India, China, Britain, America, Europe, or anywhere else.

To begin with, it's bad politics because there are many people worldwide who practice religion. Also, when we abandon the field of religious discourse, we ignore the debate about what it means to be a good Christian, Muslim, Jew, Hindu, Sikh or Buddhist. In the process, we discuss religion only negatively rather than in the positive sense of what it tells us about our obligations towards one another. Of course, organised religion doesn't have a monopoly on virtue, and one need not be religious to make moral claims or appeal to a common good. But we should not abandon any reference to our rich spiritual traditions, especially those that serve humanity well. Our fear of becoming "moralistic" may also lead us to ignore the role of shared values and culture in addressing some of our most urgent social problems.

Now, I am not suggesting everyone should suddenly latch on to religious terminology and worship or that we abandon the fight for institutional change in favour of divinity. What I am saying, the problems of poverty, racism, homelessness, loneliness, unemployment, mental health, social mobility are not simply technical but due to societal indifference and individual callousness. Despair and self-destructiveness are often caused for those at the bottom of the social ladder by the desire of those at the top to maintain their wealthy status at whatever cost. Solving these problems will require fundamental changes in government policy ignored over decades; it will also require changes in the attitude of individuals, as we found out during the Covid-19 pandemic, to our detrimental cost when places of religious worship were closed. The severe impact it had on mental health on top of our livelihoods and lifestyle, the psychological effects, when many festive occasions we take for granted got cancelled or not celebrated from *Christmas, Eid, Vaisakhi, Diwali, Jewish* New Year. Also, social events like sports, concert venues, weddings got cancelled; it affected everyone, whether a Christian, Muslim, Jew, Hindu, Buddhist, Romany, even those of no faith. It's because of the common thread that runs through every one of us as members of the same species; namely, we are human beings, irrespective of race or cultural identity.

How to reconcile the lessons learnt is up to us. What was most remarkable was how we missed our religious festivities and social events. We realised the value of religious festivals, traditions, and various social events, only when we could not celebrate with family and friends. How much we missed them? So, on a positive note. The lesson to learn from Covid-19, the "new normal," should be instead of just setting aside religious festivities for a couple of days or a week, we should extend the spirit of goodwill as a part of our daily life. Not necessarily spending money buying gifts and partying. But in the true spirit of human endeavour, addressing injustices at home and abroad. The 'Love thy Neighbour' spirit. If we look more closely, all these events and festive occasions have a common theme running through, getting together on specified dates and times of the year. Wouldn't that serve society better if we extend some goodwill messages throughout the year and extend it to others? Maybe the much talked "new normal" should be about bringing humanity together.

Some people spend their lives all alone. Only when Christmas and other religious festivals got cancelled did we realise how important those hugs and kisses, which are part of our daily lives, mean. How greatly we missed those family visits? Which led the government to decide not to cancel Christmas in 2020 despite dire warnings.

Why? Because people were worried about being lonely, about their well-being and mental health. Wouldn't it be great to remember what we missed, what we did, and learn to lead lives in social harmony in the "new normal"? Some of the changes forced upon us during the pandemic may turn out to be a blessing in disguise can be turned to our advantage. Like we shopped less, wasted less, appreciated what we had, improvised, spent more time with loved ones, cared for others, how lucky compared to others we were who lost their lives and livelihood.

As we also found out, loneliness doesn't discriminate; it can happen to anyone at any age. We need to end social isolation, provide emotional support and social opportunities that can help lift the spirits. Loneliness can be a very challenging experience for many. It is not always to do with material possessions or age. It is more to do with human contact. Compared with the deprivation we see nightly on our screens from refugee camps worldwide, the elderly British people I speak to are well-off materially. They all have shelter, a telephone and a television, they don't feel threatened with starvation, but all the same, they are suffering from the most terrible poverty – loneliness. Kindness should not necessarily be reserved, set aside for *Christmas, Eid, Jewish* New Year, *Diwali, Vaisakhi*. Kindness is a gift everyone can afford. Kindness is about making others happy. Kindness is about kindness that stands out.

*

We all like to have heroes and baddies in our life to apportion blame for our failures or regrets. Which often means defining an enemy or the 'other tribe'. One commonly held view when tackling racism is that Britain is the baddy, a legacy of a colonial master that ruined what it touched. Yes, there is some truth. Also, Britain gained far more than it spent on the colonies, and there were also some very dark moments such as slavery, a dirty foundation from the colonial past on which Britain built its wealth. But in life, history should not hold us back because of our past mistakes, however unpalatable it may be to the victim.

A change of attitudes works both ways. The record to date of ex-colonial countries is no different. They may be independent; however, it makes one wonder if there is reconciliation and understanding underneath because within each of us, there are the seeds of ills, and we cannot blame others for that. Are we all prejudiced, somewhere deep inside? I am not sure some of the ex-colonial countries can look at their track record with pride. Those who have emigrated from those countries can honestly agree with those horrible injustices inflicted upon the minority and the power grab by corrupt politicians. How long can those ex-colonial nations pretend that they are saints, better than everybody else! It's about time the citizens of those countries stopped kidding themselves, or else they will be at the mercy and whims of others, not liberated except pawns in the political game. But this time around, under their own political leaders, not their ex-colonial masters.

Similarly, those of us from those countries need to speak out. Otherwise, we would not have emigrated and stayed if they were not that bad. Or if it is not so bad now and improved, why not go back, if they still believe it's their home. Frankly, not many, no one I have heard, has gone back to settle other than hold dual citizenships to make it easy to travel. Over the years, we have witnessed from a safe distance in those countries an endless list of grotesque acts of underhand dealings, corruption, genocides, conflicts, violations of fundamental human rights, ethnic cleansing, poverty and racism. We have seen in countries known as the "breadbasket" people struggling to scrap an existence, seen educational establishments like the University of Makerere well on a par with the University of Oxford, now in ruin or total decline.

Many ex-colonial countries are still struggling with the stains of war, brutal conflicts, racism, prejudice at the core, and political power based on tribes, religion, and caste - a form of apartheid playing incessantly in the background. What is now becoming more fashionable for political leadership in those countries with an excellent past record of democracy is to inflict suffering on their citizens, people of the same race, the only fault they belong to a different faith or social underclass. As I have already pointed out in Kenya, India, Myanmar, Darfur, Nigeria, Rwanda and elsewhere, various communities lived in social harmony for so many years. Kenya and India were shining examples of post-independent countries in Africa and the sub-continent, where people from all backgrounds lived in peaceful co-existence. It was a lesson on the merits of secularism, not only for its citizens but the rest of the world.

Yet today, we witness politicians encouraging people of the nation with divisive 'populist political agenda' for self-serving interests. People of the same race are at loggerheads, killing each other or living in fear because of tribal, religious or caste differences; neighbours who had been living next to one another for many years are suddenly becoming sworn enemies. In these countries, the alternative for the minority has been a post-colonial history marked by racial, tribal and religious conflicts. A perspective of fact for those who complain about statues of wealthy, white colonialists slave traders to consider. If white people should feel guilty about Britain's colonial past, shouldn't the non-white people equally feel guilty about the ethnic cleansing-a form of apartheid- in their mother countries? Similarly, what about modern-day slavery in the twenty-first century of recruitment, movement, harbouring or receiving children, women or men through force, coercion, abuse of vulnerability, deception or other means for exploitation?

Sadly, the story in ex-colonial countries is no different: war, modern slavery, wealth, poverty, and conquest to produce those who win and those who lose. Under the pretext of democracy, political leaders target minority groups, excluding them from state services unless they convert to the "Hindu race" or "Buddhist race". No different from the vile beliefs of groups like the Taliban, Al-Qaeda, Boko Haram and Christian Crusaders. Yet, before independence, in countries like India and Kenya, people's race was an acceptable, much more flexible concept when I was growing up for example, in the 1950s and 1960s in East Africa, unlike in Britain with the signs of *no Blacks, no Irish, no dogs* displayed on doors. One could say the atmosphere in East Africa and India was more 'civilised' not based on skin colour or faith but mitigated by people working together to the best of their abilities.

*

The Iraq war uncovered it was more about oil, greed and geopolitics than the "war on terror", exposing Britain's "special relationship" with America as a one-way affair. Britain's role in the "coalition of the willing" left Britain responsible for being in Iraq with no authority, and it is hard to see any future British prime ministers going to war on such terms. It is even more imperative for Britain to regain its position as a Beacon of Hope, fairness and justice. Lost by yielding to America and the divide and rule politics during Brexit has undermined our position on the world stage, a place once served to guide nations.

Britain has always been a tremendous multilateral, working together with other countries, looked upon as the clever person in the room, people looking to us to see what we had to say. But regrettably, Britain's status has been undermined by the lack of political leadership and double standards over the last few decades. You can bet your life that there are plenty more dirty deeds carried out in the name of democracy. What an example to set for the kids, eh? Why on Earth do we think we have a right to criticise other countries or leaders when we behave otherwise? Never mind the politics; this is a matter of integrity which is also reflective of our country. Our politicians have lost the trust of the people, making Britain a laughing stock in the world. Britain gave justice, Hope, education, and more to the people of the Commonwealth and the world, yet at home, people are struggling. Yes, there were some very dark moments; however, many good things also happened during colonial rule. There is a lot to gain; build upon by learning from history, even part of that history some might regard as painful.

Studying the history of the British Empire should be the intrinsic part of any Commonwealth citizen and should not be learnt as a means to seek retribution but as a platform to build a better future. No one pretends that the British Empire was without its faults; we have all experienced it in some form; of course, many have had far worse experiences than others, and people still suffer from those colonial mistakes in some parts of the world. We can only heal the wounds by moving forward, not by more carnage, harbouring resentment against the past morals of the British Empire. Although we have advanced, many wrongs put right, but if we don't progress more, evolve, learn from history, we are still in the same position, harbouring hatred.

What good is history if it doesn't enable us to see the actual picture, help learn from the past, and not get controlled by myths? An average British and Commonwealth citizen doesn't know or even care about their history. Like politicians, those who do not want to learn from past mistakes and gains remain blinkered with their racist ideologies and prejudices 'learnt' from only listening to propaganda. As the name suggests, if the Commonwealth functioned more on the lines of 'what it says on the tin', we would get nearer to solving future conflicts and dangerous migration journeys. Our participation, role in the UN, World Bank and International Monetary Fund needs revisiting, not forgetting the ongoing purge of natural resources from Third World countries, stifling the growth of poorer nations so that the West and China can thrive. Just like it happened during the colonial era, but now under the pretext of deploying various 'civilised' financial institutions and mechanisms, like the IMF and the World Bank, that still control's their destiny.

I think that both the bright and dark moments should be leaned as a subject in school openly so that the future generation can learn from the good and bad history of the Commonwealth. If taught with honesty, in the spirit of exploration, just like our own family ancestry, history can explain so much and should unite, not divide. However, we have to be prepared to learn with an open mind, free of prejudice, envy, free of harboured grudges, as well as a willingness to build for the common good. If we think about it, the ordinary British people also did not escape the atrocities of conflicts. Even people in Britain were effectively 'deprived and exploited' when their lands got confiscated, sons and husbands got recruited to join armed forces during both world wars, with no compensation for their suffering and loss of life.

It is true that over the years, nations have chosen their destination, politicians are suspicious of each other, not only in the UK but in the whole Commonwealth. However, what is at stake here is the interest of humanity, both at home and abroad. It may not be possible to bring all the Commonwealth nations on board at the same time. Still, we can start the process by setting a good example. Leading from the front with clear intentions, not exploitation, but mutual benefit, so that all can progress, even if it initially starts with one or two countries, we can then build on this for others to see. Once people see the conviction, integrity, vision and benefits, others would also join. A unified Commonwealth will harness, unleash its vast potential, human resources, natural wealth for mutual advantage, address people's expectations of Hope.

Britain can play a crucial role in leading the way in serving humanity, but first, we need to put our house in order by being good role models for others to follow. Education means not to be afraid to discuss, reason, respect, even agree to disagree. The British Empire is relatively fresh in the minds of many people born in the twentieth century. I have no disillusions about the many benefits I had, also the blatant and subtle practices of colonial discrimination. It will be a great shame not to capitalise on the good things that happened before it gets forgotten. It's one of the main reasons why past achievements from civilisations – like Egyptian, Greek, Inca, Roman, Babylon, and Abyssinian – have got forgotten - regrettably, the main reason why many people in those countries still face poverty and conflicts. All those great civilisations have disappeared, just living behind ancient physical constructions, most now in ruins, without capitalising from the moral, cultural and economic advances.

So, salvaging the good things from the British empire is imperative before it is too late. The Commonwealth has excellent potential to become a brotherhood of nations. Even today, after all the mistakes and horrors from colonial history, there is still the possibility of seeing a better future. It's because of a deeper awareness of the bonds that unites and grips the young and old when we witness the pain suffered by fellow human beings during manmade atrocities and natural disasters. There is a profound awareness of the sanctity, dignity, and needs in our hearts, regardless of race or religion. We should look below the surface, the framework of communities and nationhood, so that a peaceful existence belongs to every member of those communities. Britain and the Commonwealth nations are fortunate to share a unique bond that has the potential to become a robust force, capable of better trade deals worldwide. It can also lead the way. Develop a stronger unified international voice of reason, justice to tackle poverty, conflict, migration, illiteracy, health, global warming, environmental issues and other disasters, not only for the good of Commonwealth citizens but for the whole of humanity. Think about it; if America had not become a confederation of fifty individual states, it would not have reached the superpower status that it enjoys today.

By combining the force of the whole Commonwealth, we can make a considerable difference based on equals, Hope and fairness, without a 'US' or 'THEM' attitude. We all have to give and take in life; not everything will suit everyone, but we can become a family of productive nations with suitable adjustments. Life-changing endeavours take time to build; it may take fifty or a hundred years. So, we just have to be patient, work towards a better future. It took a long time to build the British

Empire, but less to destroy it because of the short-sighted decisions made by the political leaders of the time.

After the dismantling of the British Empire, I believe there was a missed opportunity to bring the newly independent ex-colonies even closer by working together, not sharing the burden, but sharing the decision-making in the true spirit of the Commonwealth Charter (established 1931). The charter recognised the need for peace, security, democracy, human rights, broadened economic opportunities, a compelling force for good, an effective network for cooperation, and promoting development. I feel passionate about the Commonwealth and believe it is still not late to grasp new opportunities by working together, healing past ill feelings, and learning from them. As a purposeful body, the Commonwealth can lead the way in the world for the good of all humanity. With lots of effort, hard work and visionary political leaders, we can turn it around to become a powerful force.

Perhaps it may not seem necessary because the political turmoil of the twentieth century has primarily disillusioned us with the notion that the world has reached some sort of utopian 'end of history'. We are also in an unprecedented era of peace and progress, with perhaps less likelihood of WWIII because of a growing consensus that war between superpowers is most unlikely, unthinkable due to their weapons. It may sound like an optimistic idealist narrative, as we see ourselves today living in a safer, more prosperous environment than our ancestors and suffering less cruelty. I say this because when we look from a high enough vantage point, violence has declined after centuries of hostilities, except in a few places. Our lives get reshaped in every aspect. Even spanking our children is now seen as a cruel act, especially in the West. It's because we think we are more 'civilised' and have come a long way from our 'uncivilised' predecessors and comrades from other parts of the world because of our true moral values and democracy to uphold justice in all aspects of life. Therefore, it goes against the grain to inflict suffering and carnage on other human beings for the vast majority of people.

In a way, it's true that throughout history, humanity has shared similar 'civilised' values, namely hard work and respecting each other, as 'world citizens'. No different from when my ancestors embarked upon their perilous journey in search of a better life. We even see it happening today, people searching for a better life for their families. I am not saying there were not any bad people around. Of course, bad people are always everywhere to inflict pain on others. But what is different is the type of suffering and the overall effects. For example, all forms of deplorable acts, such as apartheid, war, religious or political bigotry intolerance, class bias, slavery, and other forms of barbarism over the past millennia, were entirely different in terms of the magnitude and pretext we see today. In the past, such atrocious acts were blatant, with a clear separation of boundaries and foes. Today, they are concealed and subversive, carried out in the name of democracy by 'civilised' politicians with double standards, inciting hatred amongst people and nations, or tarnishing a whole faith as radicalised terrorists. The scale of suffering by innocent people as collateral damage in the present-day far outweighs those of the past, in terms of numbers, as well as having longer-lasting consequences, a result of prolonged bullying, threats of economic sanctions and use of lethal weapons. So even if we believe that the chances of WWIII are minuscule, however, the scale of suffering inflicted upon others continues unabated in one form or another despite considering ourselves as 'civilised' people are far more significant!

*

Life should not be a utopia but a reality, learning from past mistakes instead of repeating the same mistakes. On the whole, in comparison to other countries, we in Britain have successfully fostered a broader cultural diversity in terms of harmony and mutual respect. But we need to take further advantage of these gains to overcome the pockets of racism and handicaps faced by non-white people. Understanding how it undermines social harmony will prevent exploitation by religious and political leaders to fuel hatred and anger to alienate communities.

Equally, the responsibility should also be on Black and Asian people. They need to acknowledge, not take, the goodwill of the white British people for granted. Stop listening to backward thinking religious and political leaders - democratically elected or not- with evil agendas, whether back in their home countries or here in the UK, preaching hatred and division. My main criticism of those who believe otherwise will be if you disagree, why live here? But they still do. Why? Because they know too well that despite racism and structural inequalities, they enjoy better civil rights in Britain, and they will be treated even worse in their own countries of birth because of high levels of corruption. And to seek justice comes at a price, with innocent people ending up in prison and forgotten.

Likewise, we all like our mother countries of birth to be a hero as I have mentioned. Something we would like to boast about: but we need to be honest with ourselves. We should not see the world through the prism, blaming others while turning a blind eye to the atrocities by making unsubstantiated stories and cover-up failings of those ex-colonial countries with a diabolical human rights record. Before questioning others, we should also speak out against those malpractices, not keep quiet if we want to be listened to as a credible voice. It is only by going abroad - 'back home' as some like to describe it – that by being honest, we can understand, admit where 'home' is and how British we are. Not the 'other' at all. The grass is not greener on the other side, despite what people may think.

We also need to realise that seeing somebody every day is not the same as knowing them. And ask whether we appreciate the civil rights we enjoy in the country we live in and call our home. If not, should take the trouble to learn, not just take them for granted. Reading about our countries of birth with nostalgic sentiments or visiting them by filtering out the nasty events does not mean it is better than Britain, your home country that you live and earning livelihoods. Because these same questions on racism and human rights afflict the minority in those ex-colonial countries, perhaps we should learn by interacting more with those affected to break the social barriers even more in those countries we originated from.

Yet, I remain optimistic for my adopted country because whichever political party is in charge, the resolute British commonsense in the end seems to prevail. Britain is the best country in the world to live, work and study. Of course, there is always room for improvement, and as long as we recognise voids in our society and communities and are prepared to address them, all will be well. Most importantly, the older generation born in the twentieth century, white and non-white people alike, need to overcome their prejudices, self-serving political and religious egos not to ruin it for future generations but leave a better legacy. As it is, they have enough problems to address and pay for the failed policies of unaccountable twentieth-century politicians.

After Covid-19, the millennials now face even a bleaker future regarding employment, homeownership and not forgetting severe disruption caused in their education because of government failures in handling the Covid pandemic. Especially for those from disadvantaged backgrounds. We can achieve anything if we set our minds on it. We have seen similar endeavours in local communities during the Covid-19 outbreak, the public coming to each other's aid. We also realised the crucial role played by the ethnic minority in all walks of life. Especially in the frontline low-paid, high-risk occupations public service jobs. Like in the NHS, cleaners, carers, transport and shop workers, coronavirus deaths amongst ethnic people were starkly over-represented by 27% dying in disproportionately high numbers compared to white people.[19] We owe it to all workers who have passed away at work during Covid-19.

Equally, I feel it is imperative that the 'silent majority' of law-abiding, ordinary people, the *voiceless*, not only non-white but also white people, should raise their heads above the parapet. We need to speak where appropriate to alleviate tension to diffuse the situation in a pragmatic, peaceful manner instead of promoting racism, segregation, and killings, which only harms humanity. We should all respect those whom we meet, just as we must respect the country in which we live and its traditions. It is hardly a difficult task, and it is a formula for success in all walks of life and one's personal life.

I am not saying differences do not exist or did not exist before; of course, they have and always will because man is destined to fight, even with his neighbour and family, at the slightest provocation. Another crucial British characteristic is that people never shirk one's responsibility but help address the problem when it matters most. We have already seen British values not succumb to bullies during the two world wars and other conflicts. We need to look to the future, learn from past mistakes and build on good things from the shared history developed from the Commonwealth bond and the respect for HM The Queen. One thing I can say with confidence about the British people but regrettably not the politicians: is that they have better benevolence, virtues, justice, standing up for the underdog, honesty and selfless acts of charity to help the disadvantaged, far outweighing anything elsewhere that I have experienced or seen.

No one expects to agree with every word someone utters or indeed to agree with every custom of any land. We are all obliged to allow people to hold their views, follow their traditions, and most importantly, respect the law of the land. We all have to abide by the rules. A family unit cannot function without basic rules; even animals follow a set of rules; otherwise, we should ask ourselves how we can call ourselves 'civilised' if we cannot follow simple rules of life?

# EPILOGUE

It was one beautiful sunny summer day in August 2020 after the first national Covid-19 lockdown. My wife and I took our two-year-old grandson Taher to Goldsworth Park, who had just relocated to England with his parents. The same park, we took his mother, her elder sister for Kumon classes and other activities. It also features a picturesque lake with many outdoor activities, an ideal site for a young boy to play and run around.

We spent some quality time together, walking side by side, doing whatever a boy his age does, gets distracted by. He had fun in the playground, loved feeding the Swans, enjoyed running and mucking around. It made me think. Although I don't recollect what I did in Tanga when I was his age, one thing is for sure; it must have been no different other than the environment, activities, the people I encountered, was surrounded by, or who loved me. Suppose it will be the same for him. He will have no recollection when he gets older of the time we spent together.

As we walked around enjoying ourselves, looking at other children engrossed in similar activities with their parents or grandparents, many thoughts went through my mind, from when I first came to Britain forty-eight years ago in 1973, aged twenty-two. Then I was in my prime, a proud Tanzanian, eager, equally ambitious to start a new life. Now aged seventy, approaching old age, a proud British, equally enthusiastic and optimistic about the future goals. I reminisced why I came to the country; I now call my Home; the country we were; the country we are, the country we could be, when Taher reaches my age, which is a long way off. And hope that Taher fulfils his aspirations in life like any parent or grandparent would wish the same for their own. A universal dream, no different to that held by the many worldwide.

My deep-rooted gregarious nature not only on that day but generally allows me to make friends, talk, get along effortlessly with people from all walks of life, whether we agree or not. A trait my late Professor Ted Trueman, research colleague late Dr Mike Earnshaw, PhD supervisor Dr Keith Marriott and good friend David Evans noticed I did with ease. One of the many people I spoke to or said hello to on that day in the playground were Clive and Estelle King, who were with their granddaughter. It transpired they were from Kenya visiting their daughter and had got stuck because of Covid travel restrictions. Not only that, but they lived in Mombasa, the birthplace of my wife and my late mother. Besides, they knew the stationery business next to the old Regal Cinema, owned by my late father-in-law and brothers until the 1990s. They also knew or had heard of people I mentioned.

It made me think, what a small world. Moreover, the coincidences did not end when Clive mentioned that he had attended a Catholic mission school near Soni, a small village in the Usambara mountain range in Tanzania. I asked if he recalled the sandalwood distillery, Usambara petrol station, Mombo Hotel and the timber sawmill from his 1950s school days, businesses established by my family at Mombo, which he fully remembered. The same sleepy little village where my great-grandfather and grandfather, one hundred fifty years ago in the late nineteenth century, discovered sandalwood in Africa and extracted oil for it, now a thriving town. Then a tiny village, with a handful of African inhabitants and dwellings, nestled at the foot of the beautiful Usambara Mountains, remembered by most as the start of the long winding hill road to Soni, Lushoto in the Usambaras and beyond.

What is significant about this chance meeting has a much deeper message. Clive was born in Kenya and Estelle in Angola. Both are white British whose home is in Kenya with their white circle of friends. Whereas their daughter and granddaughter are born in Britain, home is Woking. They are both white, and like me, live in Woking. But I am a brown British of Indian origin born in Tanzania, so are my two daughters and grandson, except born in the UK, and we meet in Goldsworth Park despite living five thousand miles apart in our everyday lives. However, what we have in common is we are British, a bond shared with many millions. Like the late murdered MP, Jo Cox, said, "We are far more united and have far more in common with each other than things that divide us."

I must concede, I am something of an Anglophile. I was born in 1951 when Tanzania, then Tanganyika, was a British colony, later granted independence in 1961. I grew up under the British education system. It was the very model of education, justice, the get-up-and-go, never-say-die-attitude in me and my forefathers, no different to that shared by many others. Yet, the history also reflects the dark times during the colonial rule that helped inflict a malicious injustice on fellow human beings based on racial differences. The consequences of those decisions are still felt by people today, cruelly manipulated by right-wing political groups and democratically elected politicians for self-serving egos.

It is because, as a country, we have not been honest about our colonial past and historical ties. The excessive benefits Britain had reaped from the colonies and its inhabitants. We have also failed to appreciate the sacrifices made by the people of the ex-colonies during the two world wars and the hard work of those who accepted Britain's invitation to help rebuild its war-torn infrastructure after WWII. Hence, Britain now has a non-white immigrant population from the Commonwealth who have the right to call Britain their home. Not acknowledging their significant contribution is one of the main reasons we have struggled to understand immigration, its close relation, race, and racism.

Maybe it's a deliberate ploy exploited by those politicians and the' establishment' born in the twentieth century to govern the country in such a way to maintain dominance over the rest of the country by fuelling a culture war. Because subconsciously, they find it hard to let go of their colonial mentality, power and privilege. And the main reason the nation has never had an open, inclusive, honest debate on racism. A country that has allowed those in power to uphold conversations by the worried pessimists, not the hopeful optimists. A country that has not explained to those concerned that immigration of non-white people was a direct result of Britain's past when the Sun never set in the British Empire, and we didn't complain then about the wealth it brought. Britain, therefore, has a reciprocal duty to welcome the non-white immigrants as they have a legitimate right to be in Britain just like the white Commonwealth immigrants who have come over or white British who settle abroad in search of a better future. And if we look hard at the hypocrisy, the right-wing groups and the media do not complain or object to the arrival of the white Commonwealth immigrants or white British emigrating abroad!

Another point to ponder is that after Brexit, immigration from the EU will fall. After all, that's what many people voted for. But let's be honest with ourselves. We will still face the ever-increasing labour shortage and costs of a country with an increasing population that is ageing. At the same time, further advances in research, medical, Artificial Intelligence will push the boundaries of life expectancy even further. As a country, we will need to create wealth to pay for that now and in the future. Hence, the conversation about immigration and race will have to change. Also, Britain will need young people from whatever part of the world because of a falling birth rate. Just like after WWII, when people got invited from the Commonwealth to rebuild Britain, we might have to rely on others, especially after post-Brexit and post Covid-19. No one can predict the effects it will have on the economy.

So, why not develop more meaningful ties with the Commonwealth based on shared values harnessing the good bits from our colonial past by discarding those nasty bits after learning from those mistakes. By that, I don't mean an open-door immigration policy. But a grown-up debate. Whereby, while we despise those dark times of British imperialism, such as the slave trade, apartheid and pillaging resources of those countries, we should also never reject the trappings of progress made during that time. The living proof today, a multicultural Britain with a great potential to lead the way in the world, setting a better example of British values by bringing prosperity to the whole of the Commonwealth working together, to alleviate some of the pain of past colonial mistakes.

Significant events are those that endure, offer Hope for each new generation to consider, and carry new standards forward, especially in a globalised world where the multiple identities of gender and sexuality will be as much a part of who they are as the colour of their skin. In a globalised world, distances and borders are no longer physical barriers because of advances in digital technology. It is easier, even quicker, to speak to someone on the other side of the world than to somebody on the other side of the street or the next-door neighbour. As a result, we may have got too much engrossed about who we were in the last century? Why do I like this race and not that one? Who is British, who is not? Therefore, it's about time race and divisive identity debate, which dominated the twentieth century, takes its place well behind in the twenty-first century globalised world facing more challenging times like climate change, migration crises, poverty, genocide......

We need to seize the moment to cast new light on things we got wrong. Programmes that were not working before the pandemic: we now need an ambitious plan to address structural inequalities like skills, affordable homes and social housing to regenerate derelict town centres. The Covid virus didn't ask us for permission to come in, yet we can use this time to think. Learn how we can move in a direction to correct things. Put them back on the right track. The top priority should be quality education to open one's mind, not the same mundane approach to get a job. Instead, equip an individual with quality education to encourage public duty and mutual respect to give a broader outlook. Equally, education at home would be a good starting point, not necessarily academic but a conversational one that builds noble moral values of acceptance irrespective of skin colour. Also, we can learn by looking back to how parents of those children who never attended school, read or write managed to raise children who not only did well academically but developed a spirit of respect for property and the wider community.

Here is the reality of the situations I would like the reader to consider who has come this far: the blame culture has got us nowhere. Two wrongs don't make a right. By remaining in denial, the problems will not go away. Adopting a confrontational approach will only cause added harm, fuel further division, stir up civil unrest, more resentment than good. Instead, wouldn't it be a peaceful future for our white and non-white children and grandchildren if those twentieth-century born politicians and grown-ups with colonial nostalgia stepped aside and admitted that they are just making it worse for the younger generation. The millennials are the innocent party who have not experienced the mistakes of the colonial past. So why corrupt their minds with those practices that are best left behind. Racism will only recede by working together towards a common goal.

Also, why make it difficult for the young? They have enough issues to resolve of somebody else's making. The second and third no-white generations of British immigrants see themselves as no different from their white counterparts regarding ambitions, music, sports, social life, etc. Still looking back at what past generations had to overcome, the BAME parents did not transmit anger. Or the bitterness of racist experiences they had to endure to their children. The degree to which such emotions have ebbed is full credit to them, a testament to their resilience to live in social harmony. Likewise, if the parents of the white British children played their part in combating racism by upholding moral 'civilised' values, the millennials and subsequent generations of theirs will reap the benefits based on their shared British values. Equally, living in a multicultural country will also offer them so much, an opportunity to achieve more, unhindered by discrimination or civil unrest.

What's also remarkable is not the number of white and non-white people from disadvantaged backgrounds who have failed to climb the social mobility ladder but the number who have succeeded against the odds. It shows if we want, we can do it. It just needs good people to come together to tackle what they find disgusting and ugly, not worthy in twentieth-first century multicultural Britain. It may be too late for the many millions subjected to religious and racial hatred who have suffered or lost lives; therefore, why continue making it worse for future generations?

I want to give credit where it is due. Tanga, my place of birth, is where I learned the rules of life, the far-reaching benefits of social harmony. I never felt different because of my faith, colour and creed. From an early age, while growing up in Tanga, I was brought up to respect people irrespective of race, religion, creed, sex and age. To this day, I see people as fellow human beings with shared values. So, it has always been easy for me to talk to people whether I agree or disagree with them. I believe we all have something to offer, provided we are honest with one another, not suspicious of each other. I always put myself in the other person's shoes. How would I feel if someone maltreated me? I first became aware that I belonged to a different race, faith and creed after arriving in Britain. Even then, I do not look at people any differently.

Walking side by side with Taher, I thought wouldn't it be better to pass on the wisdom of old age. Learn from past mistakes, yet harness the progress made by the twentieth-century generation. The twenty-first generation can build even a better future for themselves and put the Great back into Great Britain, not by repeating mistakes of the last century; hatred based on race, creed and faith, but by building on the positives. It would be a far better legacy to leave on the young shoulders. As it is, apart from paying the colossal national debt, they have to face an uncertain future post-Covid and post-Brexit, a direct consequence of the twentieth-century-born politicians' mistakes, so why burden them more. We wouldn't wish it on our own children, so why should politicians be allowed to burden others?

Isn't old age about the application of wisdom assimilated when young? Isn't growing old all about leaving a better legacy? Isn't life about giving our children a better future than us, which we all aspire to provide by instilling Hope and optimism? Isn't growing old about learning it's better to drop the ego than break relationships because my ego keeps me aloof, whereas I will never be alone with good relationships? Wouldn't it be better to accept that all the people who live on our island are British, instead of hatred, cynicism and suspicion towards each other? Wouldn't such wisdom be worth passing to the future generation for a better tomorrow than it was yesterday?

# AUTHOR'S NOTE

After years of writing to politicians, journalists and eminent people since 1992, very often ignored, not even receiving a courtesy thank you note, it finally dawned on me. The reason most voters have lost trust in politicians could be similar to my experiences.

I have remained undeterred to tell my story by taking advantage of the positive aspects of social media and self-publishing to inspire, motivate and encourage others not to give up on our shared values, whether rich or poor, literate or not. I hope this book, in its modest way, drags the *voiceless* a little further as we bend and stretch towards the light to get heard.

There are many biographies, books (fiction and non-fiction) written by eminent authors, politicians, journalists, entrepreneurs, celebrities. But seldom are books based on real-life experiences narrated by the average person. Hence, the inspiration for both my books has come from two sources: one, real-life experiences; the other, to narrate it as an ordinary person.

I knew very little about politics other than to make sure to vote. However, until recently, I always trusted the politicians because of my belief that they have people's interests at heart. After about thirty years when I wrote my first letter to a politician in 1992, although my interest has increased, I am sad to say; my trust has waned. More so, since my MP told me not to waste his time and I am "at liberty to stand for elections if I felt strongly about local and national issues." I have since also realised I am not the only disenchanted voter.

Likewise, journalists don't want to delve into the underlying causes of structural inequalities in any meaningful way. Except only seem interested in a terrible outcome or a happily-ever-after story and just like politicians, nothing in between other than the subtle undertones that treat specific sectors of society as second-class citizens. But quick to misquote somebody to make up the story with eye-catching front-page headlines, an experience that can leave an innocent person tired, scared of the media, fearful of speaking out due to the ensuing consequences.

So, after decades of futile attempts writing to politicians, collecting little bits and pieces of experiences by talking to many people, the first inklings of an idea began to form to write a book to get heard. The outcome of all that somewhat chaotic process resulted in my maiden attempt as an author. In 2020, I wrote my first book on behalf of the *voiceless* to reflect reality to help restore trust in politics and public institutions, inspire others not to give up whatever the cause, however difficult it may be to get heard. I also felt that although many top-class political commentators and journalists report daily with countless books on bookshelves worldwide written by some brilliant people on the subject, there is a distinct vacuum, a lack of direct interaction between the political class and the electorate.

The thought of writing a book felt daunting. Writing the first draft was the easy bit. Finding someone to help get it published was the hardest part. I approached many people for guidance and assistance. Not surprisingly, all attempts got rebuffed. Either I did not hear further from them or got informed that I had to be famous to generate market demand. A polite don't call us; we will contact you. Others quoted colossal amounts for their editorial expertise, well beyond my small budget, a financial risk I could not take with my life's savings if the book were a failure. But I persevered because I thought it would be more meaningful if an ordinary person wrote the book.

And that's what I did. Self-published my first book *Hope and Shared Values: A reality check* as a *people's author,* making no particular claims of an established author. I went to a state school and an unknown university in Tanzania. Obtained PhD from the University of Manchester and performed to the best of my ability, for which I am most grateful for the opportunities. Equally, I could have easily given up because I'm quite content with my life, enjoy retirement, leave it to others. But I can't because I feel if I give up now, how will I ever try to accomplish what I started in my small way three decades ago.

*Hope and Shared Values* is about a less well-known aspiring individual and his ancestors growing up in an African country during the colonial and post-colonial era. The primary objective has always been to help people like me lead lives of freedom, empowering them to break free from the chains that bind them to live in full expression of their democratic rights by making those they elect more accountable. Not through civil unrest but more by who they are, what they stand for, shared values to highlight what inhumanity does to humanity. Freedom means Hope, living in the present, not distractions for the *voiceless* worrying about the future or the past. The only question I asked myself was, what can I do next to help the *voiceless*? Because, after my first book, I had a feeling of anti-climax, not knowing what to do next. Not even felt like reading books or writing. A sense of emptiness and failure, thinking it is somebody else's responsibility. But I soon realised that it would not help the *voiceless* get heard by remaining in denial.

I am an optimistic individual, not afraid of failure, and try to do my best. I like to have a go, as I'm not too fond of regrets, especially regrets without trying, which I would say I did not learn from anyone because it is in my genes. So, I decided not to walk away, however slight difference my contribution may or may not even make, and the hard work that lay ahead in my quest to get the *voiceless* heard. I believe in commonality. Since we are born free, we have infinite possibilities for how we can lead our lives. We grow up believing in Hope, shared values, hard work, fairness, not taking things for granted, and most of us abide by the laws enacted by the 'establishment'. I also believe that political and religious leaders are best placed to make life better for ordinary people. The freedom we need is social harmony to make a difference in the world, feel free to do good to others, and liberty from selfishness without an US or a THEM attitude.

Luckily my anti-climax was temporary. Yet again, my real-life experiences inspired me to write to encourage others to speak. Tell the story as I see it from the bottom of my heart, which has remained my main focus to raise awareness. As someone who has experienced first-hand what it feels like to be ignored by the 'establishment'. And now, I have reached a stage in life where my top priority is to help the wider society. To get heard and writing books is one way of achieving it, and also a satisfying experience.

So, here is my second book, *Reflections of the Voiceless British*. Don't worry; I haven't got delusions of grandeur of an accomplished author. I don't claim it to be a perfect article. All I have to sell is my very common upbringing. And it's that experience of a *voiceless* person that has made me more determined to do something as a *people's author*. So just like I did in my simple language in the first book, here's a sequel to it to share. All I have to offer is my ordinariness, no local, national or international accolades or awards in journalism or literacy. And I don't consider myself an 'expert'. Not as if I have suddenly discovered a cure for cancer! Anybody could be me. Because all I have aimed to do is to reflect the real-life difficulties. I accept the literacy levels may not be of high standards and lacks professional touch as I have had no support whatsoever. Even to get someone to read the final manuscript, let alone an editor or an agent, to champion my proposal to the attention of a publisher.

I reflect in simple language in my books to inspire those who want to speak out and make a difference when many feel the world isn't listening. It is very topical, relevant in the present climate, lifts the lid on how difficult it is for people to get heard by the "establishment" despite claiming that they entered politics to serve public duty. It gives a new take on why people have lost trust in politicians, feel there is one rule for them, another for the rest. The two books attempt to recount extraordinary efforts and extra loops an ordinary person must jump through to get heard. Obstacles to overcome, for example, to get the local library to stock donated copies at no cost to the taxpayer, required a mindboggling effort. Whereas, books by celebrity perverts Rolf Harris *et al.* are still sitting on library shelves across the UK, including those by politicians with a sinister track record, e.g., illegal wars, political chicanery, inciting racial hatred, tax evasion. It seems to publicise a book; it helps to be famous, even for the wrong reasons.

Both books give authenticity that it is written based on real-life experiences of the man in the street. It is more important now than before to restore trust in democracy post-Brexit and Covid-19. Despite the constraints, even if the literacy levels may not be like other literary scholars of high standards, I have done well to reflect honesty, conviction, passion, and truth. I hope to inspire others not to give up their rights to get heard. The two books reflect universality based on personal efforts and disappointments by staying true to convictions and not being fickle but remaining positive when engaging with career politicians.

# ACKNOWLEDGEMENTS

D uring various conversations with people in my life, they have often told me I have solid convictions with a lot of history based on real-life experiences in vast-ranging fields, which I must record somewhere. I guess this is where I got my inspiration after all these years to put together all those different experiences into two books.

I have therefore relied on the knowledge of real-life experiences while writing this book, and here I'd like to give my special thanks to those *voiceless* people like me who have inspired my thoughts and emotions during the writing process.

Similarly, my upbringing will invariably be my shadow in the background watching over me, always my guiding angels, the best one born out of love to live in social harmony. From an early age, my late parents, teachers, friends and others taught me to respect everyone, most importantly, work hard, never take anything for granted for dreams to come true, however difficult at times it may seem to place trust in those values. Hence I am grateful to them all for shaping my life. Also, within the UK, I am thankful to those remarkable people I have made friendships with or have had the honour to know; too many to name individually, but they will know who I mean.

There were many moments in the composition of this book when I had difficulty because of my basic literacy skills, and at times struggled to believe in myself. But I persevered and produced a manuscript to the best of my ability. I, therefore, ask for forgiveness for editorial mistakes; however, one thing is for sure the book is written from the bottom of my heart. I have loved writing, feel humbled by the experience, and am immensely grateful for the opportunity to write both books and to those who will find time to read them.

Inevitably, I need to say a huge thank you to my family. First and foremost, to my wife Femi, who has always supported whatever I have done, our lovely daughters Naamah and Ummehani, and their respective husbands Husein and Mustali, not forgetting grandson Taher. I can't thank them enough.

# ADDITIONAL READING

[1] Society, culture, sport and business - Impact of immigration in the Modern Era 1900 - present - OCR A - GCSE History Revision - OCR A - BBC Bitesize

[2] Coronavirus: Gove defends £7,000 day rate for test-and-trace consultants | Politics News | Sky News

[3] Microsoft Word - ETHNOS_DECLINE OF BRITISHNESS_OS.doc

[4] Wolverhampton South West (UK Parliament constituency) - Wikipedia

[5] In praise of David Lammy, a true Englishman | The Spectator

[6] Prince William attacks BBC over handling of Bashir interview with Diana | Financial Times (ft.com)

[7] BBC sets up separate complaints page for Israel-Palestine coverage | Metro News

[8] Daily Mail slammed for article claiming there are 'no go areas' for white people in Britain (msn.com)

[9] Andrew Sabisky: minister urges review of No 10 hiring process | Boris Johnson | The Guardian

[10] Priti Patel calls rapper Dave's claim at Brit awards that Boris Johnson is racist 'utter nonsense' | Daily Mail Online

[11] Conservatives apologise to victims 'hurt by' Islamophobia and racism in party (msn.com)

[12] 10,000 people could be working in slave-like conditions in Leicester's textile factories (telegraph.co.uk)

[13] Calder Valley MP Craig Whittaker makes "no apology" for his comments about BAME community | Halifax Courier

[14] NHS Test and Trace (England) statistics: 24 December to 30 December - GOV.UK (www.gov.uk)

[15] Jacob Rees-Mogg 'ignored government guidance' by crossing Covid tiers to attend church The Independent

[16] Coronavirus: 38 days when Britain sleepwalked into disaster | News | The Sunday Times (thetimes.co.uk)

[17] Home Office failed to comply with equality law when implementing 'hostile environment' measures | Equality and Human Rights Commission (equalityhumanrights.com)

[18] Bullying inquiry 'found evidence Priti Patel broke ministerial code' | Priti Patel | The Guardian

[19] Runnymede Trust / Ethnic inequalities in Covid-19 are playing out again – how can we stop them?

[20] Bame label has 'outlived its use', says a Government race commissioner ahead of major report (inews.co.uk)

[21] Equality watchdog raised concerns about UK race report, documents show | Race | The Guardian

[22] Failures of State: The Inside Story of Britain's Battle with Coronavirus by Jonathan Calvert and George Arbuthnott. HarperCollins Publishers 2021

[23] Lord Kilclooney accused of racism over tweet about Kamala Harris - The Irish News

[24] Ollie Robinson's England suspension is over the top, says culture secretary Oliver Dowden | Sport | The Times

[25] Greg Clarke slammed for "racist" language before resigning as FA chairman - Sports Mole

[26] Martin Luther King: 'We Can't Keep On Blaming the White Man' - WSJ

[27] Which ethnic groups are most affected by income inequality? (parliament.uk)

[28] Black professionals 'twice as likely to be turned down for a pay rise' says major study | The Independent

[29] Racial murders: nearly half the victims are white | UK news | The Guardian

[30] Ethnicity_gender_and_social_mobility.pdf (publishing.service.gov.uk)

[31] UK ministers accused of turning blind eye to any Russian interference | Financial Times

[32] Trump's impact on the tone of political debate, important characteristics for elected officials | Pew Research Center

[33] Boris Johnson urges Europe to get behind Trump and end 'whinge-o-rama' | World | News | Express.co.uk

[34] democracy_report.pdf (v-dem.net)

[35] NatCen Social Research

[36] Tory rebels expect to defeat government on overseas aid cuts | Conservatives | The Guardian

[37] 'We were complicit': Lawyer who worked for Trump administration pens op ed apologising to US The Independent

[38] Schools and England's second lockdown: further closures would have adverse effects on children and a wider effect on family life | British Politics and Policy at LSE

[39] Covid-driven recession likely to push 2m UK families into poverty Society | The Guardian

[40] Fact checking claims about child poverty Children's Commissioner for EnglandChildren's Commissioner for England (childrenscommissioner.gov.uk)

[41] Spotlight-structural-inequality-in-the-UK.pdf (resolutionfoundation.org)

[42] Poverty in the UK: a guide to the facts and figures - Full Fact

[43] Poverty rates among ethnic groups in Great Britain – Joseph Rowntree Foundation https://www.jrf.org.uk/file/37256/download?token=H5-umlv2&filetype=findings

[44] You Cannot Fool All the People All the Time – Quote Investigator

# INDEX

# ABOUT THE AUTHOR

Dr Hassan Badrudin Akberali was born in Tanga, Tanzania, where he attended school. He came to study for PhD in marine biology in 1973 at Manchester University after completing a BSc (Hons) at Dar es Salaam University. He left the world of scientific research in 1985, went into business in Woking, making Knaphill his home, and became interested in politics. Since 2017, Hassan has contested elections as an Independent. He is retired and continues to focus his energy to serve public duty. He often writes in the local press and published thirty research papers in reputable scientific journals, including Nature.

Printed in Great Britain
by Amazon